Abe Koogler Selected Plays

T0243556

Abe Koogler Selected Plays

Deep Blue Sound
Fulfillment Center
Aspen Ideas
Kill Floor
Advance Man

ABE KOOGLER

methuen | drama

LONDON • NEW YORK • OXFORD • NEW DELHI • SYDNEY

METHUEN DRAMA
Bloomsbury Publishing Plc
50 Bedford Square, London, WC1B 3DP, UK
1385 Broadway, New York, NY 10018, USA
29 Earlsfort Terrace, Dublin 2, Ireland

BLOOMSBURY, METHUEN DRAMA and the Methuen Drama logo are trademarks of
Bloomsbury Publishing Plc

First published in Great Britain 2024

Cover design and illustration by Rebecca Heselton

A catalogue record for this book is available from the British Library.

A catalog record for this book is available from the Library of Congress.

ISBN: HB: 978-1-3504-4422-5
        PB: 978-1-3504-4421-8
        ePDF: 978-1-3504-4424-9
        eBook: 978-1-3504-4423-2

Series: Methuen Drama Play Collections

Typeset by RefineCatch Limited, Bungay, Suffolk
Printed and bound in Great Britain

To find out more about our authors and books visit
www.bloomsbury.com and sign up for our newsletters.

For my parents

Contents

Introduction

When I'm starting a new play, the rhythm comes first. I felt the spare, clipped lines of *Kill Floor* before I knew what words they contained. *Advance Man* and especially *Aspen Ideas* came to me as a torrent of sound. The first scene of *Fulfillment Center* arrived as a series of sharp bursts: the rhythm of the shipping center. As I started *Deep Blue Sound*, I felt the lines overlap and flow into each other like one continuous thought. If I follow the rhythm for long enough, then the characters emerge from that.

Once I learn who the characters are, I try to let them be themselves. When I allow them to speak freely, without forcing them to serve me or the play, I am often surprised by what's on their minds. They make the play stranger and more surprising. They are funnier than I am. When necessary, I guide them gently back towards the plot. But the main thing is to surrender.

Writing in this way involves a lot of false signals, rhythm without content, language impulses that don't collect into characters, characters who don't want to be part of any organized play, and partial plays that take a turn and can't find their way back. There is a lot of wheel-spinning and waiting. This wasted time—seemingly wasted—can last for weeks, months, or even years. Then it ends, and a new play is there. It's a mysterious process. I am addicted to it.

Deep Blue Sound is about life on a small island in Puget Sound, off the coast of Seattle. (I grew up on Vashon Island, for those who know the area.) The islanders in the play are all grappling with loneliness and unrealized desires. At the same time, they are working together to figure out what has happened to a pod of whales that used to visit the water near the island every year. This play is a loving depiction of my hometown, loosely fictionalized. The culture of the island is distinctive to the Pacific Northwest. But the islanders will, I hope, be recognizable to anyone who has lived in a close-knit community, struggled to figure out what to do about environmental change, or questioned whether they are living a meaningful life.

At the heart of the play is Ella, a woman dying of cancer. We were lucky to have Maryann Plunkett in this role when the play premiered as part of Clubbed Thumb's Summerworks. She gave a stunning performance, as did the entire ensemble. Really, the production was a dream—I had always wanted to work with Clubbed Thumb, a downtown theatre company that has produced some of my favorite writers. Our cast and design team were world-class, Arin Arbus directed beautifully, and audiences were extremely enthusiastic about the piece. This was especially gratifying as it was my first production after years of pandemic, during which I wrote almost nothing and often felt hopeless.

Fulfillment Center was anchored by another beautiful performance, this one from Didi O'Connell as Suzan, an itinerant folk singer who takes a job at an Amazon shipping center in the New Mexico desert. I grew up with a lot of women like Suzan, who carried with them the anti-capitalist spirit of the 1960s and found it difficult to adjust to the values and speed of our present-day economy.

I wrote *Fulfillment Center* after becoming fascinated by the intricacy of Amazon's vast shipping centers and the relentless efficiency the company demands from its workers. Like everyone else, I love convenience. In my work, I am interested in the costs of that convenience. *Fulfillment Center* is in some sense a companion piece to *Kill Floor*. Both are about people struggling to retain their humanity while working jobs that require them to suppress it.

The premiere of this play at Manhattan Theatre Club took place on a long bare platform with audience risers on both sides. There were no other set pieces, just a few chairs and props. The starkness of Andrew Lieberman's set design evoked the New Mexico desert and left the actors with nothing to play off of except each other. Pat Collins did the eerie lighting, one of her last projects before she died. The play was very well served by Daniel Aukin's sensitive, subtle direction.

In 2012, I took the first of several trips to the Aspen Festival of Ideas. I attended as a guest of an organization called Theatre Masters, which was previously run by Julia Hansen and is now run by her daughter, Vicky Hansen. Their kindness and support of my work has been a gift, and I hope they will forgive me for the fact that I found the festival fascinating but dystopic: a surreal melting pot of celebrities, artists, politicians, and CEOs who come to this elite resort town every summer to discuss the world's problems, and—ostensibly—make progress towards solving them. The veneer of virtue, paired with the extreme wealth and celebrity, gave rise to *Aspen Ideas*.

Aspen Ideas was scheduled to premiere at Washington DC's Studio Theatre in June 2020, in a production directed by Les Waters. Then the pandemic hit and the production was cancelled. It has not yet been produced, and so I haven't figured out how it sinks or swims in front of an audience. For that reason, it is the most untamed play in the collection—the shaggiest. A little blunt in certain areas, and scattered in others. But I like the sheer force of its relentless, looping language. The play's absurdity feels like an appropriate response to elite gatherings like the Aspen Ideas Festival. And I remain interested in the anxiety that builds over the course of the play . . . the sense that underneath all the conversation, something just isn't right.

Kill Floor was my professional debut, thrilling and nerve-wracking. It premiered at Lincoln Center Theater in 2015, in a production directed by Lila Neugebauer and starring Marin Ireland—my dream casting when I wrote the play in graduate school. Marin played Andy, a woman who gets out of prison and takes a job at a slaughterhouse. The job is Andy's ticket to stability. Her biggest hope is to reconcile with her fifteen-year-old son B, who is furious at his mom for her long absence from his life. B also happens to be a vegan who is horrified by his mom's new job.

I wrote the play after becoming fascinated by the architecture of slaughterhouses—the way they are designed to keep cows calm and unafraid until the last possible moment before they are killed. I was interested in the racial dynamics of American slaughterhouses, and in how slaughterhouse workers process their jobs. I was thinking about the violent, hidden systems that create our easy lives.

When I wrote the play, I felt deeply connected to B, a sensitive soul who is struggling to define his sexuality and navigate a world that doesn't seem to have a place for him. I still feel that connection, but the scenes between B and Simon feel different to me in 2023 than they did in 2015. I would write those scenes differently now. My sense of what it means to be a white writer—writing roles for actors of color—has changed. I am grateful to Nicholas Ashe for bringing B to life with such grace in the Lincoln Center production, and to Sol Patches for their similarly beautiful take on the role in the subsequent production at American Theatre Company in Chicago. This play continues to feel alive to me.

Advance Man may be the most unusual play in the collection. It may also be my favorite. Like *Deep Blue Sound*, it is about a small island community in the Pacific Northwest, where people are navigating their own personal challenges while trying to solve a communal problem. The problem, in this case, is how to prepare for a rumored visit from the President himself.

I wrote the play in 2012 and 2013. At the time, American drone attacks were causing civilian casualties in the Middle East, Eric Snowden had revealed that the US government was working with private companies to spy on American citizens, and US government support for repressive regimes was continuing, despite President Obama's rhetoric in support of human rights. The structure of American power remained unchanged even with progressive leadership. This got me thinking about Americans' relationship to politics: our unquestioning love for certain political celebrities, the way we articulate our beliefs, and how values are passed from one generation to the next. The question of generational transfer is at the heart of the play, as Marcy is transformed by Advance Man from an idealistic young person into . . . something else.

This play is loosely inspired by Gogol's *Government Inspector*, as well as by the musical, dense language I was encountering in plays by Suzan-Lori Parks, Samuel Beckett, and others. Despite the serious subject matter, there is a sweetness and even a silliness to *Advance Man*. It is as much a portrait of my island—and its idiosyncratic characters—as it is a play about politics. The director Will Davis staged a beautiful production during my final year of graduate school at UT-Austin. The students and local actors who made up the cast found the sense and the melody of each line, and the play felt like a funny, strange song.

These five plays would not have been possible without the support of many people. I am deeply grateful to my playwriting mentors: Steven Dietz, Kirk Lynn, Marsha Norman, Sherry Kramer, and Julian Sheppard, and to writing teachers Anne Fadiman, Suzanne Bottelli, and Mark Sheppard. Karen Chamberlain, my Meisner teacher, taught me how to listen. Liz Watters-Impett was an inspiring first acting teacher, and Jan Smith let me take classroom time to write and stage my own plays.

Many actors and designers made key dramaturgical contributions. I am grateful to my directors: Arin, Daniel, Les, Lila, and Will, and to the artistic staff of these theatres, including Michael Bulger, Elizabeth Rothman, Scott Kaplan, Elizabeth Sharpe-Levine, Nicki Hunter, Annie MacRae, Adrien-Alice Hansel, and Natasha Sinha. Paige Evans gave me my first professional production and Lynne Meadow gave me my second. Maria Striar saw the potential in the ten-page sample that became *Deep Blue Sound*. My agents at WME—first Scott Chaloff and now Emma Feiwel—have been skilled advocates and friends. Karim Dimechkie is always my first reader. Rachel Katz was my solid ground during ten years in NYC. Playwrights Katie Bender, Gab Reisman, Nathan Alan Davis, Josh Harmon, and Max Posner, songwriter Miranda Jones, fiction writer Gina Lalonde, and poets Katherine Noble and Corey Miller continue to be sources of artistic inspiration and encouragement. Many of these plays were developed at the Lark Play Development Center, which shut down in 2021. I am grateful to Andrea Hiebler, Krista Williams, Lloyd Suh, and other former Lark staff for providing a welcoming home for artists for many years.

Shortly after *Fulfillment Center*, I met Luca, whose love softened my life and deepened my work. Now we have August, our amazing son. I love these sweet people.

This collection is for my parents, who fed my mind, came to every show, and gave me the courage to pursue something that really mattered to me.

Abe Koogler
New York, NY
December 2023

Deep Blue Sound

Deep Blue Sound opened at Clubbed Thumb in New York City (Maria Striar, Artistic Director; Michael Bulger, Producing Director), where it had its first performance on June 5, 2023.

Ella	Maryann Plunkett
Joy Mead	Natsuko Omaha
John	Thomas Jay Ryan
Mary	Tala Ashe
Chris	Armando Riesco
Ali	Brittany K. Allen
Mayor Annie	Crystal Finn
Leslie	Jan Leslie Harding
Gary	Bruce McKenzie

Director	Arin Arbus
Set	dots
Lights	Isabella Byrd
Costumes	Emily Rebholz
Sound	Mikaal Sulaiman
Choreography	David Neumann
Props	Natalie Carney
Stage Managers	Caroline Englander, Matthew Pezzulich

Characters

Ella, *sixties, dying of cancer (this actor also plays* **Islander F***)*

Joy Mead, *fifties to seventies, the newspaper editor (this actor also plays* **Islander D***)*

John, *fifties to sixties, used to run an art gallery on the island (this actor also plays* **Islander G***)*

Mary, *thirties to forties, a massage therapist (this actor also plays* **Islander A***)*

Chris, *thirties to forties, a carpenter (this actor also plays* **Islander E**, **Alexander the Dancing Boy**, *and* **Voice of an Oceanographer***)*

Ali, *twenties to thirties, daughter of Ella (this actor also plays* **Islander B** *and* **Karl Who Runs the Pharmacy***)*

Mayor Annie, *the unofficial mayor (this actor also plays* **Islander H** *and* **Mo**, *the mother of Alexander)*

Leslie, *a horse groomer (this actor also plays* **Voice of a Therapist***)*

Gary, *a drifter (this actor also plays the* **Whale***)*

Don't worry too much about keeping track of all this doubling. Whether you're reading the play or performing it, just dive in! You'll figure it out as you go.

Actors can step in and out of roles without too much rigamarole. In general, no costume changes are needed. Things may not be as clearly delineated as we're used to.

* indicates a change in location or time, or just a shift to another character. Mostly these shifts should be instantaneous, as if the play is one long connected thought.

Time

The present.

Location

An island of several thousand people in the Pacific Northwest, accessible only by ferry boat.

Scene One

Lights up on a half-circle of chairs.

*The **Islanders** enter, greeting each other with little whispers and hellos or awkwardly avoiding each other or doing a "Hey, how you doing?". The effect of this is a little symphony of gestures and relationships between all these people, happening in near silence—they are also aware of us watching them.*

Someone does a prayer gesture to the room when they enter.

Someone does a "So good to see you, my heart goes out to you" gesture to someone else.

Two people are really *surprised and happy to see each other there.*

Whispering: Oh my God

In response: Hey hey heyyyyyyy!

At the same time two people who don't know each other that well but maybe like each other say:

(Hey there!)

(Hey!)

(So good to see you . . .)

Someone stubs their toe getting to their seat: GODDAMNIT!

Sorry

Someone has a Nalgene, someone else takes a few quick bites of something from a Tupperware.

When everyone's kind of settled:

Everyone ready?

You ready?

Yup

Yes indeedee

Good to go—ope, hang on. Sorry. Good to go.

Someone enters late

Sorry! Sorry. (*Seeing someone they know:*) Hey how are you!

Okay.

A moment when everyone is still.

Then they speak to us:

Islander B   The whales!

Islander A   We're gonna tell you what's going on with the whales.

Islander C   The whales? I thought . . .

Islander G   What's going on with us. (And the whales.)

Islander H   What's been happening here on this island.

Islander C   In this moment.

Islander F   In our lives.

Islander C (*with great seriousness*)   In *this* moment . . . in our lives.

Islander B   They just said that.

Islander H   About the whales *and* about sort of *us*. Islanders.

Islander G   Everyone plays more than one person.

Islander F   I play Ella, who's dying of cancer.

Islander G   I play John, her dear friend who doesn't know that.

Islander A   I play Mary, the three of us are friends, and I just split up with my husband Chris.

Islander E   Who's not doing so good right now. I play Chris.

Islander C   I play Les, or Leslie for long: a horse groomer with a new pen pal.

Islander H   I play Mayor Annie. *Recently* elected.

Islander B   I play Ali. Just moved back from Brooklyn to take care of my mom.

Islander D   I'm doing Joy Mead. Editor of the paper. Just takin' it all in.

Islander B   Secondary roles! I'm *also* doing Karl who runs the pharmacy, a local business.

Islander H   I play Mo, a local mom. That's all we know about Mo.

Islander E   I'm playing Alexander her son who *just* wants to be a dancer.

Islander C (*into a microphone so we just hear her voice*)   I play a therapist with a practice on the island who *tries* to be discreet when I see my clients out and about.

Islander E (*into a microphone so we just hear his voice*)   And I play a German oceanographer currently living in Switzerland for work. Many years ago I had intercourse with someone in this group.

Islander B   That's who we're playing. And we're all a separate third thing.

Islander F   Islanders.

Islander C   People who live here. The people you saw walk in.

Islander A   A lot to keep track of. Don't try and keep track of it. Just give up now.

Islander G   If you get mixed up, let it go.

Islander F   What you need to know, you'll come to know.

Islander H   One thing you do need to know: we are all worried about those whales.

Islander E   Where the hell are those whales?

Islander B   Okay let's do a general overview of us, circle back to the whales. Okay?

Islander E   . . . Okay.

Islander D   Sure.

Islander G   Yup.

Islander H   Yah.

Islander A   We've been living here, on this island

Islander F   Some of us longer than others   **Islander G**   Some of us for decades now

Islander C   Some of us were descended from those who'd settled it

Joy Mead   And some of us had moved   **Islander E**   For the water and the
over from the city after our divorce   woods . . .

Ali   And some of us had come back because our mom got sick

Islander H   But you were here as a kid

Ali   Yeah but I left.

Islander H   You left and had a great career

Ali   Well

Islander H   She went to New York, and had a great career, as an / artist

Ali   Graphic designer

Islander H   A brilliant career as a

Ali   Freelance graphic designer

Islander H   In New York!

Islander F   The island is

Islander G   We're talking Pacific Northwest, take a ferry boat to get here

Islander F   Not too far from Seattle, can see the lights from the

Islander A   Far enough to be somewhere really different

Islander E   Thirty minutes or so by ferry—does something to ya

Islander D   The water the light

Islander H   In terms of layout there's a town center

Islander C   We *have* a grocery store, and a bookstore, and I love to read

Islander E   A couple *great* restaurants

Islander F   I wouldn't say "great"

Islander G   There's an art gallery . . .   **Islander C** Historical fiction . . . you
name it!

Islander D   Where *I've* shown my work.

Islander H   She does these wonderful, how would you . . .

Islander E   They're conceptual . . .

Islander H   They're very *dense*, they sort of . . . *collect*

Islander F   But it's a beautiful island

Islander D   (How've you been? Haven't seen you at the uh)

Islander A   (Yeah I've been kind of . . . .)

Islander D   (Sure, sure . . .)

Islander A   (But I'll stop by, I should stop by . . .)

Islander D   (Stop by, yeah, not the same without you . . .)

Islanders A & D   (Sorry)

Islander H   The grocery store is a major meeting place

Islander B   Accidental meeting place, sometimes

Islander G   You have to keep your head down, if you want to get in and out

Islander F   You have to really *move*, to escape a conversation

Islander D   For example, I was in there   **Islander G**   (Are you comfortable?)

Islander H   —and we ran into each other, and we had a little tête-à-tête

Islander D   And it was / good   **Islander F**   (I'm good!)

Islander H   It was good to catch up!

Islander B   But sometimes you see someone and you think oh no: I'm going to
browse the soups intently. I'm going to see what *kinds* of *soups* they *have*.

Leslie   It's funny because people often do that to *me*

Islander B   Oh yeah? Well, that's . . . .

Leslie   And I'm Les, or Leslie for long, which is how I say it, and I'm a horse
groomer! / (*Sudden anxiety:*) Did I say that already?

Mayor Annie   And I'm the Mayor

Islanders A & B   Annie is the "Mayor"

Mayor Annie   I ran for it, and I won

Islander A   It's not really a position

Mayor Annie   It's an elected position

Islander A   Well . . .

Mayor Annie   People vote

Islander F   Every year, at the Strawberry Festival

Islander D   Long story short: it's a summer festival, there's a parade and booths.

Islander F   The island is known for its wild strawberries

Islander G   (Do you know I once worked for a summer as a migrant worker?)

Islander C   (What a rich experience that must have / been!)

Mayor Annie   The Strawberry Festival is where I was elected Mayor.

Islander A   Symbolic mayor.

Islander C (*to* **Islander G**)   You're always having *adventures*

Mayor Annie   It's an *elected* position.

Islander A   It's an elected symbolic position

Mayor Annie   It's an elected position, with powers

Islander A   There's no powers

Mayor Annie   There *are* powers

Islander A   Annie, but okay . . . what are the powers?

Mayor Annie   To convene

Islander A   Oh *okay*

Mayor Annie   To bring people together, to start conversations. And I've done that

Islander A   It's true you've started a lot of conversations

Leslie   I always thought there was a point in my life at which I would go hiking . . . I mean throughout Spain.

Islander F   Every year people vote a dollar based on which charity they want to support, and Annie was the candidate of the Island Humane Society

Mayor Annie   I happen to love dogs

Islander F   And so she won

Islander C   And I ran on behalf of homeless youth, and I *didn't* win

Islander B   Because there's no homeless youth on the island

Islander C   Yes there was Rachel Braha's daughter Melissa who was um

Islander B   She wasn't homeless   **Islander F**   Wonderful girl.

Islander E   Pain in the ass

Islander C   *Very* creative. Now *she* was creative.

Islander B   She was having a fight with her mom, so she went to stay with Lisa Hartford

Islander E   She went to school with my daughter—

Islander C   She was *functionally* homeless

Islander E   —and she was a pain in the ass

Islander C   Well, *I* think there's a homeless problem, among youth, and that's just my opinion!

Islander B   There's homeless adults, for example . . .

Gary   Wood? Anyone need wood chopped?

Islander B   No we're good

Islander E   We're good, Gary, thank you

Islander G   (That's / Homeless Gary)

Islander A   Homeless Gary, he's

Islander D   A little local color

Islander H   Let's not condescend

Islander B   He walks around the island carrying his chainsaw

Islander G   It's a little threatening   **Islander F**   Have you ever hired him?

Islander A   *He's* not threatening, he's just weird

Islander B   He wouldn't use it   **Islander H**   That's condescending!

Islander A   He just uses it to cut logs

Islander E   That's true   **Islander F**   I would *hope* that's what he uses it for

Islander D   I've hired him

Islander G   Did he do a good job?   **Islander C**   Oh wonderful!

Islander D   I'll tell you this: he was very thorough.

Mayor Annie   The power to convene.

Islander G   Oh right

Mayor Annie   And I'm using it. For example to deal with the problem of stray dogs

Islander A   There are a lot of stray dogs on the island   **Islander B**   *So many*

Islander F   And no one knows where   **Islander H**   There's not *that* many they're coming from

Islander B (She just takes herself so seriously)   **Islander H** A bit of background:

Islander E There are all these stray dogs on the island, that seem like wolves? Stray dogs that look wolf-y. They live in the woods.

Islander D My theory is that when Bob Hartman died

Islander C And that was a beautiful memorial

Islander F Thank you, I'd been practicing

Islander C Do a little bit

Islander F (*singing*) 'Tis a gift to be simple   **Islander C** So beautiful

Islander D That when Bob Hartman died, his dog went out there and mated with the wolf.

Islander B There's a Wolf Haven on the island

Islander A There's a very strange woman named Star

Islander H Star's not that strange   **Islander F** Star's wonderful, she's unique

Islander B A wolf sanctuary, she takes in strange wolves

Islander A Strange wolves?

Islander B *Stray* wolves, from around the country

Islander D Local color   **Islander H** "Wolf Haven"

Chris She tried to fuck me once.

Islander G And a wolf escaped, and Star didn't want to admit it, for political reasons

Chris I mean fuck me *over*, I'm a carpenter? Didn't pay me.

Islander G She gets a lot of money from the government for those wolves

Islander F Which is a whole other

Islander G Turns out if you own a wolf you can make out scot-free on the taxes front

Islander F It's something to do with the Endangered Species Act

Islander H Oh wonderful!

Islander B So *I* think when Bob Hartman died, his dog went out there

Islander H The Endangered Species Act has been *so* important, *so* / important

Islander A It was sort of a gruesome

Islander G Sad   **Islander E** Really sad

Islander B Case, of Bob Hartman

Islander A   He'd been dead for a while, and sort of decomposing, and his dog

Islander F   Don't tell this part   **Islander H**   Oh, come on

Islander A   His dog had been eating? Um? Eating Bob Hartman?

Islander C   Do we have to

Islander H   (This isn't part of the main story, it's just background)

Islander D   (What *is* the main story?)

Islander H   (About the whales!)

Islander B   And the dog, when they found it, was full-on crazy

Islander A   I'm a volunteer paramedic, and it's true, the dog had gone crazy

Islander C   And I'd met this dog   **Islander G**   *Sweet* dog, I mean originally.

Islander D   Bob was a regular, around town, with this dog

Islander E   Cup of coffee and a scone!

Islander F   He was Mayor, for a year, actually   **Islander B**   (Good impression!)

Islander A   (Symbolic mayor)

Islander F   Running on behalf of veterans

Islander E   He'd been in WW2

Islander B   Cranky   **Islander A**   A complete asshole

Islander F   He was *very* conservative

Islander E   There's a difference between being conservative and being an asshole

Islander B   Is there?

Islander E   Hey now!

Islander H   We respect your beliefs

Islander A   *I* don't   **Islander F**   Do we?   **Islander C**   (I like that: "WW2")

Islander F   The fact is that Bob was both conservative *and* an asshole. Two things that may or may not have been related.

Islander E   But that's irrelevant   **Islander B**   They're related

Islander A   So I get there, and the dog is eating Bob, or has recently eaten Bob because the dog has Bob *on his face*, and the dog snarls at me, and I thought *something has gone wrong with this dog, here in this closed house, with the windows shut*, and the dog ran away towards the woods, and *some* people think

Islander D   That the dog mated with one of Star's wolves, who escaped years ago

Islander G   She claimed it had died but everyone was like: where's the proof? SHOW US THE CORPSE

Islander B   And now there's a problem, of little dogs that resemble wolves, and can be seen, sometimes, at night, in the woods, with their eyes.

Islander E   I think they're just coyotes, come over from the mainland

Islander G   How, they swam?

Islander E   Animals are good swimmers

Islander C   Well that's a generalization

Islander A   Those aren't coyotes. Those are dog-wolf hybrids. / *Trust* me.

Islander H   But anyway this is all neither here nor there.

Islander A   Half-dog, half-wolf

Islander H   The point / is . . .

Islander E   Right the point is

Islander B   . . .

Islander H   But um . . .

Islander B   The whales.

Islander D   Yes.

Islander E   Here we go.

Islander F   The whales. For many years

Islander C   So my great-great-grandmother was one of the original settlers here, and her name was

Islander G   We don't need her whole backstory

Islander H   (There *were* already people here)

Islander C   I'm just saying, her name was

Islander H   (There were Native Americans here)

Islander D   Just let her say the name

Islander C   EDNA ST. VINCENT MILLAY.

Islander H   (I just want people to know that *we* know that there were Native Americans here)

Islander C   But not the one you've heard of: different one. Different Edna St. Vincent Millay. They happened to have the same name. But my great-great-grandmother was quite a trailblazer in her own right. She came over in a boat, she was pulled by the Native Americans, and she wrote about it in her journal, she was a diarist, she was a great diarist

Islander F   She was a great chronicler

Islander C   She was *the* great chronicler, the great diarist

Islander B   Well . . .

Islander C   Of the island

Islander B   Right.

Islander C   And what made a *particular impression on her*, living here in the 1800s, was that if you stood on the beach at just the right time, you could often see a family of whales, of Orca whales (Do you know them? Black, with the . . . white . . .)

Islander G   People know Orcas

Islander C   I'm just checking! . . . moving through the water, and you could see their fins, moving in strange patterns, oh and certain members were born or would die, but this family of orcas had come every year for generations, up until the current day. And sometimes they'd leap!

Islander F   They'd leap into the air, at dusk

Islander E   The most beautiful thing

Islander D   You'd see it, out of the corner of your eye

Islander B   If you were driving by the water

Islander F   As if in slow motion

Islander A   Emerging . . . rising . . . cresting . . . falling

Islander E   "Did I see that?"

Islander D   Splash!

Islander H   ("Did *I* doooo thaaaat"—is that a quote from something?)

Islander G   And then another, and another

Islander A   Emerging . . . rising . . . cresting . . . falling . . .   **Islander E**   (Some TV show)

Islander B   Whales

Islander D   Our whales   **Islander E**   (Jim Carrey?)

Islander F   Our beautiful whales

Islander A   In the water around our island.   **Islander H**   (No . . .)

Islander G   But something was different this year.

Islander F   I would often go down to the beach, and look over the water, at night, holding a glass of white wine

Islander D   And I'd do the same, with mint tea because I *don't* drink

Islander B   And I'd drive with my mom, to the beach, we don't have beachfront property

Islander G   There's a slight division here, between those who don't and those who do

Islander C   A *huge* division

Islander E   ("Did I do that . . .")

Islander H   ("Somebody *shoot* me": *that's* Jim Carrey)

Islander C   I've worked at Thriftway, for *thirty years*. I've rung up your groceries I don't *know* how many times. And do you *ever* ask about my back?

Islander D   And I'd stand on the edge of the ferry boat, after a long day in the city, and we'd all look out, over that still water:

Islander B   Nothing

Islander E   Why weren't they coming

Islander C   They had disappeared.

Islander H   And I was upset

Islander E   Because our island without the whales

Islander A   It's still beautiful

Islander G   Without the whales it's still beautiful but it's

Islander F   Little prayers, I'd sometimes say, walking down, to the edge of the water, my arms raised, as the sun fell, to the whales, for protection against harm

Islander H   When my son got really sick

Islander C   It was said that if you came down to the water, and asked them, that they'd

Islander H   And it was true, I asked them and after that he was

Islander F   Did they need *us*?

Islander D   Were they sick somehow?

Islander B   Maybe they were teasing us

Islander E   "Ya Dirty Bastards"

Islander H   (Is *that* from a movie?)

Islander E   (No)

Islander A   Point was: they'd gone missing

Islander F   And it was unacceptable

Islander C   And we'd have to find them

Islander B   As a community

Islander G   We'd have to come together

Islander A   In a common mission

Islander D   To find the whales

Islander E   Because without them

Islander G   The empty ocean

Islander B   (There'd be fish, sure)

Islander A   No whales?

Islander D   They've cared for us, I think, over the years

Islander B   As best they could

Islander A   And now it's our job

Islander E   To care for *them*.

Islander F   I mean, what the hell?!

Mayor Annie   WE JUST HAVE TO FIND THOSE WHALES.

Scene Two

John   It's very "of the 90s"

Mary   Yes

John   "Save the whales"

Mary   Yes

John   It's almost quaint, isn't it?

Mary   But now it's *find* the whales

John   It's different, isn't it: the *finding* is more about *us*

Mary   Maybe they don't want to be found
Maybe they're somewhere else

John   The great blue beyond . . .

Mary (*re: a sad little rack of sunglasses*)   What do you think?

John   We might need to go off-island for sunglasses

Mary   Or order them on—(   )

John   Don't say it! I like to shop local

Mary   The pharmacy has such a limited selection

John   It's nice to have limits

Karl   You folks finding what you need?

John   Oh hey there, Karl

Karl   Just another day in paradise   **Mary**   You got it! / Oh, what?

John   Awesome. Doin' good.

Karl   Hey let me know if you need me to order anything, anything we don't have we can order . . . just because you don't see it, doesn't mean we can't get it. Odds are? We can.

Mary   Fantastic!   **John**   Cheers! That's great to know

Karl *leaves.*

Mary   (It's so sad)

John   (Shhh) Bill Clinton

Mary   Hmmm?

John   90s stuff . . .
(*Re: sunglasses*) Ooooh

Mary (*re: sunglasses*)   Eh

John   The primary boy bands, and the secondary boy bands . . .

Mary   What was the one with Nick um

John   And then the tertiary boy bands, whose names are lost to history . . .

Mary   Save the rainforest was very 90s, too

John   As a movement? / (Le-shay?)

Mary   As something on our minds

John   I think that was more 80s

Mary   Was it?

John   No 80s was hole in the ozone

Mary   No that was very early 90s, I think

John   Ah

Mary   And then we solved that, and we moved on to the rainforest

John   And did we solve *that*? / (Lah-shay.)

Mary   I don't think so . . . global warming sort of came to encompass the rainforest, and the whales

John   Well, then, it seems very retro doesn't it? To pick one species and be concerned

Mary   I mean . . . *are* you concerned? Personally?

John   I love those whales! Don't you?

Mary   Sure. But doesn't it seem like maybe they've just . . . gone somewhere else for a while?

John   Could be

Mary   People get too scared about things, everyone's so nervous

John   On the other hand . . . there's a lot to be nervous about

Mary   Jodi's been trying to get me to come to Quaker Meeting . . .

John   I went once, I thought that might be the answer

Mary   And?

John   You just *sit* there

Mary   But you're in chairs, right? Zen des*troyed* my knees.

John   You're in chairs, yes, but people are *constantly* sighing, there's half an hour of sighing followed by thirty minutes of looking at the clock

Mary   Hah, well. So that's not the answer.

John   Sidebar: were you living here when the county tried to build a bridge to connect the island to the mainland, to replace the ferries

Mary   Good God

John   I chained myself

Mary   You did not

John   I did! I chained myself to the thing. To the whatever. To stop it.
I had a different internal sense of who I was . . .
I'm getting more and more confused as I get older about who the hell I actually am.
All of a sudden I'm thinking am I man who wears jewelry? My whole life my fingers have been unadorned, *as* has my neck, but *now* I'm thinking I want to do a sort of pirate thing, like I want my hands to flash when they move through the air

Mary   I support that, John

John   But no it was actually a blast: it was me, and Brock Taylor and his son who did *not* want to be there, and the Benedictine monks

Mary   This was before my time.

John   We didn't know each other yet! Sad

Mary   I was still living in Seattle, still pursuing the dream

John   Which dream was that?

Mary   Massage school . . .

John   Was Chris in the picture

Mary   *Can we not talk about Chris?*

John   Sorry

Mary   Sorry.
He keeps calling me, he keeps showing up! I said don't show up unless it's your day to take Carrie, but he wants to talk, I said I don't want to talk, and then he's positioning himself like he's pro-dialogue and I'm anti-dialogue, the fucker, when it's like no I just don't want to be with someone who is physically uh aggressive towards me. That's a clear boundary for me.

John   Mmm

Mary   Subject change because I know what you're thinking

John   Nothing you want to—?

Mary   No. I can hear your thoughts.

John   Mkay.
Shall we head out?

Mary   I'll just get these, what the hell

Karl   You found something you like!

Mary   Love these!

Karl   We try to have stuff that people want

John   There no better place than the pharmacy

Karl   We love to hear it!
I'll just bag these up

Mary   I'll wear 'em!
(*To* **John**) I have to pick up Carrie soon but I was thinking of grabbing groceries briefly can you stand it

John   I'll come I need dinner stuff hey have you seen Ella?

Mary   I was supposed to get together with her but she canceled

John   Yeah I've been trying to reach her but she's not responding she's

Mary   Maybe she's busy with her daughter she's

John   I feel like ever since the chemo she's been keeping her distance it's

Mary   I'm worried about her I want to know what the doctors

John   We should call her together we should

Mary   Yeah maybe if we contact her together it'll

Karl   Now you take care now!

*

Mayor Annie   Editorial from the Mayor, from Mayor Annie, for this week's paper . . . In this moment of . . . when everything's, ah . . . in this difficult moment, when we, ah . . . it's just *crucial* that we . . .
I can't think of what to say!

*

Karl   Fucking endless supply of sunglasses. We have as *many* sunglasses as I can *afford* to *have* in *stock.*

*

Chris   Hi.

Mary   What. Hi.

Chris   Fancy running into you here

Mary   Imagine the chances.

Chris   Browsing for soup

Mary   Yeah well it's cold out and I'm seeking comfort.

Chris   Can we talk

Mary   About what

Chris   I want to see Carrie more

Mary   It's not in the agreement

Chris   I know it's not in the agreement but I want to see her more

Mary   You're not kind to her

Chris   That's not true

Mary   The things she tells me

Chris   I set *rules*

Mary   Oh okay

Chris   And she interprets that as not being kind

Mary   Don't tell *me* I *don't* set rules

Chris   I didn't say that

Mary   You said you set rules

Chris　I do set rules

Mary　Which implies that I don't set rules

Chris　No I didn't imply that, I said I set rules, I'm not speaking to whether you set rules

Mary　Just saying that implies that you think I don't set rules

Chris　Name one rule that you set, and enforced, around the house.

Mary　"Respect."

Chris　Well, that's just incredibly vague.

Mary　The rules weren't the issue, it wasn't an issue of the rules. It was an issue of you and me.

Chris　I want to work on it, I told you that.

Mary　Yes, well

Chris　I think we can *work* on our communication

Mary　It's not about our communication it's about your explosive, frightening / anger

Chris　Can I come by? Sometime? To see you? To / talk more

Mary　No. I don't know. Maybe. Not right now.

John *walks up.*

John　I found my tempeh

Chris　Hello, John

John　Chris

Mary　. . .

John　. . .

Chris　. . .

*

Karl　Do you want an empty downtown broken windows grafitti everywhere total desolation or do you want to SUPPORT LOCAL BUSINESSES

*

John　Through a pen pal service

Ella　What is a pen pal service

Mary　Oh my God she is so DUMB

John　She's not dumb, she's—

Mary   Head in the clouds

John   (Well, she's a little dumb)   **Ella**   That's a nice way of putting it

John   So she met him on this service that's um, they set you up with pen pals, based on your common interests

Mary   What are her common interests?

Ella   Horses?

Mary   Every time I see her she goes on and on about those horses

Ella   Horses to me are very boring

Mary   I know!

John   Apparently she's had different pen pals over the years, some of them romantic, and she writes to them by hand which is sort of I think sweet

Mary   Does she send a picture?

John   Stop it!

Mary   I'm just saying

John   I know what you're saying.

Ella   Maybe she sends a picture of her horses

John   They have the same issue.

Ella   Oh dear.

Mary   You comfortable, Ella?

Ella   Yes I'm fine stop fussing, and both of you need to stop looking at me like that

Mary   Like what

Ella   With concern I told you I'm feeling much better

Mary   Okay sorry

Ella   I just want to not talk about all that now, it was horrible and embarrassing and painful and *boring* and it's OVER and I want to just be here with you both and gossip. That's what I want.

Little beat.

John   Alright then back to making fun of Leslie. As far as I know she's never met any of these men. They just have these protacted correspondences. Correspondence—

Mary   -es. Correspondences?

Ella   I actually took a writing class with her, with Leslie

Mary   Oh did you?

John   (They correspond.)

Ella I did, at the library, a poetry class, it was

Mary How is her poetry?

Ella Well, it's not good

John Oh no

Ella It's very actually terrible

John Well, I'm not surprised

Ella But you know what? *Everyone*'s was terrible

John Ha! Well, sure

Ella *Mine* was terrible.

Mary Oh stop it

Ella (*to* **Mary**) I read you some of it!

Mary It wasn't bad!

Ella We both agreed it was bad

Mary You were just starting out

Ella Everyone's was bad. Which took the pressure off.
Except for Joy Mead, you know her?

Mary Joy Mead . . .

John She edits the paper

Ella She brought in a poem and you know we'd sat through all these other poems, that were very terrible, when I'm there I'm just thinking thank *God* one of you isn't there or I would die of the giggles, but then Joy Mead reads hers and I thought—this is a *real* poem. Which ruined the class, actually. It was a fascinating poem. It was about being—I think—in a cult?

Mary I don't know her.

John Yes you do   **Ella** You do

John She writes that column for the Beachcomber? "Talking Island"?

Ella I think it's "Island Talking"

John I think it's like "Talkin' Island"

Ella She's actually . . . I'm working with her on something. With Joy Mead.

John Oh on what?

Ella Oh just on a project . . .

Mary . . . Okay . . . .   **John** Mysterious!

Mary So they really say you won't need any more treatment?

Ella   That's what they say, yeah

John   Well, that's wonderful   **Mary**   God that's good, Ella

Ella   Yes! I'm very relieved.
Tests every six months, but other than that: done.

Mary   Wow.

Ella   Yeah.

John   Thank God. Or whoever.

Ella   Right.

Mary   Knock on wood.

Ella   I say a little prayer to the forest sometimes, or the water.

Mary   I like that.

John   So . . . life goes on?

Ella   Life goes on.

She runs her finger around the rim of her glass.

*

Joy Mead   It's an interesting project for me, I've never collaborated on an obituary with the person who might soon die. Usually we get the notice, that someone has died, and then I write them, or the family writes them . . . but it's wonderful that you

Ella   Well, my daughter thinks me doing it myself is weird. But she thinks everything I do is weird or bad or

Joy Mead   That's having kids for you

Ella   Exactly! Anyway the nice thing about this project is that there is a clear deadline! A very firm deadline. (I'm doing an assisted sort of)

Joy Mead   Oh you're having it

Ella   Having it done, yes. Legally. They're sending a nurse to help.
I'm sort of—not telling anyone right now though? Don't tell anyone. If you don't mind.

Joy Mead   Of course.

Ella   It's wonderful that new law, that we can just

Joy Mead   But you look so well!

Ella   I know. But this thing is spreading inside me. You wouldn't know it. Sometimes *I* don't believe it. And at the moment I feel okay! It's I guess this brief window. I've emerged from several *brutal* rounds of chemotherapy

Joy Mead   Oh goodness

Ella   Which was very nightmarish and you know? Didn't actually work. So much for modern medicine.

Joy Mead   Should have stuck to the supplements.

Ella   Yes! Should have done the goat milk technique.

Joy Mead   I had an aunt who had cancer, forgive me if this story is

Ella   No I love the stories about people who have had cancer, truly

Joy Mead   Good, well, my aunt had terrible, you know metastatic sort of and she *refused* treatment she said I'm going to think positive thoughts! And I'm going to eat *completely* vegan. Not a *thing* that has been produced cruelly will touch my lips.

Ella   And did it work?

Joy Mead   Briefly.

Ella   Right. I've been resolutely avoiding positive thinking, I figure why start now.

Joy Mead   Ha!

Ella   Anyway. Thank you—

Joy Mead   Yes, shall we / begin?

Ella   —and I have to tell you that ever since we took that class

Joy Mead   Oh goodness I am not a poet

Ella   Oh my God. That poem you brought in about moving to the island and taking the ferry boat across the ocean from the city for the first time with the wind in your face at night and the phosphorescence in the water and the connection you made between that and your *divorce*?
I still think about that poem.

Joy Mead   Well, thank you.
I thought *your* poetry was—

Ella   No.

Joy Mead   Okay.

Ella   Thank you, but.

Joy Mead   Well. Shall we get started then?

Ella   Yes. God. How do we

Joy Mead   Why don't you tell me where you

Ella   Oh where I—?
. . .
No but why don't you tell me a little about you first. I mean how did you get into reporting? What a fascinating / profession

*

Mayor Annie   Rules

Islander A   Rules?

Mayor Annie   We need rules, for speaking, for who speaks when, if everyone's going to show up, we need a moderator. I'll moderate, obviously, as mayor. How many people do you think will show up. A hundred? Hundred and fifty?

Islander A   I think we should plan for ten

Mayor Annie   There are more than ten people on this island who care about our whales

Islander A   People get busy

Mayor Annie   This is the whales we're talking about here!

Islander A   Alright, let's plan for twenty. In the past everyone has voted to elect a moderator at the beginning of the meeting.

Mayor Annie   Well, I think that system in the past has led to chaos. Bad people get elected moderator. Stupid people.

Islander A   Happens every day . . .

Mayor Annie   Ha ha. But okay. So I'll moderate. Obviously if there's a community meeting, the mayor should moderate.

Islander A   Well, I don't know that that *is* obvious

Mayor Annie   Well, what's the point of a mayor then?

Islander A   Well, I don't know that there *is* a point

Mayor Annie   That's not my point, my point is

Islander A   You're a ceremonial mayor elected because people like dogs

Mayor Annie   And goddamnit, I'm gonna make use of my time in office. To do some goddamn good. I mean no one else is stepping up to the plate to figure out this goddamn whale situation, I mean we've got to get some scientists out here—Joe's a scientist right?

Islander A   He was

Mayor Annie   What do you mean *was*

Islander A   Joe moved to Minnesota about eight years ago

Mayor Annie   Well, that's why I haven't seen him!

Islander A   You have to pay attention. You have to be more aware of everyone around you. I've been trying to tell you that for years.

Mayor Annie   You have?

Islander A   You're wrapped up in your own head. You can't see the people around you. You have to improve on that. If you're going to be a good mayor.

Mayor Annie   Well

Islander A   Yeah

Mayor Annie   That's good, no, thank you for that I will work on / that

*

Joy Mead   Involved very briefly in um well I guess I have to call it a cult

Ella   That's fascinating

Joy Mead   Although of course when you're in the middle of a cult you don't call it that

Ella   Of course not!

Joy Mead   Have you ever been part of a cult?

Ella   Well, let's see. There was a period in my life where I was going to Curves every day, you know the, the . . . . women's gym?

Joy Mead   . . .

Ella   But that wasn't really a cult   **Joy Mead**   Sounds like more of a hobby

Ella   That was a hobby, yes, so *no*, I suppose, I haven't . . .

Joy Mead   So I was living in a house alone, I had just gotten divorced, and it wasn't the whole cult, it was just a family, who were members of the cult, and every weekend they'd spend on the compound in the woods, where the actual cult was located, but during the week they were just living their normal lives as a family, so I lived with them in this house in Seattle, I had the bottom floor and they had the top. And they were *very* sweet people.

Ella   Well, did they ever try to recruit you?

Joy Mead   Well, that's the strange thing they really *didn't*, and I was very on guard against it, but the fact that they didn't seem interested in having me as a member, made me kind of interested. So one weekend finally, they invited me to come out, to the compound

Ella   Oh this is fascinating

Joy Mead   We get there and the leader walked right towards me. I'd seen photos of him and always thought what a dumpy white man who'd taken this Indian name you know, but he walked towards me and there was indeed some powerful *thing* around this person, and I thought uh-oh. Even me, skeptic: he was magnetic. There was a whole meal, and everyone was—their faces were shining and they sat me right next to the leader and there was something alive in the room that in spite of every skeptical bone in my body I felt something inside me start to—open.

Ella   How was the food?

Joy Mead   Terrible! This massive communal lentil loaf

Ella   Good God

Joy Mead   And then these strange vegetables. I asked someone what *are* these vegetables? Never got an answer.

*

Ali   Being weird about it

Ella   I'm not being weird about it, I've just gone and had my obituary done, well we didn't get to it because we started talking about other things—have you ever talked to Joy Mead? She's a *fascinating* / person

Ali   I find her column to be very boring

Ella   Boring? No, it's

Ali   It's very local

Ella   Well, it's a local paper

Ali   Yes but even within the context of a local paper, the issues she covers are very / local

Ella   Okay, well, I mean for those of us who *live* here, it's nice to have things be local. I know it's not *New York*

Ali   Don't do that

Ella   Listen I understand what you're saying. But she's a big city reporter at heart—she was in a cult!

Ali   Well, good. I think it's good that you're doing this.

Ella   You do?

Ali   Yeah, I do. I mean I offered to sit down with you and write about your life, I think that could be really / nice

Ella   No no, it's better this way. It's easier to do with someone else.
But I agree that it's good. I think it'll help . . . making everything real. I mean I know it's real. But then other times I keep thinking: maybe they made a mistake, mixed up the scans

Ali   Uhhhh

Ella   These things do happen!

*

Mo   Alexander?

Alexander   What, Mom?

Mo   We're having dinner

Alexander   I'm not hungry

Mo   I'd like you to come down

Alexander   I'm practicing for my dance recital

Mo   I can see that

Alexander   It has to be perfect

Mo   I know, honey, but you have to take breaks, for meals

Alexander   Dance is my priority

Mo   I know it is *now* but

Alexander   Dance will *always* be my priority. I'm going to be a dancer.

Mo   Well . . .

Alexander   I'm *going* to be a dancer, Mom. I'm good.

Mo   Why don't you show me a little bit then.

Alexander   No! It's not ready.
Okay fine. I'll show you just a tiny part of it.

He dances.

Alexander   There. Mom? What did you think.
Tell me for real.

Mo   It's . . . it's very nice.

Alexander   Well it's not *ready*, I *told* you it wasn't / good yet!

*

Ali   Need to have some kind of plan for it, like for how you want it to feel on the day.

Ella   I don't know

Ali   Or any, yeah, ritual or

Ella   I don't want a ritual.

Ali   There's nothing that you want to like—celebrate your life?

Ella   Well, I want fresh flowers

Ali   Why don't we ask John to bring flowers from his garden.

Ella   I don't want John involved.

Ali   Have you told him that you're going ahead with it?
Mom.
Have you even told him you're still stick?

Ella   . . . not yet

Ali   He's your best friend.

Ella   I know that. You think I don't know that?

Ali   He would want to be there. You have to tell him. Mom!

Ella   Just leave it, okay? I need you to stop pressuring me. I need you to back off.
. . .
I want you to take care of yourself through all this. Have you been keeping in touch with your friends?

Ali   Yes

Ella   Any word from Shaina?

Ali   I told you we're on a break.

Ella   I *really* like her.

Ali   You've made that very clear.

Ella   She seems to really care about you and be up for you know your *moods*

Ali   I told you we are *on* a break.

Ella   Okay okay sorry
I'll try to be more proactive about planning my big day.
There is someone else I'd like to come actually.

Ali   Who?

Ella   I have to ask her first.

*

John   And I'm John

Gary   Okay

John   So yes. That's me and I'd like to hire you to uh

Gary   Chop the wood

John   Well, yes, actually, so uh—well, first, are you hungry?

Gary   No I ate

John   You ate

Gary   Yes

John   Seen you walking around with that chainsaw for many years, and I have all this wood, the storm, you know the storm?

Gary   No

John   There was a pretty big storm?

Gary   No

John   Okay well it brought down a lot of trees

Gary   Seen a lot of trees down

John   Yes! Probly from the storm.

Gary   Which made me kinda think that more people would be hiring me and stuff lately to chop but no go

John   Okay

Gary   Yeah no go on that, keep walking around but no one's stopped and picked me up brought me back to their place until you so—no go, yeah, no / go

John   Well, that's strange you'd think there'd be lots of offers

Gary   So I do appreciate the work

John   You're sure you're not hungry?

Gary   No I just ate about a minute or two ago

John   . . .
Listen I've always wondered, where do you stay? At night, I mean, do you live with someone, I know there's no ah shelters on the island

Gary   I don't live in a shelter

John   No I know

Gary   How come you're saying that?

John   Well, I don't know, I mean . . . aren't you / homeless

Gary   I have a home

John   Okay, yeah, great! Well, that's wonderful.

Gary   How come you're saying that maybe I'm homeless?

John   I mean your name is Homeless Gary

Gary   That's not my name

John   I guess that's what people call you, that's . . . were you not aware of that?

Gary   My name is Gary. Gary Williams.

John   Of course. I'm sorry. I didn't . . . I'm sorry . . . .
Let's go take a look at the wood out back

Gary   I gotta grease up my chainsaw

John   Okay, well, maybe I should show you the / wood

Gary   I gotta grease it up out front the chainsaw get it all greased up and then we can take a look at the wood out back

John   Okay . . . well . . . great . . .

*

Mayor Annie   Editorial from the Mayor. Ummmmmm . . . .

*

Mary   What the fuck are you doing here?

Chris   I don't know I was just driving by

Mary   I specifically said don't come here this is not charming behavior this may have been charming fifteen or even ten years ago but things have changed, culturally this is considered abusive

Chris   Is Carrie here?

Mary   It's not your day, no, she's at a friend's house

Chris   What friend?

Mary   Why are you here?

Chris   What friend?

Mary   Ainsley

Chris   I don't want her hanging out with Ainsley, her mom's a meth addict

Mary   Yeah, well

Chris   So I don't want her hanging out with her

Mary   She likes Ainsley. And I'll let her hang out with Ainsley if she fucking wants.

Chris   . . .

Mary   . . .

Chris   Garden looks good

Mary   It's winter there's nothing growing

Chris   Yeah, well, you've wrapped everything up, you've wrapped the bushes up just like I used to . . . I appreciate that. Taking care of them for the winter. That's thoughtful. That shows some real care and concern for the bushes. You kinda tied this one wrong.

Mary   . . .

Chris   But that's okay

Mary   Why did you come here, what do you want . . .

Chris   I want to try and be different

Mary   Jesus

Chris   No really though

Mary   I know that's what you want! I know you want it very sincerely, every time you want it. You *really* do.

Chris   I miss you really badly. I miss Carrie like I'm in pain. I feel sick.
I told you fifty times I'm really sorry. I fucking said it over and over, what else do you want?
I'm sorry.
I need help.
I swear to you I can be different.

*

Leslie (*deep sigh*)   I am writing you this letter . . . after a *difficult day* with my horses. I won't go into it in *great* detail but

*

Mayor Annie   Editorial from the Mayor. I so appreciate all of you who have taken the time to send your congratulations, to me, about me becoming Mayor. I must stress that I am aware that this is a ceremonial position, but in a time like now where uh—where things are going on, I must say that I intend not to waste my time in this position, and I intend to do some good. I think we've all just got to get together and see if we can get some information about those whales. Later we'll deal with the stray dog problem but at the moment they don't seem to be causing any issues and I am just much more concerned about those whales. So *please* get involved and stay involved. In closing, the holidays are coming up, so happy holidays, no matter *what* you celebrate, or whether you're just observing the change of seasons. Sincerely, "Mayor Annie." P.S. I hope some of you can make it to the meeting to discuss the whales.

*

It begins to snow.

Islanders (*multiple voices, sung*)   God bless you merry, gentlemen

Everyone sings the song but there aren't enough lyric sheets to go around and only some of the people know the words.

There's a lot of humming and sort of trying to hear what other people are saying.

But it finishes strong.

Islander F   That's *very* good. *Very* good. You've all been practicing at home, and it *shows*.

Islander B   You sounded great tonight.

Islander C   Oh did I? Well, I thought you sounded very nice as well.

Islander D   (Been hanging in there?)

Islander A   (Yeah! Doing alright, doing alright . . .)

Islander D   (You should come over some time, I'll make dinner)

Islander A   (Sure, yeah, no, that'd be fun, no definitely)

Islander G   Anyone had a whale sighting?

Islander B   No

Islander H   Sadly, no

Islander E   Not me

Islander A   Can't say I have

Islander G   (Winter came so fast)

Islander H   (I know. I barely registered the fall.)

Scene Three

Ella *is onstage, alone, in the near-dark.*

Voice of a Therapist   What do you see.

Ella   I'm on a boat . . .

Voice of a Therapist   Is there anyone in the boat with you?

Ella   I don't think so . . .
I'm alone.
There's a paddle in my hand . . . I'm going somewhere, but I don't know where
The island's in the distance, getting farther and farther away and
I don't know where I'm going

Voice of a Therapist   Say more.

Ella   It's not bad to be out on the water
It's nice to be away from everything, I have always dreamed of being completely
unreachable.
But I do miss my daughter.
I feel a clear feeling of—missing her.
Do you mind if we stop now? I'm tired.

Voice of a Therapist   Of course.

Ella   So uh . . . I'll see you next week. If I'm feeling up to it. I think things are about
to turn.

Voice of a Therapist   Why do you say that?

Ella   I just feel it coming.

Voice of a Therapist   Ella.

Ella   What.

Voice of a Therapist   It's okay to be scared.

Ella   I know that.

Voice of a Therapist   It might be helpful to say it.

Ella   Say what.

Voice of a Therapist   . . .

Ella   I am . . . scared.

Voice of a Therapist   Say more?

Ella   I am angry

Voice of a Therapist   Yes.

Ella   I am angry at myself.
I am so angry.
I have *wasted my fucking life.*

A flock of birds flies across the sky—overwhelming and fast—then they are gone.

Scene Four

Islander H   Migratory patterns being such that

Islander A   Is that really the right um

Islander H   Yes

Islander A   Word, migratory

Islander H   Or whatever, patterns, such that, we can tell

Islander F   Very old school isn't it (the map)

Islander E   I like it, kinda vintage

Islander H   Such that we can tell that

Islander G   And I've really looked into this online, so I'm happy to confirm

Islander H   Oh okay would you like to

Islander G   No, sorry

Islander H   Great so anyway

Islander B   Yes let's

Islander H   *I* can actually confirm that

Islander C   Do you want the

Islander H   No no I'll do it without the

Islander B   Would you like me to

Islander H   Only if you'd

Islander B   I find that it can

Islander H   Sure then. Sure. I find that the

Islander A   Talk about the seasons

Islander F   We know about the seasons

Islander A   Talk about the currents then

Islander B   We'll get to the currents

Islander H   We're just doing a general overview of the

Islander F   Okay lemme

Islander H   Here is the West Coast. Of the United States. So the whales begin here, when the weather is warm, all the way up by Alaska, and then they come down, following currents and temperatures—nearly the whole height of the world, from top to bottom, eating fish all the way, and sleeping on one side of their body at a time—which is amazing—(*demonstrating:*) sleep/awake, sleep/awake—and then they end up here. In Mexico. And then they come back for a while and hang out outside of San Diego. And then when August is kind of turning into September as I understand it they begin to make their way back all the way up here, to the Pacific Northwest, and they arrive here just as fall is ending, just as it's getting cold. Here in the water around our island. At least this pod does. And that's when we see them jump

Islander C   Which is my favorite thing

Islander A   I love going down to the water just as twilight is setting

Islander D   Coming?

Islander A   Twilight is coming, the sun is setting

Islander G   Golden

Islander D   Or sometimes in the morning, just when the sun is

Islander C   Spreading its um its fingers

Islander F   *Love* that language yes in those moments when the day has um before it's started or when it's about to end

Islander B   And the light is kind of

Islander D   And everything's just

Islander B   Exactly

Islander D   Suspended and still

Islander C   The way sometimes in the water there will be nothing, nothing . . . and then they'll JUMP

The **Islanders** *imagine it.*

Islander H   Anyway. So that's the situation as it stands now. And I know all of you need to get home to your kids and to dinner if you have kids and just to dinner if you don't have kids. So now that we're all on the same page, maybe next time let's focus on developing a plan of action to find them. Sound good?

Islander C   Go team!

*

John   Getting dark

Gary   Yeah
But I'm not done with the wood

John   I get it
But you've done a really good effort and I think maybe you could stop now

Gary   Yeah, but I'm not done

John   No I get that but I hired you and I'm telling you it's okay

Gary   I can't stop if I'm not done. You hired me to do a job

John   No yes but listen I'll pay you the full amount it's just

Gary   Do you not want your wood chopped?

John   I do! I do but it's just that this is plenty of wood and it's I'm making some dinner and I was wondering if you want to

Gary   Oh

John   You're welcome to, if you'd like, I'm going to

Gary   I have to finish this wood.

John   Oh, well, alright.

Gary   . . .

John   . . .

Gary   Chop chop

John   Making of the dinner

*

Mo   Alexander?

Alexander   Yes

Mo   You have to come down for dinner

Alexander   I'm dancing, watch me

Mo   I can't right now

Alexander   Watch me I'm getting better, right? Watch me for a second

Mo   Honey

Alexander   For a second

Mo   Okay, for one second

He dances.

Alexander   I'm getting better right

Mo   I don't know, to be honest

Alexander   Mom!

Mo   What matters is you're having fun but I want you to keep up with your schoolwork

Alexander   I don't care about my schoolwork

Mo   That's what I'm concerned about

*

Joy Mead *and* **Ella** *have dinner. Delicious, comfortable. A candle.*

Joy Mead   There was something really wonderful about the community of the cult: to be connected to God *all of the time* during every moment of the day

Ella   I can't imagine, it sounds wonderful

Joy Mead   I mean I've tried to do that my whole life feeling like every moment matters or whatever but up until then I'd failed

Ella   It's hard to do

Joy Mead   My mind is always racing, regretting the past or imagining different kinds of lives I could have had or

Ella   Me too!

Joy Mead   There was something about that environment where I was able to just—settle. It could have been the natural beauty, you had to drive a very long road to get to the main building, the fellowship hall, the sides of the road were strewn with wildflowers, the drive was truly endless and then you emerged to see this beautiful green field and beyond it the vast blue ocean, sound of wind and birds: two women in robes came out to meet me with slices of fruit.

Ella   Incredible
Would you like some more?

Joy Mead   No but this is a fantastic

Ella   This is my special

Joy Mead   And this salad!

Ella   These are the first greens of spring

Joy Mead   Thank you for having me over by the way

Ella   Oh I'm so glad you said yes!

Joy Mead   And at some point we have to get to that obituary

Ella   Yes but tell me more. First. About the cult. So you get there

Joy Mead   I was so entranced by the place that I didn't actually go home for weeks. I stayed there for several weeks. We had a very strict schedule I always knew where I had to be and when. At 6 a.m. we prayed, 7 a.m. a simple breakfast. Work for four hours, more prayer. I felt like a different person: amidst all the work I was at rest. There *were* weird things about it too I mean having sex with Robert (the cult leader, I could *not* call him by his Indian name even when I was deep in it) was interesting he had the smallest penis

Ella   Oh God!

Joy Mead   I've ever seen in my life

Ella   That's wonderful, I mean as a detail, that's a funny detail

Joy Mead   Really microscopic a um—how do you say it

Ella   A micropenis

Joy Mead   Yes, almost invisible, there amongst the—voluminous

Ella   Stop it!

Joy Mead   Waves of his pubic hair, really a *very* full bush

Ella   You are too much!

Joy Mead   And we were supposed to worship it! Not all of the time, it wasn't

Ella   Sure

Joy Mead   A phallic cult and he was very careful to worship our vaginas

Ella   Naturally

Joy Mead   I mean me and whoever else he was sleeping with

Ella   Were there threesomes?

Joy Mead   No no no hahaha it wasn't *that* bad.
Have you ever had a threesome?

Ella   Who me? No no. I never did.

*

Leslie (*talking to her pen pal*)   Nice to talk to you on the phone I've very much been enjoying writing back and forth, by post, it's rare, isn't it? Rare and wonderful. Oh, you know, I just finished feeding my horses and now I'm making dinner for myself. I like to snack for dinner, I like to pretend I'm having just a bunch of little snacks, as if I'm in Spain . . . well, that's how I imagine they do things in Spain, have you been?

No me neither! That's wonderful well um. . . . well we'll have to go! Maybe we could meet for the first time in Spain . . . if you want.
Listen I've written a new poem, and I'd love to read it to you, if you'd . . .
It's called "Life."

Joy Mead (*still at dinner with* **Ella**)   And he leaned forward and whispered to me—"if you're very quiet, you might hear it."

Leslie   Life.

Ella   Hear it?

Joy Mead   If you're very quiet, you *might* hear it.

Leslie   Life is funny

Ella   What is *it.*

Leslie   Some say it's funny

Joy Mead   *It.*

Leslie   But as for me

Ella   I don't understand.

Leslie   Life has been a bitter fruit.

Joy Mead   If you're very quiet, you might hear it.

Leslie   With sweet seeds

Joy Mead   If you're very *still*, you might *see* it.

Leslie   Hard to find

Joy Mead   You *might* hear it.

Leslie   But *very* tasty

Joy Mead   You *might* see it.

Leslie   When you do.

Joy Mead   It might be in the room.

Joy Mead *and* **Ella** *sit in silence—waiting to hear it.*

*

Mary   Communication, okay! It's these sudden it's lashing out, suddenly, at me, as if you're

Chris   Well, I get frustrated

Mary   I know that I mean my God this whole marriage has been an immersion in your frustration—and things have been good, often they've been good, I love raising a daughter with you, loved

Chris   I do too

Mary   But don't you think it's hard on her, I mean you're so kind, when you're kind, but then the screaming

Chris   I know. Don't you think I know? That it's a problem? I don't like—I mean I'm *aware* of it as a problem, don't you think I *know* / that?

Mary   You're building to it now

Chris   I'm not building to it

Mary   Yes this is how it happens, don't you remember the last time that / it

Chris   Yes of course I do

Mary   Don't you see that that's a problem?

Chris   Fine well, yeah well . . . I can see / that.

*

Ella   Listen I uh this has been the most wonderful evening, thank you for coming

Joy Mead   I hope hasn't been too tiring, to have me

Ella   No! This is exactly what I need right now.
There is something uh—I need to ask you.

Joy Mead   Uh-oh.
When someone says they need to ask me something

Ella   Oh

Joy Mead   Am I in trouble?

Ella   Not like that! I um—I
I wanted to ask you if you'd—be in the room when I do it.

Joy Mead   Oh.

Ella   I know we've just met and this is . . . I know this is a big ask, but I feel so connected to you and I think us not knowing each other that well will be a good thing? You can just come, it'll only take an hour or two, and you can sit there, my daughter will be there too so I promise it won't be too awkward, and if you wanted to read something you could, or write a little something you could . . .

Joy Mead   Oh.
Well . . .
I don't think so.

Ella   You can think about it if you want.

Joy Mead   No, I don't think so.

Ella   Oh.
I thought maybe you would say yes.

Joy Mead   . . . this has been wonderful, to get to know you, and it was such a pleasure to work on your obituary

Ella   Well, we're not done

Joy Mead   No

Ella   We've barely even gotten to it, the conversation has been so wonderful, hasn't it?

Joy Mead   It's been very nice . . . but, you know, it's mostly been me talking

Ella   Oh

Joy Mead   Sorry . . . I'm a very direct person

Ella   Of course

Joy Mead   And you know, I don't even know you really . . . don't you have people who know you?

Ella   Of course I do, I have my daughter, and my friends, but

Joy Mead   They might be more appropriate, don't you think?

Ella   Of course

Joy Mead   You should be with your loved ones right now. That does seem—that does seem important.
. . .
Thank you again for having me over though. This was truly an amazing meal.

*

Joy *leaves.* **Ella** *begins to clear the table.*

During the following sequence, she may change her clothes, or be helped out of her normal clothes and into a gown—transitioning from well to sick.

Mary   Haven't heard from you

Ella   Been busy

Mary   With what

Ella   Getting back to everything! After the treatments, getting back to my life, and my daughter's been here, so, from New York, so that's kept me busy

Mary   Are you avoiding me, for some reason

Ella   No! Not at all

Mary   I just feel as if we had a very intense experience, all of us, taking care of you, through the chemo, and now you're

Ella   You weren't taking care of me

Mary   I drove you back and forth to the hospital

Ella   And I really appreciated that

Mary   But now I feel this . . . distance, it's very strange. . . . I mean what is going on? I've been texting you, calling, wanting to get together . . . John said he came by and you pretended not to be home?

Ella   I just need a little space right now. I'm sorry.

Mary   Ella.

Ella   What.

Mary   Are you still sick?

Ella   I need some space.

*

Voice of a Therapist   How are you feeling today, Ella?

Ella   Incredibly energized. Incredibly wonderful

Voice of a Therapist   That's interesting

Ella   Yes. I mean there are problems, my pain is increasing, and I've had to go to the hospital a couple times

Voice of a Therapist   Who's taken you?

Ella   My daughter

Voice of a Therapist   Do you have more of a support system than that?

Ella   Not right now.

*

John   Ella

Ella   What

John   What are you doing

Ella   What do you mean

John   Why don't you call me, you're sick, I want to be there for you

Ella   I feel fine

John   You have to ask for help

Ella   Goddamn you. Why do you keep telling me I'm sick when I'm not. I'm not sick. I have so much energy, there are so many things I want to do. I want to clear out all my boxes, I want to empty out the house. I want to think back on my life and remember it and I want to go walk on the beach and I am praying—praying—that the whales come back so I can see them one more time. I'm seeing friends

John   Mary says that she tried to come see you

Ella   Other friends! Other friends I have a lot of people here who care about me who want to see me when I
Oh

John   What

Ella   Pain

He helps her sit down.

*

Chris   It just washes over me, it's like this wave and I feel it rising and can't stop it.

Voice of a Therapist   Can you remember the first time you felt like that?

Chris   Not really. There was a lot of anger in my house when I was a kid. My dad used to um hit me. He hit my mom too, she got it the worst. I feel proud that I haven't turned out like that, that I've . . . stopped the cycle. At least with my kid. I've *never* hit my kid.

Voice of a Therapist   Have you been in therapy previously?

Chris   I don't believe much in therapy. I mean today has been good but

Voice of a Therapist   Well it doesn't matter too much whether you believe or not. It matters if you keep showing up. Are you going to keep showing up?

Chris   Sorry. I just had a memory. About my dad.

Voice of a Therapist   Do you want to tell me about it?

Chris   Uhhh
. . .
Yeah so my dad was not someone who I

*

Gary   Been a strange life. Walking back and forth with my chainsaw, on the island.

John   Well, for me too it's been a strange few years. I was living with a man: Santiago, and we had a little gallery, on the island? Just showing local island painters, mixed quality—some good ones, some I'd be happy to set on fire. I'd met Santiago about ten years prior, he was a little younger than me—Venezuelan by birth, very kind eyes, *very* attractive, and he actually came into my gallery, and at that *exact* same moment

*

Mayor Annie   Can we have a meeting? Can we please have a meeting? Can we? Can we have a meeting.

Islander G   We're busy, Annie.

Mayor Annie   Don't you care about the whales?

Islander G   We do care but it just seems . . . out of our hands.

Mayor Annie   No. We can't think that way. That's lazy. No. We will step up to the plate, we will be responsible stewards of this island, for the next generation.

Islander D   It's probably something to do with climate change

Islander H   To do, are you British?

Islander D   I spent time in Europe, in college

Islander H   Okay that's great

Islander E   Probably picked up some of the affectations

Islander B   I mean they're out there in the water, somewhere, / hopefully

Islander D   If they're still alive

Islander E   Oh stop it

Islander C   They're still alive

Islander A   Don't be a Polyanna

Islander C   I'm not being naive, I'm saying, what, a whole family of whales is just going to die?

Islander A   Sure

Islander C   From what would they be dead?

Islander E   Disease

Islander B   Maybe they got chopped up, by a boat

Islander D   Maybe they got too warm from global warming, and they sunk

Islander A   Or their food sources are gone

Mayor Annie   Basically . . . we need to come up with a plan.

Islander D   Can we do Roberts rules of order?

Islander E   What's that?

Islander C   I know what that is

Mayor Annie   Well, a lot of us don't know what that is

Islander B   I think we should just take turns

Islander C   I think we should have what's known in tribal cultures as "a speaking stick"

Islander A   Don't be an idiot

Islander F   Hey!   **Islander D**   Harsh. No need to be harsh.

Islander B   I think we should go around the circle, and everyone should have two minutes. Keep it simple.

Islander E   Can I pass?

Islander D   Of course

Mayor Annie   No. You can't pass. Everyone must participate.

Islander E   Well, I don't know if I have an opinion

Mayor Annie   Well, form one. Form an opinion. If you want, you can go last and listen to other people's opinions and pick one. That's fine. But it's your duty to have an opinion. Otherwise why are you here

Islander E   I wanted to be a part of it

Islander B   Okay I'm going to speak. What I think is

Islander G   (And we developed a plan of action.)

Islander B   Okay so

Islander D   My sense—(I was on the phone with an oceanographer, he was from Germany although his accent was so light you could barely tell with whom I'd had a brief relationship when we were both in our twenties living in Monterey California at the time have you been there? Wonderful aquarium)—my sense is that there are larger forces at play

Voice of an Oceanographer   Well, obviously there are larger forces at play

Islander D   Such as global warming, my sense is that there are temperature changes

Voice of an Oceanographer   Well, I'm aware of that I'm an oceanographer

Islander D   And I know you're aware of that, I'm not trying to / condescend

Voice of an Oceanographer   You're explaining global warming to / me

Island D   I'm just giving you my sense of things! Now listen: why isn't the whole oceanography community down here

Voice of an Oceanographer   Because there are systemic disruptions, it's happening all over . . . I mean my God we've lost nearly all of the minnows, shrimp are nearly kaput, except for the ones in factory farms

Islander D   Shrimp fields

Voice of an Oceanographer   Exactly

Islander D   Heard a podcast about that

Voice of an Oceanographer   To say nothing of the dolphins, porpoises are just about kaput

Islander D   Well, I know that

Voice of an Oceanographer   What we're seeing here are truly crazy disruptions, species are behaving in ways that could disrupt vital food chains and send the whole ocean spiraling towards collapse

Islander D   Well, why isn't anyone covering this, why isn't anyone sounding the alarm

Voice of an Oceanographer   They have been! People have been sounding the alarm for years! I mean my God they've been sounding the alarm for years

Islander D   Well, they should have said it louder they should have been more insistent and stuff!

Islander D *storms off.*

*

Islander G   Dream of ah of being ah a whale, of one of our whales, funny to think about it / that way

Islander F   No but I do, I do too, / our whales

Islander G   It's funny to think about it that / way

Islander E   No but I do too

Islander G   Do you?

Islander E   Yes I feel a sort of, not / fatherly but

Islander F   I feel a very motherly sort of

Islander B   I want to hug them. Can you hug a whale?

Islander G   I think it would be challenging

Islander A   They'd be slippery

Islander B   They're very large

Islander B   If you could somehow sort of secure them in place

Islander G   Of course you'd have to ask for consent

Islander A   You would wouldn't you

Islander E   How would you do that

Islander G   Can people speak whale language?

Islander B   There is a language, I don't know / if

Islander G   Aren't there words and things, in whale language

Islander F   There *are* words

Islander B   No

Islander F   There are I studied it

Islander B   No come on

Islander F   I took a very bad class on—this is embarrassing but—sonic meditation?

Islander E   What's that

Islander F   It's where you're trying to meditate, but there's someone in the room playing a didgeridoo

Islander E   Ah

Islander C   It's wonderful that you did that

Islander F   I had to drive into the city, it was a pain in the tukkus

Islander C   No but you're always doing that, you're taking these courses

Islander F   Well, I always see you at the library!

Islander C   I love to read but I always wish I was taking more *courses*

Islander F   Well, in this class I was like—must this digeridoo player be a very attractive young woman? Who I have nothing against, as an older woman I love younger women: except this one. I found her annoying. There was a weird sexual vibe in the air, as if the teacher, who was a man with long hair and very bad body odor, he wove this feather into his hair

Islander E   Oh I think I know him he didn't pay me for some / contracting work

Islander F   Yes he actually lives on the island part time but anyway, as part of the class we were all supposed to learn whale sounds together, so I actually do speak whale.

Islander C   Wow

Islander F   Pidgin whale, not well, I mean

Islander C   Not *whale*

Islander B   Ha!

Islander A   Well, what can you say?

Islander F   I can say um . . . well, there's not really meanings, well, there's sort of meanings but okay, well, they think this is a sort of greeting . . . . . *blaassssshhhaaaaaaaorrr* . . . . . or no it's more like . . . *maaaassssorrrrroooooooooo* . . . ah, well, I was never

Islander G   So I guess we won't be able to ask them for consent

Islander D *returns with a latte.*

Islander B   You're back!

Islander D   Yes   **Islander A**   Hi   **Islander F**   Welcome back

Islander H   What did your friend say, the oceanographer, from Germany

Islander D   Well, he wasn't much help.

*

Islander B   That at no point in my life have I had certainty at every moment I've been plagued by doubt, at every moment I feel as if others are so clear on what they want to do, as if they're so clear and I am always like what the hell should I do I mean is this clear to other people about what the hell to do about *anything*

*

Islander D   Well, what else can we do?

Islander A   I don't know, we could call the city

Islander B   I called the city they said they're not sure

Islander C   The um the EPA

Islander A   The EPA has their hands full, there's a lot going on

Islander D   Apparently lots of different kinds of animals are going missing

Islander G   Is that true?

Islander F   That's what they're saying on the news

Islander G   Well, that's upsetting

Islander A   The people at the university

Islander B   They say they're trying to find them but they don't know

Islander C   We could go out there in a little / boat

Mayor Annie   What, and look for them? How would that help. That's the worst idea ever. That's truly the worst idea ever. I mean that is the worst idea ever. I mean talk about bad ideas: that's one of the worst ideas I've ever heard. I mean that is truly bad. That's a bad one. That's a terrible fucking idea. Go out there in a little boat? *Spit.* I'm sorry. I've lost control of this meeting.

*

John   Stay here at my place if you want, Gary.

Gary   Why would I need to stay here

John   Well, I'm not saying you / need to

Gary   I don't need to

John   I'm not saying you *need* to I'm saying you *can* stay here, if you want. If you want.

Gary   But why would I want that?

John   Gary. I have a suspicion that um . . . that you are in fact homeless. That there is nowhere for you to live. I have that suspicion. And you seem like someone who is . . . very proud, and I respect that, believe me, that internal sense of dignity.

Gary   People don't need houses. They don't need houses. There's actually lots of ways to live. I'm not homeless. I do good for myself. I've found my own ways.

John   Okay, well. Sure. Of course.

Gary   Let me know if you have any more wood that needs to be cut.

John   Yes I will. I think it will be a little while, because you chopped all of the existing wood. But I certainly / will.

Gary   Well, let me know when you *do* have more wood, I'm not saying there's more now

John   No no I know

Gary   I'm saying let me know when you / do

John   Yes. When I do. I will find you.

*

Islander D   Hey

Islander A   Yeah

Islander D   I know this is crazy but I was thinking about taking my boat out tomorrow, just seeing if we can spot any whales—do you want to um . . . do you want to come?

Islander A   Oh

Islander D   Could be fun, bring a couple beers?

Islander A   Yeah, no, that could be um. . . . sure. That could be good. That could be fine.

Islander D   Tomorrow afternoon?

Islander A   Yeah sure. Yeah no sure, no. No that sounds fun.

Islander D   Oh look

Islander A   What

Islander D   Bioluminescence

The sea is alive with bioluminescence.

*

Leslie   Hey haha thought I'd reach out over email just to say that I was thinking of calling but it did seem too late so I'm emailing. I'm just looking out the window at my horses. They're restless tonight they can't sleep I don't know why. I've tried everything I sang to them I brushed their manes I gave them more food I inspected them for fleas I told them how beautiful they are I stood right in their sightline so they'd know I was there . . . but they're so restless *something* is off. Anyway it's been tough to connect with you recently, I mean it's been hard to track you down . . . It *was* wonderful to get that photo of you, you're very handsome, the beard *does* suit you. And I hope that you liked my photo . . . I sent it a couple days or so ago so you should have gotten it . . . and I haven't heard from you since then . . . I've lost a little weight since that photo I think I said, but . . . it's been such a joy to communicate over letters mostly, and some phone calls, and some emails like this one haha . . . anyway I hope you're okay my darling, can I call you that? . . . and I look forward to hearing from you soon . . .

*

Ella (*asleep*)   No . . . God . . . please . . . that you . . . off me get . . . GOD—off ME get OFF ME get off you OFF me OFF. . . . . . .AHHH

Ali   Mom

Ella   They let you on the boat thank God, my sweet

Ali   Mom, no it's—you're dreaming

Ella   I'm what?

Ali   You woke me up, you were calling out

Ella   Oh I'm

Ali   You're

Ella   Sorry I'm confused—bad dream I'm

Ali   Do you want some water?

Ella   Yes please water

Ali *brings a glass of water.*

Ella *gulps it down—so thirsty.*

Ali   Are you in pain?

Ella   No worse than usual

Ali   Do you want me to come sit in here?
Or I could rub your feet

Ella   No that's not necessary go back to sleep I'm sorry to / wake you

*

Ali   Fucking waking me up screaming. She is so scared. I mean I would be scared, I get it but she won't *say* it she changes the subject she's fine talking about the past or about *my* life but when it comes to what is actually happening now she—yeah.
Won't.
For it to be over.
Horrible to say, but yeah.
I just—miss my life.
I want to get back to my life.
I miss you, actually.
I've been missing you a lot.
It's nice to hear your voice.

Hey I know I said I wasn't coming back to New York after this was over but um—
what if I came back?
Oh.
No, that makes sense. I get that.

*

Ella   I was born in Seattle in 1955.
Went to high school at Roosevelt, studied Art History at [the] U-Dub.
Spent a summer in Italy—incredible.
Had my beautiful daughter, sweet daughter.
Moved to the island.
Worked for thirty years as an administrator at the high school, in various roles.
Grew a garden.
Voted in every election.
Threw great birthday parties for my friends.
I was diagnosed with cancer two years ago in June.

*

Alexander   Mom

Mo   Yes, Alexander

Alexander   Can't sleep

Mo   Why, honey?

Alexander   I'm worried about the dance recital I'm worried I'm not going to be good

Mo   Oh, honey

Alexander   I've been practicing a lot

Mo   Yes you have and it's been wonderful to see

Alexander   I'm worried that even though I've been practicing a lot, and really trying to do my best, that I'm not good. I'm worried I'm still not good. Am I good? Mom? Do you think I'm good?

Mo   Of course you are

Alexander   But not in general, I mean at dancing. I mean am I a good *dancer*?

Mo   . . .

*

Gary   Follow me

He moves across the stage, trailed by a few, then tens, then hundreds of small dark forms.

Follow me, dogs

Come with me, dogs, come with me
Come with me, you dogs, you wolves . . .
Deeper and deeper . . .
Deeper and deeper and deeper . . .
Deeper and deeper and deeper . . . into the woods . . .

Scene Five

Ella   Day I had chosen to die

Ali   Mom

Ella   Hi

Ali   What are you doing?

Ella   Just woke up

Ali   Do you want some water or anything?

Ella   Water here

Ali   How are you feeling?

Ella   Pain

Ali   I'm sorry, I don't know what to do.

Ella   [*Come*] —here.

She does.

Ella   Nurse called?

Ali   She said the ferries are all messed up.

Ella   Going to be late?

Ali   Probly

They sit there for a moment.

Ali*'s hand is on her mother.*

*

Leslie   I've booked a trip to Spain. Yes, well, it was always something I wanted to do. I'm going hiking! I've booked a hotel for each night. I'm going to go in summer, so the grass will be golden, I'll stop for a beer somewhere in the late afternoon, I'll sip my golden beer looking out at the golden grass, with the wind blowing . . . I'm very excited. I'm going by myself.

*

John   Santiago. It's me, John. I know it's been years since we but I was thinking that I just have to tell you that I before it's too late that I

*

Mary   Hi

Chris   Hi

Mary   I told you not to come by

Chris   I know
You guys eating dinner?

Mary   Yeah

Chris   What are you having

Mary   Macaroni and cheese

Chris   My favorite

Mary   . . . .
. . .
Do you want to come in?

Chris   Yeah

*

Mayor Annie   Speech from Mayor Annie.
Well, it looks like our effort to find the whales has failed as of now. But still I think
they might come back or some of them might come back if we keep our eyes open.
Maybe on certain issues, there's not a great deal that can be done, except to keep your
eyes open and be aware.
And I know this isn't an elected position. I know it's not a godamn elected position
like President, or Governor, or even member of the US House of Representatives
Or Local State Representative or State Senator
Or even county council member
Or even the water board, for chrissake, which I know is an actual elected position.
But my God: I want the record to show. At my end of first year as Mayor (symbolic
Mayor), that although I was elected on a platform of the Humane Society because
people like dogs, that I have nonetheless governed with an expanded mandate.
To do good *everywhere* that I could. And that I have thought about personally and
tried to get everyone else to think about on a kind of group level about how we
can thrive as a community, taking care of ourselves, but also of each other, and also
of the natural world around us, which in turn takes care of us, giving us clean air
and water, and food and stuff like that. We are not separate from the earth. We are
of the earth. I mean I don't understand what's so goddamn hard about that to
understand.
So I don't know who will be next symbolic Mayor
But I hope for God's sake that you don't stick to the issue on which you were elected
But that you view your mandate as expansive
As I did mine.

So I guess I'm signing off now. And giving up my powers, or lack of powers.
So in the words of one of the greats:
Good night
And goddamnit:
Good luck.
Sincerely,
Former Mayor Annie

*

Islander D   Hey

Islander A   Hey

Islander D   You wanna take that boat out?

Islander A   Yeah sure

Islander D   It's a beautiful day

Islander C   They take the boat out.

*

John   Hello

Ali   You came

John   Yes

Ali   She's sleeping, I'm sorry. It's hard for her to stay awake right now because of the medication. And now we're just waiting for the nurse, there's something fucked up with the ferries

John   That's alright, we should let her sleep. Is she in pain?

Ali   Last night she was but I gave her a lot of the pain medication and this morning when she woke up she seemed pretty um blissed out or calm, I guess, relatively, although she did tell me she was in pain.

John   I hate knowing she's had to experience all this pain.

Ali   You brought flowers!

John   I hope that's okay. I know she didn't want me to come and I wanted to honor that but I thought. I looked out at my garden and I thought: I have all these flowers. I was supposed to take them into the city to sell at the Pike Place Market. I thought it would be good to have something to do today, to keep on working. But then I thought goddamnit. My friend is dying today. My lifelong friend. And goddamnit I don't want to go to work. I don't want to not come just because she asked me not to come. Fuck her wishes. I matter too. And what I want is to cut all these flowers from my garden and bring them to my friend. To my lifelong, my dear, maybe my dearest—yes— friend. And that's what I'm going to do. So fuck the market, and fuck her. Anyway I have all these flowers now. Will you help me bring them in?

Ali   That's very kind of you

John   I'm warning you –there's really a lot. I started cutting and I couldn't stop.

They bring in bucket after bucket of flowers.

*

Alexander   Mom mom watch me
I'm nervous for the performance today, for everyone to be watching me
Can I do the dance for you, before we leave?

Mo   We don't have much time, Alexander, we have to get there

Alexander   Just once, please
To practice

Mo   Alright, just once
And then we have to go
But don't wear yourself out
Save it for the real thing!

*

Ella   I'm awake
I can see the flowers
I can see outside the room
The house . . . the garden . . . the road . . .
Luckily I can see through my eyelids now
Luckily I'm hearing through my fingers now
Luckily my head is opening towards the sky

*

A whale enters.

No special costume.

Whale   I am a whale, and I have always been a whale.
There's nothing cute about it.
If I could somehow show you how big the ocean is, and how great it is to be inside it.
Everyone says it's getting polluted, and that's true. The trash is okay, we don't notice
that too much. Even the temperature is okay, the changing temperature. It's making
some of us sick, and affecting our food supply, and that's not so good. But we can
deal with that. Death is no problem, if all of us die, that's no problem, not for us.
What scares me is the loss of silence. There are more noises now, and I hate that.
Weird booms in the distance, engines, you have no idea how far the sound of engines
travels, when you're a whale underwater.
But still there are stretches of the ocean where you can just swim and swim, and hear
nothing except distant fish and
Faint rustles and movements on the surface of the ocean floor

Very far below you.
My group of whales and me used to go every year to the water outside the island.
It was a tradition.
But this year we split up, we were like, let's just do our own thing.
Mothers split from their kids, friends were like take care, maybe we'll cross paths again down the road.
I wandered around for a while.
And then I decided to swim back up towards the island. I'm nostalgic, I guess, and I missed it.
There's something about the water there that's so beautiful.
I swam for a long time to get there.
And finally I saw it
And as I got closer and closer
I remembered what it was like to be a kid there, when my mom was around me, and my brothers
What fun it was to be a whale
My swimming got faster and faster
And all of a sudden
I was overcome with a feeling I could not describe
And it was so overwhelming
That I couldn't help it

Islanders D *and* **A** *see something in the water*

Islander D   Hey, look!

Whale   I leapt into the air.

Somehow, the whale leaps from the water, his massive body turning in the air, just as:

Something happens to **Ella***, just as:*

Alexander *does the last few moves of his dance.*

He's dancing his heart out—he's really been practicing.

He finishes, breathing hard.

Alexander   Mom
How was it?

Mo   Oh, honey

Alexander   How *was* it

Mo   Oh, honey
My darling
It was

It's more than she can express.

End of play.

Fulfillment Center

Fulfillment Center opened at Manhattan Theatre Club (Lynne Meadow, Artistic Director; Barry Grove, Executive Director), where it had its first performance on June 6, 2017.

Madeleine	Eboni Booth
Alex	Bobby Moreno
Suzan	Deirdre O'Connell
John	Frederick Weller

Director	Daniel Aukin
Set	Andrew Lieberman
Lights	Pat Collins
Costumes	Ásta Bennie Hostetter
Sound	Ryan Rumery
Stage Manager	Kyle Gates

Characters

Madeleine, *thirty-one, Black.*
Alex, *thirty-one, Latino.*
Suzan, *sixties, White.*
John, *forty-two, White.*

Time

The present.

Locations

An apartment
An alley behind the shipping facility (or "fulfillment center") for a large online retailer—you know the one
A campground
A bar
A sculpture garden
A highway
. . . all in New Mexico.

A Note about Dialogue

A "pause" can be as short as a quick beat, or as long as a full rest.

An ellipsis is a pause owned by that character.

Overlapping lines are indicated in two ways: with a slash (/), or like this:

Alex Of course   **Madeleine** And that's

Scene One

Sound of a buzzer.

Lights up on **Suzan** *and* **Alex** *in the alley behind the fulfillment center.* **Alex** *is holding a clipboard and an iPhone, which he'll use as a stopwatch.*

There are several orange cones set up.

Alex   Go.

Suzan *runs between the cones.*

Alex   Okay don't run.

Suzan   What?

Alex   Don't run.

Suzan   What?

Alex   *Don't run.*

Suzan   I can't / actually hear you.

Alex   You can't run.

Stopwatch beeps.

Suzan   How was that?

Alex   Yeah, you can't run.

Suzan   What?

Alex   You actually, *you can't run.*

Suzan   How did I do though, did I make it?

Alex   You made it within the time limit, yeah

Suzan   Great! / God that's great

Alex   But as I said, you can't actually

Suzan   What?

Alex   Run.

Suzan   I wasn't running.

Alex   That was a pretty quick walk.

Suzan   That was a jog I think

Alex   Uh . . .

Suzan   Think that was a jog!

Alex   You're completely out of breath.

Suzan   Well, *that's* true.
You got me there!
Hang on
Whew
Okay.
Hahaha

Alex   We just have a policy that you can't actually run.

Suzan   What about jogging?

Alex   Or jog, yeah, jogging, yeah

Suzan   Well, why is that? Hahaha
You said it was a time, uh, time-based sort of   **Alex**   Well, it's just—
. . .   . . .
                                                                                     System, yeah, so—

Suzan   So did I make the time?

Alex   You made it, yeah, but—

Suzan   Well, great! So that's great!

Alex   The policy is in place because the job is a seven-hour shift.

Suzan   Uh-huh.

Alex   It's not, you know, the running thing is in place because you can't actually *run* for seven hours, so we need people who

Suzan   Right, well, I'm a little older

Alex   Uh-huh

Suzan   So that's, of course there's gotta be a *slightly* different policy for a "woman of a certain age," right?

Alex   Actually, no. I'm sorry. Thank you, though, for—

Suzan   I've just been traveling, was on my way from Tucson up to Maine, but then my car completely conked out on me, just sitting over there at the campground, and I saw the posting for this job, and I thought this will be perfect: short term, pay's pretty good, work through the holiday, get my car fixed, continue on my journey, and I'm in good shape for my age, so

Alex   I actually have to go back inside now, / it's a busy

Suzan   Lemme try it one more time, k? Hahaha, one more time, come on. Holidays are coming up, I bet you could use the help . . .

Alex   Uh . . .
Alright. / Once more.

Suzan   Oh thank you
Oh that's nice of you

Alex   Then I gotta

Suzan   Sure, great, of course. I understand.

Alex   You ready?

Suzan   Hang on, gimme a minute
Haven't done something like this since um

Alex   Ready?

Suzan   Yup, alright, sure, so

Alex   Go.

She goes.

Alex   Now you're going too slowly

Suzan   I'll run

Alex   You can't run

Suzan   I'll jog then

Alex   Jogging is running

Suzan   Well, am I gonna make it how fast am I

Alex   You have to walk
That's a walk

Suzan   To me these terms feel
Very
Slippery

Stopwatch beeps.

She's breathing hard.

Suzan   How was that?

Alex   Uh

Suzan   I made it?

Alex   Yeah . . .

Suzan   Great, oh that's great
Hahahaha / "Trying to murder me?"

Alex   But it's not, listen, you have to do this—
It's seven straight hours of work.

Suzan   I know that

Alex   You have to do that for seven hours.

Suzan   With breaks.

Alex   It's eight hours, with an hour of breaks.

Suzan   Eight hours with an hour of breaks
Well
That's good   **Alex**   Spread out.
That's a lot of breaks
I'll rest up during the breaks!
I promise you
I'll do a good job, I swear.

Alex   . . .

. . .
Okay.

Suzan   Yeah? Oh great.

Alex   Alright, yeah, um

Suzan   Oh great, that's a relief. God, thank you.

Alex   It's—

Suzan   It means a lot to me. Thank you.

Alex   It's not a favor

Suzan   No, of course not.

Alex   It's—we need the help.

Suzan   Great, of course.

A buzzer sounds inside the fulfillment center.

Suzan   Feel like I'm late for class

Alex   Yeah that's to keep us on track, gotta get a certain amount of packages out within each of those time frames, then they shorten or lengthen the time-frame depending on how we're doing center-wide

His phone buzzes.

Alex (*looking at the phone*)   Ah shit
They need me back inside, so I'll just orient you real quick

Suzan   Oh, I'm—

Alex   You wanna start now?

Suzan   Yeah! I—

Alex   You brought all your paperwork, all that?

Suzan   Of course, here . . .

Alex   They'll uh—they'll take care of that inside

Suzan   Okay
Sorry, not the most organized

Alex   Lemme just give you the quick overview,   **Suzan**   Papers everywhere
then I'll take you inside   Sorry

Suzan   Okay.

Alex   My colleague usually does this but we're moving quickly here, welcome to
November

Suzan   Ready to go.

Alex (*reading from a script*)   This is a fulfillment center.

Suzan   I'm gonna sit down.

Alex   Don't do that

Suzan   Oh

Alex   Just

Suzan   Sorry

Alex   Yeah, just stay on your feet for a minute.

Suzan   Absolutely.

Alex (*back to script*)   This is a fulfillment center, um, so this is the main distribution
center for the greater New Mexico region, every order that needs to go out to Santa
Fe or Albuquerque, believe it or not, comes through here.

Suzan   Wow!

Alex   . . .
So that's approximately 10,000 packages a day, each of which may contain multiple
items located at different points around the shipping floor. And those volumes double
or sometimes triple during the holiday season, as New Mexicans depend on us to . . .
make their holiday dreams come true.

He closes his eyes, takes a deep breath.

Suzan   You alright there?

Alex   —holiday dreams come true. So that means we have an important job here. An
important responsibility

Suzan   Lots of gifts

Alex   Especially during the holiday season

Suzan   I would bet, lots of gifts going everywhere, I bet

Alex   Sorry, could you actually just let me get through this?

Suzan   No problem.

Alex (*back to script*)   You've ordered from us?

Suzan   What do you mean?

Alex   As a customer, you've—been on the website, you've—

Suzan   Uh yeah, I'm sure at some point . . . yes.

Alex   Great, so you know how satisfying that is to um receive the thing you ordered, in good condition, on time or before you expected it. That's a good feeling, right?

Suzan   The best feeling.

Alex   Great. So that feeling is our business. We need to create that feeling every time, for our customers. That means the lowest prices on the front end, and on the back end, here, that means *relentless*, ah, relentless, ah . . .
Sorry.

Suzan   Senior moment, huh?

Alex   I've just . . . been getting these headaches

Suzan   Oh gosh

Alex   . . .
Give me a second.

Suzan   Do you wanna sit down?

Alex   Yeah
I'm sorry

Suzan   No problem!

Alex   Tell me if anyone's coming?

Suzan   Oh! Okay
Pain is the worst
My back has been
(*Realizing she shouldn't mention her physical problems:*) Well.

Pause.

Suzan   I know a trick actually

Alex   It'll pass it's   **Suzan**   Used to be really yeah,
                                          into bodywork and stuff
                                          Bend down?

Alex   Uh, no.

Suzan   Trust me, it'll help.
Bend over?

Alex   Uuuuh . . . .

Warily, he puts his head between his knees.

Suzan   Just like that, yeah, just like that

She puts her hands on his back.

Alex   What are you, you can't / touch me!

Suzan   Shhh

Alex   You really can't touch me

Suzan   To make it work, you actually need to be quiet.

She touches him.

Alex   Oh God that's

Suzan   You have to

Alex   So. Good.

Suzan   You have to be quiet.
You have to be really quiet, if you want the pain to go away.

She continues to touch him.

A buzzer sounds far away inside the fulfillment center.

It becomes clear that **Alex** *is crying.*

Suzan   Oh, honey.
Oh, it's alright.

Alex   I'm sorry.

Suzan   Are you kidding?
It's good.

He finishes crying.

Alex   Oh my God.

Suzan   Yeah

Alex   I don't know what happened there

Suzan   You released something.

Alex (*standing*)   This is a fulfillment center.
I did that part.
Thank you.

Suzan   Sure.

Alex   I'm sorry.

Suzan   No.

Alex   Listen you're gonna be fine here. It's not that hard.

Suzan   Oh, that's nice of you to say. I appreciate that. I do.

And hey—
Maybe it'll even be fun!

Scene Two

The apartment, that evening.

Alex *and* **Madeleine**.

Madeleine *has just arrived.*

They're drinking wine.

Madeleine   So yeah but basically it was a nightmare because I had to have like fifteen hundred goodbye drinks, different goodbye drinks, I kept trying to get everyone together at the same time, but no one was available at the same time, so I spent like my entire last week in New York having different drinks in different neighborhoods mostly with people like Brian and Elena

Alex   That sucks

Madeleine   Yeah people I don't even like, but they were like "we have to get together before you move," so I was like ugh fine, and then Sarah ended up being out of town the whole week for this work trip, so I didn't even get to say bye to her, and like I was trying to see Marta, but she had this client presentation to prepare for, so we could only meet up briefly on Monday night, blah blah. And then I woke up this morning and there was still shit all over the apartment, I hadn't even packed, so I panicked, and I was like aaah! Running around, shoving stuff into boxes, so I'm sorry in advance, don't kill me, but I'm not sure what stuff is in what box?

Alex   I thought you were gonna label them

Madeleine   Yeah but it's gonna be a surprise instead, yay. Also we have *so much junk*. The kitchen was the worst, I was like do we actually have this much silverware? I threw some of it out, sorry

Alex   Wait what did you throw out?

Madeleine   Just . . . stuff. Forks, mostly, dude, we had thousands of forks.

Alex   I feel like that's not true

Madeleine   Anyway so I'm throwing all this stuff away, and throwing everything else into boxes, I barely had time to clean the apartment

Alex   You didn't clean it?

Madeleine   I mean I swept and stuff, sort of

Alex   They're gonna take it out of our deposit

Madeleine   Well, yeah okay thanks for the feedback, I mean maybe if you'd been there to help, I mean I was doing it by myself

I mean fuck you I was doing it by myself

Alex   I know I know, thank you
Sorry

Madeleine   It's fine, but, so, I'm running late for the plane and then the Uber's late because the guy can't find me, I'm like there's a pin on the map, go towards the pin, I'm the pin, but whatever I made the flight, but I'm sweaty as hell, like I'm sitting in my seat and I can smell the sweat like wafting up

Alex   Gross

Madeleine   Fuck you! I packed my deodorant, it's in some box.

Alex   Can't wait until you find it.

Madeleine   I smell fine, fuck you!

Alex   Lemme test

Madeleine   Gross

Alex   Smell test

Madeleine   Gross

Alex   Smell test smell test

Madeleine   Gross stop

Alex   C—

Madeleine   You're an asshole

They kiss.

The fire alarm goes off.

Alex   Shit

Alex *runs offstage to the kitchen.*

Madeleine   Should we order some sushi?

Alex   I don't think they have that here.

Madeleine *pours herself more wine.*

Madeleine   So yeah and then I get here, you're not here, it's like 2 p.m., I'm alone in this fucking apartment, we gotta decorate this place

Alex (*offstage*)   Yeah I'm sorry I just haven't had time

Madeleine   And it's so quiet, I mean have you noticed that, it's so goddamn quiet in New Mexico, when I got off the plane I was like fuck. And I told work I was gonna be traveling all day, there's a conference call but I don't need to be on it, so I have no responsibilities, I'm off the grid, and I decide to go for a walk. What are you doing in there?

Alex I'm just salvaging our dinner

Madeleine So anyway I decide to walk into town.
I started walking along the side of the highway? Is there another way to get there?

Alex Yeah there's a whole path

Madeleine Well, I missed the path so I'm walking along the side of this highway, or road, I don't know, there weren't many cars, it was like some fucking Tombstone shit out there. I think I saw a tumbleweed.
There were all these weird adobe houses in the distance.
And then like twenty minutes in my phone died and there didn't seem to be any town appearing so I was like I should turn back, and I turned around, and then I kept walking and like I wasn't seeing the turnoff for this place, but then I thought I saw it but I ended up in this totally other you know land of weird adobe houses, and there was like fucking *no one* out in the yards, or not even yards, like little rock gardens. All the shades were down on the houses, and I started to get really thirsty.
And *then* I was like is this a stand-your-ground state? Like am I gonna get shot by a crazy old white man if I knock on a door? And then I was like, is this when I die?

Alex *returns.*

Alex Part of it is burnt, but the other part isn't cooked, so I cut the burnt part off and we just have to wait for the uncooked part to cook.

Madeline . . .
Anyway then I kept walking and I realized I was actually only two streets away from this place so I made it back alive in the end. Yay.

Alex There *is* fun stuff to do here

Madeleine Like what

Alex We can go hiking

Madeleine Fuck you

Alex There's supposed to be beautiful trails

Madeleine There's no trees, there's no grass, it's so bleak

Alex There's good galleries

Madeleine Yeah I bet they're really excellent galleries, really world-class art.
The world's best collection of, like, dogs playing poker. / Bucking broncos.

Alex Okay, can you like

Madeleine What

Alex I mean it's not New York

Madeleine I know

Alex You can't expect New York things

Madeleine   I know that, I'm not an idiot

Alex   It's kind of beautiful here, I don't know
And yeah, there's not that much stuff to do
So we'll have to like
Make our own fun
Maybe you should just, like, reserve judgment
See how it goes

Madeleine   I'm not making any judgments!
I'm totally open
And yeah, maybe it'll be fun

Alex   Maybe we'll become totally new people
Than our New York selves
Maybe we'll feel like totally free

Madeleine   Yeah . . .
It's only six months, I can survive anything for six months

Alex   . . . .

Madeleine   . . . the duration of this experience is six months, right?

Alex   Yeah . . .

Madeleine   Yeah, what do you mean, yeah?

Alex   If I do well. If things go well.

Madeleine   What do you mean?

Alex   I mean they've put me in this extremely high pressure situation with minimal support to see if I do well. And if I do, then I get the transfer, and we can move to Seattle.

Madeleine   Dude

Alex   What?

Madeleine   You didn't tell me it was conditional

Alex   Well, I'm just like . . . figuring this out now.
It's hard, I've never actually managed people.

Madeleine   At the start-up you did.

Alex   I got fired from the start-up

Madeleine   Yeah, well
It wasn't the right fit for you

Alex   No, they fired me because I sucked.

Madeleine   Dude

Alex   What?

Madeleine   Don't.

Alex   Sorry

Pause.

Alex   Hey I wanna show you something.
Close your eyes.

Madeleine   No.

Alex   Close your eyes.

Madeleine   I *hate* surprises.
Do *not* attack me.

Alex   I won't.

Madeleine   Do *not* tickle me. I hate being tickled. Everyone's like: it's fun. I'm like no. It's not fun.

Alex   Just close your eyes

She does.

He digs in his pocket, pulls out a ring, holds it out.

Alex   Okay open them

Madeleine   *AAAAAH—what the fuck is this a joke?*

Alex   Uh—no?

Madeleine   This is the worst fucking timing, this is—*not* romantic it's are you proposing to me?

Alex   No

Madeleine   Then what the fuck are you doing?

Alex   I'm just showing you the ring I wanna see if you like the ring

Madeleine   Well, why are you showing me the ring, what: you bought this?

Alex   Yeah

Madeleine   Well, why are you showing it to me now you're freaking me out!

Alex   I just want to see if you like it

Madeleine   That's not how it *works*, you don't

Alex   Okay

Madeleine   *Spring* this on me, you don't do that!

Alex   I thought it would be a nice surprise for when you got here

Madeleine   It's *not* a nice surprise I don't want you thrusting rings at me

Alex   I thought it would give rise to a nice discussion

Madeleine   Well, I don't want a nice discussion!

Not right now
Not just out of the blue when I just got here / Jesus Christ

Alex   Fine
Jesus

Madeleine   I'm just—
You scared me
It's just not the right time

He puts the ring away.

She feels guilty.

Madeleine   Hey, how's your headaches?

Alex   Fine, I just gotta get more sleep

Madeleine   Not gonna happen now that I'm here!
Bow chica wow wow

Pause.

Alex   I should go check on dinner

Madeleine   Hey there is one thing I want to do here, actually
I was reading online that there's this sculpture garden, this guy . . . I forget his name
. . . probly someone you would have studied in Scully's class

Alex   I don't know

Madeleine   Come on it's everyone knows him it's these huge like monolithic they
kind of dwarf the human they're set up outside in like this it's very stark. That's all I
remember. It's these very stark large huge sculptures. I was thinking we could go on
Saturday.

Alex   I have to be at work really early on Sunday.

Madeleine   Well, we can go in the afternoon, be back by the evening.
Come on I thought you wanted to explore!

Alex   Yeah
Okay

Madeleine   Yeah?
Okay good.
I think it will be fun.

Scene Three

The campground, evening.

John *is working on his car.*

Suzan *approaches.*

Suzan   Working on your car, huh?

John   Yeah

Suzan   Nice

John   Not really

Suzan   I mean, it looks like it runs!

John   Yeah, that's—

Suzan   Mine's completely on the fritz over there, totally conked out the second I arrived here, so any car that I see that looks like it runs I'm like: nice car.

John   . . .

Suzan   You sleep in the back there or you have a tent or . . .

John   In the back

Suzan   Oh great! Well, that's nice, that must be nice

John   Not really. Pretty umm cramped

Suzan   Cramped yeah I was gonna say bet it's pretty cramped there, then, yeah.

John   . . .
(*i.e. "see you later"*) Alright.

Suzan   I've got a tent over by the um the
Water fountains, the bathrooms
A little too close to the bathrooms for my taste but it's fine it's
This is a good place, I think

John   Yup, it's pretty good

Suzan   All of the amenities

John   Not a whole lot of amenities

Suzan   Right but it's got all of them!
Listen, sorry
I'm—I have this—[*bottle*]
If you   **John**   I
                                                  Don't really drink

Suzan   No, sure, I, sure, it's something I—just—to help me sleep—was looking for someone who

John   Uh-huh

Suzan   No one really here except for that RV
And they look bundled up pretty tight

John   Like I said I

Suzan   Sure

John   Don't really drink

Suzan   Uh-huh
Wondering if you wanna um
Just sit with me

John   Oh

Suzan   For a minute

John   Um

Suzan   I know it's
I just like to have a little
Company   **John**
Before I   Alright
                                           Yeah

Suzan   Yeah?

John   Okay

Suzan   It's just a thing for me I don't like to drink alone

John   I hear you

Suzan   You know?

John   Yeah

Suzan   My dad always used to do that when he got home, sit in the living room, have a drink with my mother. My sister and me on the rug, we'd be watching TV . . . course that was before he left.

John   You hear that song?

Suzan   Oh on the

John   Radio, yeah, car radio, yeah

Suzan   I love this song

John   That's all this station plays.
"Classic rock"   **Suzan**   Haha, right they just play one um—
One song

Suzan   Right that's

John   "Stairway to Heaven"

Suzan   Right that's the usual one it's

John   Nothing else

Suzan   Oh God it's these oldies stations are um

John   "One song"

Suzan   Hahaha oh that's too funny that's
You are really funny
That is really true
But I like this song actually
It's
Actually so beautiful
Course I'm a big fan of all this stuff
Joni Mitchell, she's my gal
Probly a little before your time

John   Joni Mitchell?

Suzan   She's the one with the

John   Nice voice?

Suzan   Yeah, the . . . pretty, high voice
(*Singing*) "California . . ."
You know

John   Hahaha
I like her

Suzan   She's the best.
Kind of a patron saint for a lot of us women of a certain age who sort of took to the
road with our guitars, you know, I was a singer too, back then, course I never had *that*
kind of success, but I did alright for a little while. Traveled. East Coast, through the
country, West.
Friends you'd make, on the road.
"Come stay with us!"
"Sure!"
"This is Ken," you know, "and this is Alice," or whatever, "and here's a joint," you know,
 and etcetera . . .
"Cool man, cool, sure. We'll just travel together for awhile."
Anyway
Probly a *little* before your time.

John   Not too much

Suzan (*playfully warning him*)   Uh-uh-uh

John   I'm forty-two

Suzan   Well, that's young!

John   I don't feel young
In my body

Suzan   Well, you *look* pretty young to me
Ever tried yoga?

John   Yoga?

Suzan   Yeah, you know, with the

John   No

Suzan   Oh you got to, you have to

John   Haha not really my /sort of

Suzan   No really it's
Here I'll

Johsn   Nah

Suzan   I'm serious it's

John   No
I don't
Really

Suzan   Alright

John   Go in for
That sort of stuff

Suzan   Okay

John   Just kinda like to

Suzan   Sure

John   Stick to what I know
How to do
Already.

Pause.

Suzan   "Downward dog"

John   Hahaha

Suzan   "Upward-facing dog"

John   Hahaha

Suzan   That kind of thing

John   You're funny

Suzan   Well
I can be funny, sure.
Got kind of a "wry" sense of humor.
Don't drink, huh?

John   Nah
Problems

John	**Suzan**
	Oh
You know	Sure, I—

I know some people like that.

I was living with my girlfriend
Really nice um girlfriend
Over in Albuquerque

Oh

About an hour um
Hour or so
South
Of here

Okay
Yeah

Uh-huh

Right
I drove by
On my way here

Suzan   Nice place

John   It's a terrible, terrible place

Suzan   Oh, okay, hahaha

John   Just completely
Really um
Rough, nothing sort of place.
She kicked me out.
Pretty um—so that's
Got tired of me

Suzan
Well
Guess she uh
Gosh

So I'm
Yeah

Suzan   So you came here

John   All I got is the car at this point
Some
Stuff
Inside
Guess she got tired of me.

Suzan   She's pretty?

John   What?

Suzan   A beautiful woman?

John   Yeah she's

Suzan   Gotta be

John   Gorgeous

Suzan   I figured
Gotta be

John   Yeah

Suzan   Careful of the pretty ones, minute they're tired of you they'll drop you.

John   That's what she did.

Suzan   Well
You're a very handsome

John Well	**Suzan**
Guess it wasn't	Sometimes it's not
She	But you're, you'll
Yeah . . .	

Suzan   Pretty women
Gotta be careful of them
I used to be one
So I know

His phone buzzes, he starts texting.

Hard to believe now, I know, but I used to be one.
Hard to believe I know.
 "Smartphone," huh?

John   Yeah it came with the
Plan

Suzan   I guess everyone pretty much has one now. Not me. (*Pulling out her flip phone:*) I have this little guy but not um—I just don't find myself needing any extra features. For that price, you'd have to really need them.
That her?

John   What?

Suzan   That your girlfriend?

John   No, just . . . Someone I met online.

Suzan   Oh okay, hahaha

She waits.

He finishes texting.

John   You got anyone special?

Suzan   Oh me?
Not now
Not right now
My sister lives about an hour from here

John   Oh you gonna

Suzan   Nah

John   See her?

Suzan   Nah, no, probably not

I don't
Want to bug her

John   Okay

Suzan   She's

John   Alright   **Suzan**   It's a
Long story

John   Okay

Suzan   Yeah, she wouldn't wanna hear from me
She doesn't wanna hear too much from me anymore, so

John *yawns.*

John   Well

Suzan   Oh

John   Guess I better

Suzan   Sure, you're probly

John   Tuckered out

Suzan   I gotcha.
I didn't catch your

John   Lemme know if you uh

Suzan   Oh

John   Need anything

Suzan   Oh well, that is really nice of you

John   Gonna get cold in that tent.

Suzan   Well, that is really nice of you, and I might take you up on that
Gonna get pretty cold over there
Gonna be a pretty rough—

John   Cheers

Suzan   Yup, cheers
Hahaha, okay
Night

Scene Four

Afternoon.

A bar.

Madeleine, *with drink in hand.*

John *enters.*

Madeleine   You're older than I expected

John   Haha

Madeleine   You need to update your picture, dude.

John   That's the only one I have.

Madeleine   It's pretty fuckin' outdated.
I mean—sorry.
I mean you are attractive.

John   Okay

Madeleine   In like an ugly-hot way.

John   You are also attractive
Lady

Madeleine   Uh-huh, well, this is off to a really great start.
You wanna get a drink?

John   I don't drink.

Madeleine   Warning sign!

Pause.

Madeleine   You ever feel like everyone's kind of
Staring at you?

John   Not really.
Maybe you have a um
Inflated
Sense of
Self, hahaha.

Madeleine   Oh. Okay.
You're a little different.

John   I'm quiet

Madeleine   You are definitely either a serial killer or um

John   I'm not a

Madeleine Autistic or Asperger's you know one of those Rain men	**John** I'm just Quiet

Pause.

John   Your profile said that you're looking for something kind of

Madeleine   I don't wanna get into that yet, okay?

Give a girl a chance to have a drink.

John   Big drinker, huh?

Madeleine   Says who?

John   Seems like you've had a few

Madeleine   I hide it well

John   Not that well

Madeleine   Fuck you!
So what is this for you?
You into Black women?

John   No.
I mean not more than at a normal level.

Madeleine   Educated women?

John   Sure

Madeleine   Young women?

John   Not *so* young.

Madeleine   What does *that* mean?

John   I just thought you had a nice face.

Madeleine   Nice face, wow, okay.

John   A nice energy

Madeleine   A "nice energy."
And so you work some kind of blue collar uh
You've got the whole jean jacket kind of thing going on

John   I'm a carpenter.

Madeleine   Hah!
Sorry
No, that's great, that's
Serious?

John   Yeah

Madeleine   That's like a real skill.
And you're into um so you saw me and you said
She has a nice face, she'll be fun to kill
With my like my

John   No

Madeleine   "Hammer"

John   No

Madeleine   My "saw"

John   I'm not going to kill you.

Madeleine   I guess I'll just take your word for that then

John   I'm a good guy I'm just—a little nervous I guess I'm not very articulate.

Madeleine   Well, why don't you get a drink or something.

John   Like I said I don't drink

Madeleine   You're an alcoholic?

John   No I just choose not to.

Madeleine   So it's like a philosophy.

John   Not really.

Madeleine   So what is your philosophy?

John   What?

Madeleine   Like your personal philosophy: do you have one?

John   Like a motto?

Madeleine   No not like a motto, a motto's like "an apple a day keeps the doctor away," I mean like guiding principles, like a personal philosophy. Everyone needs one. What's yours?

John   . . .
Live and let live.

Madeleine   Okay so how do you apply that.

John   What?

Madeleine   Like how is that relevant to you? What do you do with that?

John   Well, I try to . . . live and let live.
Like you let me live my life, I'll let you live yours.

Madeleine   So do you eat meat?

John   What?

Madeleine   Do you eat meat?

John   Uh . . . yes.

Madeleine   So it doesn't apply to animals.

John   I'm not sure.

Madeleine   Interesting.

Pause.

John   So where do you work?

Madeleine   Okay can we just not do *that*?

John   Okay

Madeleine   Let's just talk when we have something to say and not do the whole "interview" like "where do you work" type thing

John   Well, do you wanna go somewhere?

Madeleine   No!
I mean not right now.
I mean that, for me, at this point, would be an insane thing to do, with you.

John   I'm gonna get a glass of water then

Madeleine   Rude.

He leaves.

She is alone.

He returns.

Madeleine   So where do *you* work? What is there in this town?

John   I thought you didn't want to do a

Madeleine   Yeah, well, now we're moving on to the interview sort of portion of the

John   I don't really want to do that either.

Madeleine   Well, then, say something you know Jesus Christ keep up your end of the

John   You're kind of aggressive aren't you

Madeleine   . . .
Uuuuh

John   You're kind of a bitch, aren't you
. . .
You're kind of a little cunt, aren't you

Madeleine   *What?*

John   Hahaha

Madeleine   Okay, I'm going to go.
That is—
Wow.

John   Wait no
Sorry! I thought that maybe

Madeleine   You thought you could just suddenly call me a cunt and that would somehow be appealing to me?

John   Yeah I guess
Hahaha
Bad call

Madeleine   Yeah really fucking bad call.
I'm gonna go

John   No stay I just you have such a nice face, really, just uh just stay to the end of this song

Madeleine Oh God that's So Cheesy!	**John** I really Love This song, it's one of my favorites It's . . . Joni Mitchell.

Madeleine   No it's not.

John   Yeah it is. / I think it is.

Madeleine   It's fucking not Joni Mitchell.

John   Just—shhh—just can we just—

They listen.

The song is barely audible. It's not Joni Mitchell. But it is beautiful.

Something happens between them—a vulnerable moment.

It's too much for **Madeleine***, she looks away.*

The song ends.

Madeleine   It's not Joni Mitchell.
Joni Mitchell has a beautiful voice, that was shit.

John   Okay

Madeleine   That was a fraud.

John   I believe you.

Madeleine   This has been thoroughly weird, dude

John   For me too

Madeleine   Great, well we agree.
Good luck on your um
Your journey

He raises his hand like: bye.

She leaves.

Scene Five

The alley behind the fulfillment center.

Alex *calls* **Madeleine**.

Alex   Hey, I wish you'd pick up when I call
I mean it's fine if you're working or something, but you could text and say that
Or you could text and say you don't want to text, or whatever
I was thinking about you and
I miss you
Even though I'll see you tonight
And I'm looking forward to the sculpture garden, on Saturday
It'll be fun to do something like that, together.
'K
Bye

He hangs up.

Suzan *approaches.*

Suzan   Hey!

Alex   Aaaah!

Suzan   Scared ya!

Alex   Jesus

Suzan   Is this the right place to take lunch, or—   **Alex**
Just kidding I knew I'd um   Uh yeah no this is where the
Find you out here I   managers usually
brought you something it's

Alex   Oh

Suzan   Cookies! From the

Alex   Thanks . . .

Suzan   I'm not in a living situation right now where I can *make* them but these are
pretty good, they're crunchy and uh—
(*Reading the label*) "Chiptastic." Not sure that's actually a word, but anyway—here!

She holds them out until he takes them.

Suzan   I know you've—you're here when I get here and still here when I leave so I
know you're working really hard, I mean we're all working, and I guess you don't have
to move around as much and stuff, but the hours are probably, I mean I can't imagine.
You're captaining the ship! My generation at your age they put us on the poop deck.
Hahaha.

Alex   Well, thanks for these. That's nice of you.

She digs in her purse.

Alex   This is usually a place where the Managers sort of
Associates are usually
Take their lunch
Out front

Suzan
What?

Know I brought the uh

Suzan   Sorry, do you mind if I try one?

Alex   Oh

Suzan   I hate to ask

Alex   . . . no, please

Suzan   Thanks, sweetie, I thought I had a little granola bar, but I must have left it in the, in the . . .
These are fantastic.

Alex   Usually though you're gonna wanna take your lunch where the other associates do
Out front

Suzan   What's that?

Alex   You're gonna wanna take your lunch where the other associates do, usually, out front, because if any of the other managers saw me there'd be—it's not an official thing? It's just—

Suzan   I gotcha: they like to keep us separated.
I had a job once managing a bakery. Well, managing, I don't know. I ran the cash register, and then I was supposed to lock up at the end of the day. Put the cash in a little whatever, take it to the bank. And I gotta tell you: I hated it. Hated the responsibility. I'm bad with money, I don't like locks, I'm opposed to locks on principle I think, I believe everything should be open to everybody! Why not. Course maybe you could call that "utopian" but what the hell, I say why not try it. I never put locks on anything. Maybe that's why I'm always losing my stuff.

He gets a text.

Starts texting back.

Suzan   That your girlfriend or your wife or . . .

Alex   My girlfriend . . . .

Suzan   Oh!
You live together? Or . . .

Alex   She just got here. From New York.

Suzan   *That's* a big change

Alex   Apparently.

He texts.

Alex   Her company is letting her work from home, and so she's working from home, I keep telling her to get out of the apartment, but she doesn't like the town, blah blah blah, it's a whole thing.

He texts.

Like I told her if you don't wanna come you don't have to come, but she came anyway and now I feel like she's blaming me and I'm like don't blame me when I *told* you you didn't have to come! And like get out of the house and maybe you won't be so unhappy!

Suzan   You've been together a while?

Alex   Since college.

Suzan   Long time!

Alex   Yeah

Suzan   Well how old are you, honey

Alex   Thirty-one

Suzan   That's a long time.
That's a good age!
You're a spring chicken.

He finishes texting, puts his phone away.

Alex   And like
I kind proposed to her a couple days ago?

Suzan   Oh God! What'd she say

Alex   She screamed

Suzan   Well, that's great

Alex   Like in terror

Suzan   Oh God

Alex   Like a full-on scream of terror

Suzan   Well, that's . . .

They both find this funny.

Suzan   I almost got married, a couple times.
There was one man—Gary—this was, oh, thirty, gosh, years ago, and I've had other—but this was the first time that I really thought about it, because he was, you know my judgment can be very bad, and I'm aware of that, but this was a good man,

and I was deeply, deeply in love with him. You know how that is? Where you really would—jump into the fire, have you had that?

Alex   I think so.

Suzan   Anyway, he asked, and I was like, I need some time, and I took some time, and the more time I took, the more I thought about it, and I imagined it, and I came to feel—I had a sort of sinking feeling about it. And everything had been kind of golden before, very wonderful, but all of a sudden I started to feel very—bad when I was around him, very kind of sad. And I couldn't explain it. But I couldn't, you know, shake it. And two weeks later I said Gary, I can't marry you, and I actually can't be with you anymore, and I left.

Alex *is lost in thought.*

Suzan *watches him.*

Suzan   I'm intuitive
Which means
I just get sense of people right away.
You have a lot of light around you
And I think everything's gonna work out just fine.

Some kind of moment between them that is too much for **Alex** *– he looks away.*

A buzzer sounds somewhere inside the fulfillment center.

This is their cue to get back inside.

Alex   Listen I want to apologize about the headache thing

Suzan   The headache thing

Alex   When you did the thing on my back

Suzan   Oh God it was fine that's! Are you kidding me?

Alex   No, I, it was, I've been wanting to apologize, I—it was unprofessional of me. I shouldn't have put you in that position.

Suzan   Put me in a position! I was happy to help

Alex   No but I shouldn't have acted like that.
It was inappropriate.

Suzan   Okay

Alex   You know, under different circumstances it would be fine, but
We're at work.

Suzan   Absolutely

Alex   Sorry
You know

Suzan   Oh honey, I do. They're watching you, the big kahunas.

How are my times though, I'm doing good? Keeping up?

Alex   You're . . . getting better

Suzan   Great! Oh, great, yeah, think I'm getting the hang of it.
Those buzzers are driving me a little crazy . . . reminds me of school somehow . . .
gotta get to class! But I understand. They're necessary! Keep us on track. Everyone
running around in there, little mice . . . it's fun.

Alex   But yeah you gotta get your numbers up.

Suzan   But I'm getting better you said

Alex   Yeah

Suzan   Well, great

Alex   But you're still, yeah . . .
You need to move faster, still.

Suzan   But don't run.

Alex   You can't run.

Suzan   Can I jog?
Just kidding hahaha, message received, I will walk faster.
The thing is, honey?
I am doing my best.

Alex   I know that

Suzan   I really am. I am giving it my all.

Alex   And I see that and you're definitely improving.

Suzan   Well, that's great that's all you can ask for right?

Alex   I mean no actually, because there's certain metrics that you have to

Suzan   No I get that, but I am getting better, I will get there before too long

Alex   Right the thing is we don't have that long.
It's the middle of the holiday season, so like, and it's great that you're improving, but
you need to improve . . . faster.

Suzan   Well, I'm doing the best I can

Alex   Right totally

Suzan   So what else can I do

Alex   I mean . . .
Yeah, just keep doing your best then.

Suzan   And honey: I will.

Alex   And yeah and don't sit down.

Suzan   Well, that was

Alex   During your shift.

Suzan   I wasn't sitting, I was leaning

Alex   It just kinda looked like you were sitting on the ledge.

Suzan   And I totally get why it looked like that, it's just that I wasn't sitting, I was leaning because I stopped for a second because I actually got lost? It's very confusing in there

Alex   The aisle numbers are directly over the aisles.

Suzan   Right but it's very confusing, because you have the letters, and the numbers, and it's kind of counterintuitive actually, but . . .
I did stop, for a second.
I have some back issues, to be honest.
It's not that serious but some days are worse than others. And then other days are fine! But yesterday I was having a rough day.
I have a fair amount of pain on the lower part of my spine. And I have pain in my knees from—in my left knee I don't have much of a kneecap anymore, so it makes—I had a fall.

Pause.

Alex   These aren't my rules

Suzan   I know! And I popped a bunch of Advil this morning and I am feeling good

Alex   And you're getting better and I know that and I see you trying

Scene Six

The campsite, evening.

John *is standing there.*

Suzan *is crying.*

She's just gotten back from work.

She's exhausted.

Suzan   Can't do it I

John   Oh

Suzan   Can't can't do it I

John   Well

Suzan   Just so miserable to

John   Well, that's

Suzan   You ever had a job like that?

John   Yeah, sure

Suzan   I'm sorry I'm in um—so much pain I it's

John   Why don't you quit?

Suzan   Need the money

John   Well

Suzan   It's good money, and I need it
Trying, basically, to make it up to Maine

John   Okay

Suzan   Trying to make it up to Maine because there's a well a man who I used to be involved with hahaha it's a long um
Anyway he's always given me "safe harbor" when things were going *poorly*
And I'm actually I had been living with another man over in Tucson for a while but he turned out to be a bit
Anyway
Kind of "on the run" hahaha
Just need a little money to get me up to Maine until I
Because my car, it's completely, I can't *leave* it here

John   He couldn't send you money?
The guy up there?

Suzan   Well, I wanna kind of surprise him, you know, it's been a little while since I
Anyway I've asked him for money before so

John   You said you had a sister

Suzan   Yeah, well, hahaha, lot of water under *that* bridge
I mean she lives close but I
No I can't I—have exhausted that connection, I'll tell you that. That well is dry. My sister and me . . . we went kinda different directions in life so, and yeah, she doesn't want to hear from me too much anymore, so
Anyway if I can work here for a couple weeks or so I can make enough to you know take it to a mechanic, little bit longer is gas money, etcetera
So that's kind of *my* story

John   Alright

Suzan   Whew
I'm sorry I just
Had a really rough day there I was in a lot of pain.
It's not so bad
Some days it's not so bad

John   Handkerchief?

Suzan   Oh that's nice of you thanks
Got back here and I just started—bawling

John   Hahaha

Suzan   Like a kid! Hahaha
"I'm a widdle waaa waa"
Still working on that car, huh?

John   Fixing it up

Suzan   Alright! / A project

John   Yeah I've just been
Cleaning it
Fiddling

Suzan   I'd ask you to take a look at mine but I don't wanna impose

John   Ah I don't really know that much about cars, I'm just fiddling over here

Suzan   Gotcha
You could take a look at it though

John   Yeah I wouldn't wanna mess anything up.

Suzan   Gotcha, I hear ya

John   But
You wanna sit in it?

Suzan   In your car?

John   Yeah

Suzan   Well
Okay!

John   Hahaha

Suzan   Haha

They get into the car.

Suzan   Ope
Aaah
This is nice

John   Yeah

Suzan   Nice car

John   Yeah I've had this car since
About ten years ago I it's
I've put a lot of time into it
Work

Into it
It's one of my favorite things kind of a
Private space to just sit in while I
Drive

Suzan   Any interest in driving me up to Maine? Hahaha

John   Hahaha
Mmm

Suzan   Yeah could be fun!
Could be quite a trip hahaha!
I'll be fine
Couple weeks more
Three weeks more
Little spending money, get me up to Maine
Carry me to the next phase of my journey
My "life's journey"

John   Hahaha

Suzan   Haha
You're a funny man

John   What

Suzan   You are, just funny, here with your car
I don't know why that woman kicked you out
If I'da had you, I'da held onto you.

John   I'm not so great

Suzan   You're a good listener
Compassionate, I can tell that
Quiet
And easy on the eyes

John   Hahaha

Suzan   Ope! Who said that?

John   Hahaha

Suzan   Old enough to be your mother

John   No

Suzan   I am

John   No

Suzan   I really am

John   Not so old

Suzan   Well

She kisses him.

He doesn't stop her.

But he doesn't really participate.

Nonetheless, she is pleased.

John   Haha

Suzan   Ah . . .
Haha. *Well.*

She stares at him, smitten.

He turns his head, looks out the window.

Suzan	**John**
You could come up with me to Maine	So dark out there
If you wanted	
It's just an idea	
We could make a good time of it	
I know some good places	
There's this great cafe	
Where I stopped once	
Around 72, 73	
When I was traveling through	
That was a good time	
The height of my success!	
I had some fans	
Used to follow me around	
Well, a couple fans	
One or two	
One of them was the man I was involved with	
And his friend	
Big fans of me, of my music	
They used to follow me everywhere	

She sings a few bars—it's Joni Mitchell's "Woodstock."

He snores.

Suzan   Asleep!
Just like that
Beautiful man

She kisses his cheek.

Brushes his hair away from his face.

Sweet dreams

Scene Seven

Afternoon, the apartment.

Madeleine *is working from home.*

She's restless.

She considers having a drink.

Decides against it.

She walks back to her computer.

She thinks she hears something.

Madeleine   Hello?

Nothing.

Then **Alex** *is there.*

Alex   Hey.

Madeleine   JESUS CHRIST

Alex   Surprise!

Madeleine   It's the middle of the day what the fuck are you doing creeping up on me

Alex   Relax, I was just

Madeleine   Standing there watching me? That's EXTREMELY CREEPY

Alex   I'm sorry

Madeleine   What are you doing?

Alex   I took a break. To have, yeah, to have lunch with you.

Madeleine   They let you leave like that?

Alex   Someone's covering me.

Madeleine   I don't want you to self-sabotage.

Alex   I'm just taking a little break! Chill out.

Madeleine   Jesus.

Alex   So surprised!

Madeleine   Well, you scared me! I don't like that.
Do you want a sandwich or something?

Alex   Nah, I already ate

Madeleine   . . .

Alex   Is this your working from home outfit?

Madeleine   Yeah . . .

Alex   You look cute

Madeleine   You are like pathological. You believe I am always cute

Alex   That is correct. Even in these
Disgusting little sweatpants

Madeleine   Ohmygod, they're running pants

Alex   "Ohmygod, they're running pants."

Alex   Listen this is kind of out of the blue? But

Madeleine   No.

Alex   You know how you were saying you have like that fantasy?
Like the one where

Madeleine   I was *so* drunk.
That was like nine months ago!

Alex   I feel bad we never explored that.

Madeleine   Uh

Alex   I think we should explore that. I think we should do that.

Madeleine   Okay

Alex   Now

Madeleine   Why is your timing always so terrible?

Alex   It's gonna be fun.

Madeleine   Like using what metric?

Alex   Why don't you stop being a bitch for one second and just try and have a little
fun?

Madeleine   Woah

Alex   Sorry

Madeleine   No, that's okay

Alex   What's our safe word

Madeleine   Um:
Stop?
Or wait, no: roses.

Alex   Just like the word "roses"?

Madeleine   It's random

He leaves the room.

Alex (*offstage*)   Do some work, just do some work!

Madeleine   Jesus

Madeleine *pretends to work.*

But then she kind of gets caught up in actually working.

Alex *comes back in the room.*

He's wearing something different—maybe a hoodie and a hat?

He comes at her pretty aggressively.

Kissing her, trying to take her shirt off.

It's kind of hot at first.

Then the shirt gets tangled in her arms.

Everything is kind of tangled.

Alex *is very serious.*

Madeleine *starts laughing.*

She tries to contain it, but she can't stop.

Alex   Mad, stop.
Come on, stop!

More.

She laughs harder.

Madeleine   I'm sorry, I can't
I can't
I can't, I can't
I can't

Alex   You're supposed to say "roses"

Madeleine   Roses!
I'm sorry
It's better
In my mind, what is that hat

Alex   I thought

Madeleine   Oh my God, that's good

Maybe he laughs too.

Their laughter subsides.

Alex   What are you doing here all day

Madeleine   What do you mean

Alex   When you're here alone, what are you doing

Madeleine   I'm working

Alex   Are you drinking?

Madeleine   No!
Sometimes I have one right before you get home
You get home at like eight, it's totally normal to have a drink at night, dude

Alex   Okay

Madeleine   Normal people do that, I've done that the whole time we've been together, there's nothing new about that

Alex   Fine

Madeleine   You have a drink when you get home, when you're done with your workday, the only difference is, my workday ends, and I'm already home, so yeah, so I have a drink.

Alex   Just one?

Madeleine   Dude

Alex   Maybe you should find a cafe or something, stop working from home

Madeleine   I told you I don't like this town
Everyone stares at me

Alex   I just worry about you here
Spending all day alone

Madeleine   I'm done with all that stuff

Alex   Yeah?

Madeleine   Yes.
Yes.
I mean what the fuck is wrong with you why do you insist on treating me like a child and like micromanaging my life. I don't need you checking up on me. I am a grown. Adult. Woman.
I hate it when you do this it drives me batty batshit insane

He moves away, she yells after him in frustration.

Madeleine   AAAAAAH.

Pause.

Alex   I'm not doing so good at work
My metrics suck, my team is falling behind
I'm getting a bad feeling from my bosses

Madeleine   Well, have you talked to them, have you asked them for support?

Alex   It's considered a sign of weakness

Madeleine   Because I know at the start-up

Alex   I wish you would stop bringing that up

Madeleine   But it annoys me that you never thought critically about why it was that that didn't work out. I mean I feel like you had a kind of defeatist attitude about the whole thing, like you assumed you weren't doing well, and that you were in over your head, and you got down on yourself, and everyone started picking up on that, so yeah, it was a self-fulfilling prophecy, or whatever, and then you failed.
I'm trying to be encouraging here.
You're smart, man, you went to one of the best b-schools on the planet

Alex   NYU isn't really one of the best

Madeleine   It's right up there, and you nailed it, you did so good

Alex   It's b-school, the only way not to get an A is if you literally murder someone. Anyway it's all just stupid case studies, they didn't prepare us for this

Madeleine   Right so like that was school, and this is the real world, and yeah it's gonna be different.
What are you struggling with.

Alex   Just—managing people, I don't know
I'm just like: maybe this isn't even what I wanna do
Maybe I should have done music, like I wanted

Pause.

Madeleine   I moved here from New York.

Alex   I know

Madeleine   I packed up all our shit, and I left behind my friends, and I came here, to this nightmare desert shithole town, so that you could do well at this job, so that we could move to Seattle.

Alex   I know.

Madeleine   So like what are you telling me then.
You're gonna get fired?

Alex   . . .

Madeleine   I shouldn't have come.
I just honestly don't get it.
Why are you here in the middle of the day. I literally don't understand. Like go back there and figure out how to do a good job, and do it! I'm sorry.
You chose to do this.
This is what you chose to do.
So fuck.
Dude:
Do it.

Scene Eight

The alley behind the fulfillment center.

Alex *and* **Suzan**.

Alex   I have to, I'm sorry.

Suzan   Wait wait wait.
Come on.
I can do better! Hahaha
It's been a rough couple days, I think it's the weather, but once my body gets used to it—
Sometimes, okay, it takes a little while, to adjust, because I told you I'm coming from Tucson, where it is very hot, and here, I mean in there especially, it is *very* cold. I've been meaning to ask you, actually: why do they keep it so cold?

Alex   Yeah I don't know

Suzan   No really though, because I actually think if it was a little warmer, just normal temperature, we might move faster. I think people are very cold in there. You could suggest that to your bosses, might win you some points

Buzzer.

Alex *tries to leave.*

Suzan   Alex, wait
I am not the worst one in there, I will tell you that
So what, you're gonna fire all of us? I mean *that's* a good strategy, what, you gonna do it all yourself? I can see it now, running around trying to get all those damn boxes filled, "where is everything"

Alex   You *are* the worst
I mean of everyone on my team, your numbers are the worst
So this is where I'm gonna start, so
I'm really sorry.
I think you're a really great lady, and like . . . I like you.
But that doesn't matter, actually, here.
So good luck.

Suzan   Good luck, don't good luck me, that's—like it's out of your hands

Alex   It *is* out of my hands

Suzan   Why don't you take responsibility for your fucking actions, I mean if you're gonna fire me, say it

Alex   I already said it

Suzan   Say it to my face, don't blame the guys at the top, you know, like it's—don't blame the numbers, do it—

Alex   I already did

Suzan   —to my face, if you're gonna do it, own it, I mean say it right to me, say it!
Say it!

Scene Nine

Afternoon.

Madeleine *and* **John** *in the apartment.*

John *has just arrived.*

They're tense.

Madeleine   Thanks for coming

John   This your place?

Madeleine   Temporarily.
Yeah that's my

John (*looking at a photo on the wall*)   Boyfriend

Madeleine   Yeah

John   Skiing

Madeleine   Yup, we went skiing.

John   Looks like a nice guy

Madeleine   He's a really nice guy.

John   That's the old like that's the classic is that you're with someone nice so you
uh so you uh

Madeleine   Uh . . . yeah. I guess so.

John   That's a classic dynamic.

Madeleine   Well, I hate to bore you.

John   I'm not bored.
Are you?

Madeleine   Not yet.

John   Cheers.

Madeleine   Cheers.

They take a shot of vodka.

John   Cheers.

Madeleine   Skol.

They take a shot of vodka.

John   No more for me.

Madeleine *takes another shot.*

Madeleine   Cheers.

Madeleine *takes another shot.*

Madeleine   Cheers.

Madeleine *takes another shot.*

Madeleine   I fucking love alcohol.

John   Huh.

Madeleine   I love it maybe a little too much. That's what my therapist says. Said.
I had a great therapist back in the city. I miss her more than I miss my friends actually.
My friends don't really listen very well. My therapist listens very well. For a price.
In that way it's kind of a fucked-up thing it's like paying for a friend but I actually
don't mind that because I'm fundamentally a capitalist. Like I like capitalism. Like I
believe in paying money for goods and services.
Do you believe in that?

John   What?

Madeleine   Do you believe in paying money for goods and services?

John   I don't know.

Madeleine   Interesting.

John *approaches* **Madeleine**.

She moves away.

Madeleine   So yeah, this is my place, that's my boyfriend.
We met in college.
He's very patient with me.
He like, laughs at my jokes.
I like the way he smells
We have nice sex, it's not great? But it's nice
Sorry if this is TMI

John   What's that?

Madeleine   Don't worry about it.
I can picture our kids, they'd be fucking beautiful
I can picture our house
I can picture our whole life
I'll get another job, I hate working from home, maybe I'll start my own consulting
company. Rent a little office.
He'll do good at his job, get promoted, maybe, if he gets his shit together
We'll move to the suburbs, hire a gardener, I want a nice garden, but I don't want to
do it myself

Our kids will be very successful
Or one of them won't, we'll have one fuck-up, but the other two will be great
We'll each have an affair, but it'll be fine
We'll own a bunch of cool shit
We'll be happy, mostly, probly
And then we'll die.
Or none of that will happen
Maybe we'll break up and I'll move back to New York.

John   Huh

He approaches **Madeleine***, kisses her on the cheek.*

Madeleine   Okay

John   That's

Madeleine   Yeah, that's

She kisses him on the mouth.

They kiss.

Then he pulls away.

Madeleine   Uh . . .

John   Yeah . . .

Madeleine   So . . .

John   Maybe we can

Madeleine   Sure . . . that's fine . . .

John   Sorry, I—

Madeleine   That's nice, actually, maybe.
Ease into it

John   Talk a little bit

Madeleine   You should talk now
I've just been

John   Mind if I

Madeleine   Go for it

John   Thanks
Thanks for having me over

He take a little sip from the bottle.

Then a huge gulp.

Madeleine   Woah there

John   I'm forty-two

Madeleine   Okay

John   Older, I'm an older guy, that's true
Not compared to some, but to me, in comparison to my own life, I'm the oldest I've ever been.
I'm a smart guy though they used to say I was one of the smartest in my high school

Madeleine   Okay

John   Blue ribbon, all that, top of the class . . .
You mind if I?

Madeleine   Fire away.

John   The sweet stuff.

Madeleine   Nectar of the gods.

He drinks more from the bottle.

John   I don't know, it's funny.
Hard for me to remember sometimes what everything was about, what happened.
Just spitballin' here.
You had high school and then you had um, or I had, uh the period after school, in which I was—tough to say, lot of stuff I think at that point, probly some bad uh . . . bad stuff.

Madeleine   Uuuh . . .

John   Lots of images of that time, you know, of me, of what I was doing, just kind of images, not really placed into stories. Snapshots.
I'm here . . .
I'm doing this . . .
I'm kind of like this
(*A memory:*) Hahaha! And then there was . . .!
Or yeah, not.
Does that make sense?

Madeleine   Not too much.

John   Yeah I don't try to talk too much when I try to talk too much I kind of get off the rails and lose track of it.

Madeleine   We can just hang out.

John   No it's good for me to talk it's good for me I don't know.
I was living down over in Albuquerque for about two or three years
By myself, at first
And then this woman "picked me up"
But yeah she turned out to be kind of a fucking cunt

Madeleine   *Oh*kay.

John   That ever happen to you?
You think you know someone and then they turn on you?
Like in the case of this woman she turned out to be a fucking bitch, you know the type, just one of those completely stupid cunts

Madeleine Okay listen	**John** In the way she treated me.
Uh	So yeah so
This is a little bit	I had to uh
	I had to uh

Madeleine   I actually

John   Leave, actually I had to

Madeleine   I think you should go.

Pause.

John   That ever happened to you? That someone you thought you knew turned out to be a complete fucking cunt?

Madeleine   I'd like you to / go.

John   In my case it's usually women, it's almost always uh *women*

Madeleine   Yeah this is getting really—

John   Not what you expected huh?
Yeah people are always saying that to me: I thought you were gonna be different.
But I'm always like: I didn't make you any promises, I just show up, try to be myself.
But people don't really tend to like that so, but.
That's difficult for me. Can you imagine? How that would be difficult for me?
"Be yourself" and then people don't like it.
It's funny though because I just listened to you talk, and now I'm trying to talk, I thought that like, and you don't want to listen, and I just think that's funny. And I've tried to be sympathetic, you know, to listen, to you, another uh "human," right? Human animal, right? I've done that for you. I've sat here and listened while you blabbed on just like women always do, blahblahblah, shut the fuck up Jesus Christ I mean don't you people ever stop?

Madeleine   Okay get out
GET OUT

Pause.

Madeleine   I'm serious I want you to leave

John   Please

Madeleine No	**John** I need you to listen, please
No	

No I said No I SAID NO   *I've got so much to say*
GET AWAY

He lunges at her.

She is scared but holds her ground.

He stops.

John   Hahaha
Jeez
You don't need to be scared
You really
Freaked out there.
I'm not like that.

He walks to the door.

I guess I just thought that maybe
You'd be someone
To talk to

He leaves.

She is shaking.

Sculptures rise up around her.

They are enormous.

Alex *enters.*

It's Saturday.

Scene Ten

Alex *and* **Madeleine** *in the sculpture garden.*

Alex   Jesus

Pause.

Alex   These sculptures are big.

Madeleine   Yeah

Alex   They're so big.
What do you think?

Madeleine   Wow

Alex   I googled this before we came—
They're supposed to like change the way we think
Or feel

Or behave or something
While we're inside it.
Like it's not supposed to be "about" anything
It's just supposed to I think
Make us feel small
Which is kind of cool
But also like: *fuck you, sculpture*—you know?

Madeleine   I wish there was somewhere to sit.

Alex   We're not supposed to be sitting!
We're supposed to be changing our relationship to space.

He practices changing his relationship to space.

Madeleine   I still wish there was like—a chair.

Alex   We can leave do you wanna keep going? There's a cafe.

. . .
You alright?

Madeleine   Yeah sorry.

Alex   You seem quiet today.

Madeleine   Just taking it in I guess.

Alex   I fired this old woman, one of my employees.
She was one of the worst, like I've got other bad ones, but she was really bringing down our times.
And I tried to do it politely, you know, professionally, but she kind of freaked out. She was like telling me I was doing something wrong, and calling me a bad person.
And I was like: lady, don't personalize this, you know, I'm just doing my job.
She was super upset, and I mean I felt bad for her.
But I also felt weirdly, like I was like
I had this weird reaction.
I felt really empowered and kind of good. And I realized yeah, she's not capable of doing that job, and she shouldn't be there, and like fuck her for putting me in that position in the first place! I mean I was trying to be nice but she totally took advantage of that.
She's a nice lady, she just needs to find a job she can actually do.
Anyway I feel like it was an important step for me.

Madeleine   Alex, that's really good.

Alex   Yeah.

Madeleine   I'm really proud of you.

Alex   Yeah?

Madeleine   Yeah.

Alex   I've been looking at some listings in Seattle and it's not too bad, the market, I think we can get a nice place if we start looking now. Maybe even a backyard. Grass. I miss grass.

Madeleine (*suddenly overcome with emotion*)   I miss grass so much
I hate New Mexico so much it's so empty

Alex   Mad
Oh man
Do you want to talk about anything?

Madeleine   *No I don't want to talk about it I don't want to talk about everything I'm feeling not everything needs to be fucking "STATED."*
. . .
I kind of don't like these sculptures.
I kind of hate them actually.

Alex   I kind of do too

Madeleine   You do? They're just—these huge fucking stupid blocks and I hate them so so much I think they're so stupid.

Alex   The cafe here is supposed to be pretty good

Madeleine   Can we just go and get a cup of coffee or something?

Alex   Yeah

Madeleine   A sandwich or something? I'm fucking starving, I'm so so hungry

Alex   I want like a roast beef sandwich.

Madeline   I want like a tuna fish sandwich.

Alex   I want like a roast beef sandwich with tuna fish on it.

Madeleine   Like both?

Alex   Like both on the same sandwich.

Madeleine   That's so fucked-up.
I want like a chicken salad sandwich with a layer of tuna on it and a pile of roast beef on the side.

Alex   See *that's* fucked-up.

Madeleine   And Dijon.

Alex   I want like a tuna salad sandwich with chicken on it, sliced chicken, and some roast beef on the side, and some goddamn potato chips.

Madeleine   I want a goddamn potato chip salad.

Alex   I want a fucking goddamn Coca-Cola with ice.

Madeleine   Hey
I'm glad I'm here.

Alex   Yeah?

Madeleine   Yeah.
I mean, I hate it here
I can't wait to leave
But I'm glad I came.
I just—wanted to say that.

Alex   Let's just get some food.
Let's just get some lunch.
Okay?

Madeleine   Okay

Alex   Okay

Madeleine   Okay.

They smile at each other—it's tentative but real.

Madeleine   Okay.

Scene Eleven

Nighttime.

Highway.

Suzan *and* **John** *in* **John**'s *car.*

Suzan *is driving.*

She's drinking.

Suzan   Hahaha
God!
Oh God to be, you know, back on the road!

John   Right

Suzan   Driving again, the open road, back on it!

John   Yup

Suzan   It's amazing!
Dark outside, headlights ahead

John   Uh-huh

Suzan   We could stop here and start a fire, we could do that
No one would find us

John   Uh-huh

Suzan   Good to be gone

Good to be gone from that campground, that stupid job!
Forward!
Onward.
Upward.
The open road!

John *yells.*

It's frightening.

Suzan   You alright?

John   Yep

Suzan   You seem a little agitated

John   All good

Suzan   This is gonna be great.
Your car is working great, not like mine, happy to leave that piece of shit behind.
It literally stopped working. That's not right. If we drive all night we should make it by morning to this great um—
There's a campground that I know of where I stayed at once that uh—
When we get to Maine I'm telling you!

John *slams his hand on the dash.*

Suzan   Here
Maybe you should
These are sleeping pills
I take half of one
You should take one maybe

He takes a pill.

Suzan   Take two, works better actually, I usually take two

He looks at her, then takes another pill.

Suzan   Sleep through the night
Sleep until morning
I'll drive
Don't worry about the driving, I'll drive, I like to drive.
Shhh, you sleep

He doesn't sleep.

She turns on the radio.

Suzan   Joni!
Is it Joni?
No it is. This one is. I know it is.

We can barely hear the song through the static, but it is Joni: haunting, beautiful, far away.

Then the static becomes too great and she turns off the radio.

He is still awake.

Suzan   You know I went to Woodstock
Or tried, tried to go to Woodstock
I ran away from home with my sister, we were sixteen
Met these guys along the way, older, much older
And they kept saying how they wanted to marry us, you know, and we'd grow our
hair long, live on a farm, have fifteen babies, live off the earth
We were both virgins so that all sounded very appealing.
So we were driving from Pennsylvania up to New York, these guys were driving us.
Stopped at this hotel.
And we could tell they wanted to have sex with us and you know they had money,
they had a car, they had everything we needed to get to where we wanted to go
And we'd planned it so well, we were going to the festival! I could see it in my mind.
But these guys—I mean the payment was clear, what it cost to get from A to Z
So we went outside for a smoke
Me and my sister
And we didn't even have to say anything
We just looked in each other's eyes and were like—nope.
Ran down the road a ways, found a payphone, called our mother, and she drove two
hours to pick us up.
She was angry of course, furious, her hands were shaking.
And my mother was a *very* poor driver to begin with.
But I remember she brought these sack lunches for us to eat
in the back seat
on the way home.

Suzan *looks over.*

John *is asleep.*

Suzan *stops the car.*

As quietly as she can, so as not to wake him, **Suzan** *gets out of the car.*

Stands at the edge of the headlights.

Dials her flip-phone.

Suzan   It's your sister, I know.
Late, I know.
Long time, I know.
I'm sorry, I know.
Wait.
Don't hang up.
It's me. It's your sister.
I'm by the side of the road
It's the middle of the night
I'm in a bad situation

I'm making some bad choices
And I need you to get in your car and come get me.
I need you to help me.
I need you to pick me up.

Suzan *waits on the phone for her sister to speak.*

End of play.

Aspen Ideas

Aspen Ideas was scheduled to open at Studio Theatre in Washington DC (David Muse, Artistic Director; Rebecca Ende Lichtenberg, Executive Director), with a first performance on June 24, 2020. The production was cancelled because of the Covid-19 pandemic.

Anne	Mary Beth Fisher
Rob	John Judd
Jay	Eliza Huberth
Chris	Adam Poss
Sophie	Megan Graves
Director	Les Waters

Characters

Anne, *fifties*
Rob, *fifties*
Jay, *thirties to forties*
Chris, *thirties to forties*
Sophie, *sixteen*

A Note

Dialogue in brackets like this:

Anne   Oh sure could you—[*get me a refill*]
is not meant to be spoken. It's what the character would have said had they continued speaking.

Another Note

I suspect this dialogue moves quite quickly, especially at the beginning.

A Final Note

Embrace the pace and style of the language, but resist broadness in characterization. These must be real people, even when they're saying absurd things.

Scene One

A cocktail party.

Anne, **Rob**, *and* **Jay** *stand talking to each other, drinks in hand.*

Anne *and* **Rob** *are married to each other.*

Jay *looks a little more artistic, more bohemian.*

Jay   So I have a theory—

Anne   Okay

Rob   Fantastic

Jay   That explains why we're at—

Rob   Okay

Jay   Where we're at—

Anne   Uh-huh, *tell* us

Jay   Today.

Rob   So the theory explains (I just want to get clear) . . .

Jay   Why things are, the way they are, in this moment.

Anne   Oh God, good

Rob   Great, because to me

Anne   We've been saying to each other

Rob   That it's not just the president

Anne   No the problems go much deeper

Rob   They go much *much* deeper, that's clear.

Anne   I mean if we tell ourselves the problems are just this man (can't say his name), or even his party (*can't* say the name)

Rob   He's a—okay *he's* a—okay

Jay   Symptom

Rob   Yes!   **Anne**   Yes.

Anne   Of a larger, sort of

Rob   Yes! An interconnected web of

Jay   Yes!

Anne   Right?

Rob   That's been going on for years

Jay   That's it. And this is connected to my theory.

Rob   God, tell us

Anne   *Please* tell us

Rob (*strangling gesture*)   We need to know!

Anne   Rob . . .

Jay   It's pretty simple

Rob   That's great, God, tell us

Jay   Now I'm not saying it will explain everything. This theory. This *idea*.

Anne   Okay

Jay   It's just a um framing of the problem, or an explanation of, let's see: Why we are, where we are.

Anne   Well that would help

Rob   Completely, if we could umm focus on

Jay   It frames the problem: and then the solution is up to us.

Anne   That's wonderful.

Rob   God that's great
Floor's all yours!
Tell us what you think!

A micro-beat.

Rob   Oh hey before you—[*say your theory*], I'm gonna

Anne   Rob

Rob   What

Anne   She was just about to

Rob   I'll be right back!
Refill?

Anne   Alright

Rob   "Jay," did you say it was?

Jay   Yes!
And no. On the refill.
(*Holding up her glass:*) Seltzer

Rob   Gotcha.
(*To* **Jay**) I'm really enjoying talking to you.

And I can't *wait* to hear your theory.

Rob *leaves.*

An awkward moment between **Jay** *and* **Anne***. Two strangers left alone together at a party.*

Anne   Don't drink?

Jay   I stopped after college

Anne   I don't drink that much, but when I do I find it *really* cuts into my productivity the next day.

Jay   What do you hope to accomplish?

Anne   I'm sorry?

Jay   The next day, what do you tend to be hoping to accomplish?

Anne   Oh, whatever the day holds I guess.

Jay   Yes

Anne   Work, or the kids, or getting exercise.
You *have* to take time for yourself

Jay   Yes

Anne   You *have* to make time to sleep!

Jay   That's what they're saying

Anne   I'm doing this new system:
I divide the day into blocks?

Jay   Oh yes?

Anne   It's called "blocking," and it involves blocking time, for various tasks, according to how important they are to you, (blocking off time)

Jay   A block-based system

Anne   —and colors, there's different blocks, and different colors, and you sort of overlay the colors on the blocks. I get confused about the colors. Forget the colors! The blocks are great.

Jay   I guess the foundational issue though is
What are you actually trying to accomplish.

Anne   Well, that's true.
(I mean all I really want to do these days is sleep)

Jay   I hear you

Dream time

Anne   Yes

Jay   Get the subconscious—

Anne   I love to sleep in total darkness. Blinds closed tight, mask over my eyes, not a peep of light. Close my eyes and I'm gone.

Jay   Like falling down a hole.

Anne   What?

Jay   Like falling down a hole.

Anne   Yes!

Jay   I hate clocks in the bedroom. When I'm sleeping, when I'm *anywhere* near sleep, I do *not* like to know what time it is *at all*.

Anne   Oh I *love* that.

Rob *is back with drinks.*

Anne   Rob I think we we should take the clocks out of our bedroom

Rob   I ran into Jules and Barbara

Anne   Oh God

Rob (*to* **Anne**)   Oh stop
(*To* **Jay**) You know them?

Jay   Who?

Anne   Jules and Barbara Greene? They are a / nightmare

Jay   I don't know them

Rob   Ah so who's your, uh, connection

Jay   I know Chris

Anne   Oh who's Chris?

Rob   So do you live in the city or

Jay   No

Rob   Visiting then.

Jay   Uh-huh

Anne   Well, we just moved to Brooklyn

Rob   We made the move!

Anne   We're about twenty years behind, everyone else made the move about twenty years ago

Rob   Manhattan is all oligarchs now, show properties, apartments sitting empty

Jay   I read about this

Rob   Those apartments you see at night in New York? Those bright, you know, buildings? The entire goddamn skyline?
Completely fucking empty.

Jay   Wow

Rob   They're just vessels to channel money from New York, to Dubai, to the Cayman Islands, and beyond

Anne   We just moved to Dumbo

Jay   To where?

Anne   Dumbo

Jay   Sorry?

Rob   To Dumbo

Jay   Where's that?

Anne   Oh it's

Rob   Where did you say you were from?

Anne (*seeing someone*)   Oh God BLOCK ME it's Emma

Rob   What?

Anne   Turn your body and block me

Rob   Oh

Anne   Thank you. / (*To* **Jay**) Sorry, she's a nightmare, and if she sees me, she'll *definitely* come over

Rob   Dumbo is, it's a former industrial, ships, docking, used to be . . . cargo, etc. . . . . you can smell the brine

Jay   Oh great

Anne   Dumbo is where a lot of the dockworkers and also the docks used to be. At first we were unsure whether it would be good for our family, because it's a bit cold and it's a bit stark, but our daughter

Rob   She's a teenager

Anne   *She's* a bit cold, it turns out, and a bit stark

Rob   She's never home anyway

Anne   She goes to school on the Upper West Side, so

Rob   Bit of a commute

Anne   Fieldston? The Fieldston School? Fieldston? The Fieldston School? Anyway . . .

Rob   We used to hope she'd use the commute for reading but now that they've opened up the subways for reception we're worried she's just texting

Anne   Do they do anything else now?

Rob   "Millennials"

Jay   I'm technically a millennial
I'm right on the cusp

Rob   Before or after

Jay   Right on the cusp

Chris *enters wearing vintage glasses.*

Chris   Hello

Jay   And this is Chris

Rob   Ah okay!

Anne   "Chris," wonderful, and . . . who do you know here . . .

Chris   I know Jay

Anne   Oh wonderful!

Jay   Chris and I have been friends for a long time

Anne   That is fantastic

Rob   I love your glasses

Chris   They're vintage

Anne   We were just talking about millennials

Chris   What about them?

Anne   On the phones

Chris   I don't understand

Rob   But you were going to tell us your theory

Anne   Have you heard this theory?

Chris   Which one?

Jay   The main one

Chris   Oh yes I've heard it

Jay   We came up with it together

Anne   Oh wonderful, do you, in some sort of formal setting are you, professors or . . .

Chris   No

Anne   Writers . . . actors . . . "influencers" . . .

Anne   Our daughter wants to be a writer

Rob   God help us

Anne   God help her

Chris   Why

Rob   The creative life. . .

Anne   "The artist's way" . . .
I was a dancer, for a long time

Rob   She has long limbs

Anne   Dancer's limbs

Rob   Show them

Anne   Oh gosh
Like this

Anne *shows them the length of her limbs.*

Jay   Wow

Chris   Uh-huh

Anne   But the joints were the problem

Rob   Fantastic limbs, troubled joints

Anne   Eventually I said I have been *taking* fish oil, oh *yes* I've been stretching—as a dancer you stretch for *hours*, every day, I kept increasing the time, but it just stopped working. Something had gone awry.

Rob   And then we met

Anne   Which was a stroke of luck

Rob   Immediately moved in together

Anne   Really that same day

Chris   Uh-huh

Anne   Felt like that same day

Rob   Time *condensed* when we were with each other

Anne   Everything clustered together. In a good way!

Chris   And you were older

Rob   What?

Chris   You've always been older?
Than her?

Rob   Uh, yes

Anne   But you were going to tell us your theory

Rob   Oh yes!

Chris (*to* **Jay**)   Go ahead
(*To* **Anne** *and* **Rob**) It's a good one

Anne   Good! We need explanations, because, these days, I mean the president

Rob   Disgusting. The insults . . .

Anne   I've been having a dream lately terrifying about civil um civil um

Rob   War?

Anne   Thank you. Usually when I sleep it's just falling into darkness, like Jay said, and I love that, I say NO light, I say get rid of all lights in the bedroom, I'm militant about it, there *are* clocks, but you've inspired me to get rid of clocks, Rob did you hear this? Jay refuses to sleep near a clock.

Jay   It's true.   **Chris**   That's very true

Rob   Wow

Chris   And if I can just butt in here:
I love clocks. I'm extremely punctual. This has been a source of actually um

Jay   Stress

Chris   Of stress. Because anytime I wake up I want to know what time it is *right* away. It's a bit of a thing.

Jay   And I *don't* want to know what time it is. I very firmly just *don't*.

Rob   Well, and this is fascinating because this is something you really have to navigate. As a couple. Don't you find? Different uh—sleeping arrangements. Different preferences in general. / For example

Anne   It's true! But you said um . . . you're not a couple?

Jay   No no!   **Chris**   No

Rob   But you sleep in the same bed

Anne   Rob

Jay   Right   **Chris**   Exactly

Beat.

Rob   Okay, cool! Diferent um, different ah—

Anne   Forgive me if this is rude, but:
Do you ski?

Jay   Not usually

Rob   Oh it's great.

Anne   You *have* to try it.

Rob   Flying down the hill, cold air *blasting* your face / wakes you *right* up

Anne   Forget all your troubles, we love it it's
Oh and you would love

Rob   Long story short:
Every summer in the mountains in Colorado

Anne   In Aspen

Rob   (Sounds a little obnoxious, I know, but)

Anne   Have you heard of the Festival of Ideas: Aspen?

Rob   Little poscript: Aspen.

Jay   No   **Chris**   No

Anne   You would both *love* it   **Rob**   Oh wow

Anne   They bring all these wonderful thinkers, from so many backgrounds, each of whom has one single very interesting idea

Rob   For example: put locks on guns

Jay   Locks?

Rob   Little locks on the trigger, you have to unlock the lock before you pull the trigger

Jay   But the gun still fires

Rob   Yes but there's a little lock
So if you want to fire the gun
You unlock the lock

Chris   That's brilliant

Anne   Or here's another one: fight poverty, with um, what was it?

Rob   Cows

Anne   Give everyone a cow

Rob   You give everyone a cow, *if* they need one

Anne   Yes

Rob   And in other areas, it might be

Anne   Give everyone a chicken

Rob   Yes or um up in the mountains

Anne   Give everyone a goat

Rob   Voilà: goat milk!

Anne   Make the fur, into jackets

Rob   Boom: you go to a village, everyone's wearing these goat jackets, the economy is revitalized

Anne   They say it will solve poverty

Rob   Wider distribution of cows

Anne   Who knows

Rob   So it's all the best thinkers and policy makers, and artists, at the Festival of Ideas: Aspen

Anne   The artists are incredible: Tracy Chapman

Rob (*pronouncing it Bah-no*)   Bono

Chris   Boe-no

Rob   Oh uh I believe it's *Bah-no*

Jay   It's Boe-no

Rob   Okay, so, regardless, he gave a speech about something or other

Anne   He's just walking around, you're peeing next to him

Rob   I peed next to him

Anne   Claim to fame

Rob   Here's the urinals, here's me, here's Bono
We're standing there, pssssss

Anne   He loves telling this story

Rob   I'm thinking, should I say something? It's Bono

Jay   Boe-no

Rob   I'm thinking what should I say to Bono, we finish peeing, I actually cut off my flow early so I can get to the sink at the same time, we're standing there, washing our hands

Chris   He's got his shades on, I imagine

Rob   Right and I'm all

Anne   Rob says

Rob   "I love your music"

Chris   Oh wow

Rob   *Complete* lie.

Jay   Wow

Rob   Yup, *total* lie.

Anne   He hates U2!

Rob   When their album came with the phone I said: no. Get this off my phone.

Anne   He spent hours trying to delete the U2 album from his phone.

Rob   I said: I don't even accid*entally* want to listen to this album.

Anne   But in the moment, in the bathroom

Rob   I wanted to connect
And Bono says

Anne   Do the accent

Rob   "Thanks, mate"

Chris   Is he Australian?

Rob   I'm sorry?

Chris   You just did an Australian accent

Rob   I think so

Chris   I don't think so

Rob   I think he's from Perth

Chris   Hmmm

Anne   And last year at the festival there was a wonderful um who was that singer

Rob   He's from this slum and he

Anne   Very inspirational, very

Rob   Cutie X!

Anne   Yes do you know Cutie X?

Jay   No

Anne   Drums, incredible drums

Rob   Get you riled up

Anne   Your heart pumping: vigorous!

Rob   Counterpuntual, it's all

Anne   There's a famous song you'll / recognize

Rob   Ah yeah what's the rhythm what's the

He tries to do the rhythm of the song.

Anne   No it's

She tries to do the rhythm of the song.

Rob   You're sure it's not

He does the rhythm he did before.

Anne   No that's

Rob   Okay

Anne   That's a different

Rob   It's

Anne   No

Rob   Well
You'd know it if you heard it our daughter *loves* it although the lyrics

Anne   Completely indecipherable, there's a lot of passion there

Rob   There's a lot of anger there

Anne   But it's catchy its

Rob   The lyrics are completely indecipherable, he

Anne   Our daughter loves him

Rob   Cutie X
Great name

Anne   Very unusual

Rob   He plays there every year, at Aspen

Jay   We're big music fans

Anne   Oh us too we, although my daughter, I mean modern pop music is

Chris   Terrible

Anne   Yes!

Chris   But necessary

Jay   You have to keep your ears filled

Anne   But your theory your theory!

Rob   Oh wait but I have to finish telling you about Aspen first, its up in the mountains, but it's summer

Anne   It's gorgeous

Rob   There are flowers everywhere, and these fields, these

Anne   Sometimes we picnic

Rob   We're like kids up there we

Anne   Have you ever picnicked in a field, in summer? It's

Rob   Flowers everywhere

Anne   That Aspen mountain air

Rob   There's a beautiful field, in the mountains above Aspen, where we picnic And we're usually, we're dressed up like the rich

Anne   Rob!

Rob   No but we are, it's rich person casual, it's

Anne   "Summer wealth"

Anne   We were both poor, in our twenties

Rob   Up until our thirties

Anne   Until bam, at forty, we were rich

Rob   It had all accumulated

Anne   A lot of social capital and um regular capital

Rob   Hard work

Anne   Ups and downs

Rob   Inherited wealth, partially

Anne   I came into some wealth

Rob   Just as my career was taking off

Anne   Rob found

Rob   I found that if you have money, it's easier to get people to give you money

Anne   So Rob manages money

Rob   People give me money, and I manage it

Jay   Put it in different places

Rob   Sort of squirrel it away in different places, yes

But it happened so suddenly that we're still getting used to it, I mean the switch, from poor to rich

Anne   We haven't quite settled in

Rob   To us these are costumes, essentially

Anne   Are values are bohemian

Rob   We keep an ironic distance

Anne   And our daughter, we're trying to, with the values

Rob   Sometimes you get lucky
I got lucky

Anne   He got lucky, and then I got lucky

Rob   Both started out in the arts

Anne   He's a wonderful painter

Rob   I went from being homeless to being a painter

Anne   BAM: one minute he's on the streets, the next minute he's painting

Jay   Wow

Anne   The biggest canvases you've ever seen

Rob   I became known for the size of my canvases

Anne   Maybe you've—[*heard of him?*]

Rob   In the eighties

Anne   Late eighties, and New York was—were you here then?

Chris   No   **Jay**   No

Anne   New York was a wild place

Rob   Absolute chaos

Anne   There were little lighted storefronts, and you had to get out of your taxi and run, so as not to be mugged

Rob   I was mugged fifteen, twenty times per year—easy.

Anne   Assault was very common

Rob   Assault was a given

Anne   And back then the insults were very

Rob   "Jejune"

Anne   Whitey
Or Honkey Cracker

Rob   Or Pretty Boy

Anne   Fancy Boy

Rob   Fancy Pants

Anne   Gestures of a silver spoon, people would make that

Rob   Born on third base

Anne   Yes

Rob   There was a series of gestures back then that served as insults

Anne (*doing a gesture*)   Born on third base

Rob   No it was

Anne (*doing a gesture*)   Silver spoon

Rob   No it was like:
(*Doing a gesture*) Born on third base
(*Doing another gesture*) Silver spoon

Anne   But
And at the time we weren't even

Rob   We were poor

Anne   I was poor, you were

Rob   I was more than poor, I was homeless

Anne   He was the one slinging insults for a while

Rob   That's how I know them

Anne (*doing a gesture*)   Silver spoon

Rob (*doing a gesture*)   Top hat and spats

Anne   Art galleries were places of safety for me

Rob   For both of us

Anne   I was a dancer, but I loved art, it inspired me, I'd create dances based on art

Rob   Show them

Anne   No

Rob   Show them

Anne   Oh Rob

Rob   There was one, and it was brilliant

Anne   There was one based on this painting that was kind of—all these little dots, and lines

Rob   It was called "Line . . . . dot!"

Anne   I spent a *lot* of time in galleries getting inspired

Rob   They were these outposts of um of safety, for the weirdos like us, the "outcasts"

Anne   Long story short

Rob   My canvases were getting larger

Anne   At the same time as I was getting less and less work as a dancer, because of my injuries, in my joints, I thought *how many godamn hours a day do I have to / stretch*

Rob   And at a certain point everyone got tired of my work, I felt it, everyone had been looking with interest, and then one person started yawning, and then everyone started yawning. Figuratively. And literally.

Anne   He had become too dependent on size

Rob   I wanted to shock, but within a gallery there's only so much size a canvas can take up. I tried to rent a warehouse in Queens and install a single large canvas.

Anne   But he was running out of money

Rob   By then it was already too late.

Anne   I'm so hungry.
Were those brownies? That just passed?
Wait!
You guys want some?
I'll grab us all some.
Nobody move, or I'll lose you . . .

Anne *leaves*.

Rob   She'll be back . . .
Long story short, my career cratered, I spent several years homeless, on the streets actually, I was doing folk art, on a very small scale, arranging trash into patterns, hoping to get noticed, I'd stand near the trashcan begging for commissions, but people can be cruel, have you noticed that?

Jay   Incredibly cruel

Rob   I kept saying *goddamn you people, can't you see this is art?*, but they kept saying: it's trash, and the more I looked at it, the more I realized: they're right. It's literally just garbage, that I've arranged into patterns, or what felt to me at the time like patterns, gripped, as I must have been, by some sort of delusion, but out here? The next morning? Standing, on the street, next to the can? The garbage can, the "bin," as they'd say abroad? Well, now it's clear that I've just taken the garbage from the "bin," put it on the ground and tried to get people to buy it. And then cursed them for calling it trash. It is trash! It's literal trash, and it's figurative trash, by which I mean: it's garbage. I mean what a fool I am, or was, I thought, or realized, at the time, standing there, homeless, next to the trash. (You know where I'm at, Jay, with all of this, and you too, Chris, I can tell . . .)

But then time would pass. And I'd stand there, next to the trash, looking at it, cursing myself, and after some time had passed, I'd realize:

Hmmm.

It *is* garbage.

But I kind of like it.

Anne *returns, wildly out of breath.*

Anne   The waiter was walking too fast. So I found the table of food where everything stays put. It has everything that's on the trays being circulated, but it's stationary. So I thought thank God. I saw it in the distance but it was obscured by people moving back and forth in front of me, in little groups that shifted and merged and split apart. People were calling my name but I ignored them. Some of them knew me, I think, but I didn't care. I get so goddamn hungry at these parties, Rob will tell you, all I want to do is eat. I saw Jules and Barbara, but I moved right past them. I kept the table in my sights. As I got closer I could see that it was empty, it was *more* than empty, it was *decimated*, I mean they're out of *everything* over there. Crumbs, shattered plates, the tablecloth is ripped. There was a run on the food I guess. People panicked for a moment and we missed it. We should have been *fucking* watching. So there's no chance of snacks via that table. We'll just have to keep our eyes peeled for a waiter.

But the waiters walk so fast, I mean my *God* did you see him before, they're practically *sprinting*, I mean it's insane. This is the worst party I've ever been to by far. I'm so hungry, aren't you, I'm starving over here. I'm sorry to keep speaking but it's true.

The only hope is for a waiter to pass, and that there would somehow be something left, that he hadn't been somehow swarmed, like the other ones are, when they emerge from the back. We should stay closer to the door, where they're coming out. Or would it be weird if I found a way into the back? But no that's too much. Would it be weird if we moved? Closer to the doors? So we can catch them as they emerge? If they're still coming out that is . . . who knows . . . Maybe there's no more food, who knows. Oh God. But we'd know, right? Some one would tell us. Or we'd *sense* it. Right? Rob?

Rob   I don't know . . .

Beat.

Anne   There's a waiter! I'm gonna catch him!

I'll bring you back something.

I'll bring you *all* back something—if I can!

She runs away.

Rob   Anne gets very hungry at these parties

Jay   God I have to pee

Rob   Go go!

Jay   Be back . . .

Jay *starts to head off.*

Rob (*calling after her*)   But it's to the left, no it's
To the left
No it's

But **Jay** *is gone.*

Rob   God I hope she finds it

Chris   She'll look for as long as it takes

Rob   What a place . . .

Chris   Magnificent . . .

Rob   The length of it

Chris   It's a wide place too

Rob   The view

Chris   Fantastic

Rob   You can see the whole city
I love at night how it's all lit up

Chris   But they're empty you said, the buildings

Rob   But beautiful nonetheless.
"Like stars in the firmament."

Chris   What's that?

Rob   "Like stars in the firmament"

Chris   Ah.

Rob   . . .
And you?

Chris   I'm sorry?

Rob   You, you're . . .

Chris   I'm sorry?

Rob   Tell me about you, before I

Chris   Oh God . . .
"The third degree"

Rob   Ha ha ha

Chris   Ha ha ha

Rob   Ha ha ha

Pause

Rob   Funny stuff

Chris   I'm gonna go find Jay.

Chris *leaves to find* **Jay**.

Rob *sips his drink for a moment.*

Then leaves in the other direction.

Anne *and* **Jay** *run into each other elsewhere at the party.*

Anne   There you are

Jay   Hello

Anne   Have you seen my husband?

Jay   I've been in the bathroom

Anne   Ah how are the bathrooms, I haven't gone yet but I've heard good things

Jay   They're nice

Anne   I mean this whole place is . . .

Jay   Yes
What

Anne   A little . . . [*too much*]

Jay   ?

Anne   I don't want to . . . [*speak negatively*]
This isn't actually my crowd to be honest, it's my husband's, he's

Jay   Oh

Anne   Does a lot of work for people like this, whereas I tend to be friends with, artists, more, from my background as a dancer, although its been decades—do you know Helene Merill?

Jay   Helen Merill?

Anne   Hel*ene* Merill

Jay   No

Anne   I know it's, it's actually spelled Hellen, but she pronounces it Hel*ene*, which, whatever, but, she's a wonderful dancer, former dancer, and, she's a friend of mine, and she actually was maybe going to come, but then she said "I can't come."

Do you go to a lot of parties like this?

Jay   I go to a lot of parties.

Anne   Oh wonderful, because of work or

Jay   Yes because of work and I like them

Anne   That makes one of us

Jay   I like um—

Anne   No I like them, I like

Jay   Talking to—

Anne   Exactly

Jay   Meeting, new people—hearing about their life, and

Anne   Sure, interesting people, a cross-section, of

Jay   And then there's the food

Anne   Mmm-hmmm

She looks around nervously.

Rob *enters.*

Anne   You're back, I was just going to tell them, or her, Jay here, right? Jay?

Jay   Yes

Anne   Just had a moment of panic: is it Jay? But no. It's Jay. / Good.

Jay   Where's Chris?

Rob   Oh I don't know

Jay   Didn't we leave you here with Chris?

Anne   He's great by the way, how long have you two been

Jay   Oh we're not

Anne   Oh, but you're

Jay   We're

Rob   He was, we parted ways

Anne   You just, aww, we had a nice group going I was like, God, protect me from all the bores here

Rob   Okay that's not

Anne   What

Rob   I need you to

Jay   I'm just going to—

Anne   Sorry! Internal discussion, internal couple discussion, sorry, Jay

Jay   —find Chris

Anne   Come find us again! Please.

Jay *leaves.*

Rob   I need you to—this isn't just pleasure for me, this is a work event this is

Anne   I talked to all those people with you, we've made the rounds

Rob   And I appreciate that

Anne   I've been very charming

Chris *enters.*

Chris   Have you seen Jay?

Rob   Oh hey!

Anne   She went umm looking for you!

Chris   Oh that's funny and I'm looking for her

Anne   Come back when you find her, I'll be right here, we both will, I think . . .

Chris *leaves.*

Anne   They seem lovely, I love her look

Rob   She's great, I love her

Anne   He seems a little

Rob   I can't figure him out

Anne   They must be artists

Rob   They definitely dress like artists

Anne   They remind me of some of the people we used to

Rob   Listen I need you to

Anne   What

Rob   I'm going to circulate, I'm going to

Anne   *Don't leave me here!*
Please.

Rob   Well, do you want to come?

Anne   No I've already circulated I've

Rob   Okay well I have to there's clients there's

Anne   Please don't leave me I can't I can't I can't I can't please I can't do this anymore please I'm sorry please

Rob   Oh, honey
Okay
I won't go

Jay *and* **Chris** *re-enter.*

Anne   Oh God you're back!

Jay   Hello

Chris   We found each other

Jay   We brought you—[*brownies and crab cakes*]

Anne   Oh GOD, thank you!

Rob   That's sweet of you, that's very kind

As they eat:

Anne   Oh God. Oh this is good. Oh my God.
Can I just say, and forgive me if this is too much, but:
We like you both so much. Right, Rob?

Rob   It's true

Jay   Well, we like you!

Anne   So can we just stay together now? Until the party ends?

Chris   Sure

Rob   Cheers to that

Chris   Cheers

Jay   Cheers

Anne   Hooray!

Jay   We were just saying, it would be fun to continue the conversation.

Chris   Right

Rob   Oh you mean a um

Anne   An after-party?

Jay   NO no   **Chris**   No

Chris   Not an after-party, we both sleep early

Jay   But soon?

Chris   Continue the conversation, talk more?

Anne   Oh God that's a great idea

Rob   Oh yeah

Anne   Yeah that's a great idea we should—Rob we should have them over!

Rob   Sure

Anne   Don't you think? We should, we should have you over. Let's do it. It's done. How about next Friday?

Jay   Works for us

Chris   Oh you have that

Jay   No I cancelled it, it's

Chris   Oh great, well. Works for us then!

Rob   Oh great!

Jay   Cheers

Chris   Cheers

Anne   Cheers! I'm so happy we met!

Scene Two

Next Friday night.

The living room of **Anne** *and* **Rob***'s house.*

Anne *and* **Rob** *are standing there.*

Jay *and* **Chris** *have just entered.*

Rob   Little more relaxed?

Jay   Yes

Rob   Little more relaxed, isn't it? Than the party?

Chris   There's a couch

Rob   Yes!

Anne   I'm sorry about the seating arrangements, they're, I know they're unconventional

Rob   She wanted something eclectic

Anne   I wanted to be unique, la dee da, old story

Rob   She wanted people to come in here and be like wow, how eclectic

Jay   Wow

Anne   Hahaha

Jay   How eclectic

Anne   Exactly

Chris   No but really it's wonderful it's where did you get this.

Anne   Oh you're interested in chairs?

Rob   Chairs bore me, I'll be honest with you, chairs—

Anne   This is a

Chris   Looks like a

Anne   Original um

Rob (*to* **Jay**)   And you? How've you

Jay   Hmm?

Rob   God it's good to see you, that party!

Jay   Yes

Rob   You cracked me up

Jay   Oh yeah?

Rob   Fantastic give and take between the four of us

Jay   Yes

Chris   The bounce on this

Anne   You like that?

Chris   It's springy

Rob   She's obsessed with chairs, my wife

Jay   And how've you

Rob   What?

Jay   How've you—

Anne (*to* **Chris**, *re: another chair*)   Here try this one

Chris   Alright . . .

Rob   Oh well, well. Well . . . what?

Jay   How've you

Rob   Good! Oh. Good. We've—our daughter

Jay   Ah

Anne   Not as

Chris   Yes but

Rob   Problems

Anne   You could

Chris   Sure

Anne   The colors are

Chris   Oh and with your expertise I'd

Rob   Do you have kids or

Jay   No

Rob   She's at the age where

Chris   Exaaaactly

Anne   And that's what

Rob   You know what I'm saying?

Jay   Oh sure

Rob   So I'm

Anne   Can I show you the—?

Chris   Please!

Anne   Do you all have what you

Rob   Will you grab us some

Anne   Sure
Come with me, Chris! I'll show you the

Chris   Wonderful wonderful
Thumbs up

Chris *and* **Anne** *head off.*

Rob *and* **Jay** *are left alone.*

Rob   Anyway . . .
I feel like I don't know as much about you as I want to!

Jay   Oh

Rob   I want to know—well, I know very little actually, shall we

Jay   Sure

They sit.

Rob   First things first.
You and Chris.

Jay   Yes

Rob   What's the story there, friends, or, I mean these days I hear of a lot of unconventional kind of—you seem very close.

Jay   You want to hear how we met?

Rob   If you don't mind

Jay   I don't mind.
It's kind of a funny story actually.

Jay *downs her glass of wine.*

Rob   Oh do you want some more?

Jay   Oh no no

Rob   No no in our house the rule is keep drinking! Same thing?

Jay   Sure . . .

Rob *leaves.*

Jay *is alone onstage.*

Sophie *enters.*

Sophie   Hello

Jay   Oh. Hello.

Sophie *leaves.*

Jay *watches her go with interest.*

After a moment, **Jay** *gets up and follows* **Sophie** *offstage.*

Rob *comes back in with a drink for* **Jay**. *But* **Jay***'s not there! Hmmm.*

Anne *returns.*

Anne   What are you doing?

Rob   I was bringing Jay a drink. But she's gone. Where's Chris?

Anne   He's in the bathroom.

Rob   These people are always using the bathroom.

Anne   Listen:
Thank you for pretending that everything is okay. I appreciate it.

Rob   Wish we could have cancelled.

Anne   Yes well
I don't cancel.
But like I said:
Thank you for pretending.

That everything is okay between us.
Right now.

Chris *returns.*

Chris   I found the bathroom!

Anne   Oh good!

Chris   It's a long hallway

Rob   It's a lot of doors

Anne   That was my main problem when we bought it, the place is very

Chris   The width is fantastic

Anne   But the depth is very poor, exactly, it's *barely* two floors, it's got great width, *very* good length, limited depth.

Rob   The house has its limitations. In a perfect world . . .

Anne   He *loves* talking about a perfect world

Chris   Well . . . "in a perfect world" . . .

Rob   Right? "In reality . . . the world is broken!" Ha ha ha

Anne   My God, the latest *news* the news!

Chris   Oh it's

Anne   You follow?

Chris   Try not to

Rob   Well, there ya go!

Anne   [*We should*] Follow your example!

Rob   The boorishness of the / man

Anne   The—this is one thing we always agree about, I mean we fight about almost everything, except for / *politics*

Rob   Not everything

Anne   Raising a girl, and
Why are you holding that

Rob   I was bringing it for

Anne   Oh where did she

Rob   Maybe she went looking for the

Anne   Maybe I should see if she

Rob   No I'll—[*look for her*]
Here

Anne   Oh the food, I'll—[*go check on it*]
Here
Don't move, Chris.

Rob   Relax, Chris! Hang out. Turn on the music. Find something you like.
It's too quiet in here.

Rob *goes off to make sure* **Jay** *isn't lost in the house.*

Anne *goes off to check on the food.*

Chris *is left alone.*

He finds the little remote for the stereo system.

He turns it on—finds a piece of music that sounds like Cutie X. It's rhythmic, intense, a certain strangeness to it. It plays at a very low volume, almost imperceptible, through the following:

Jay *returns.*

Jay *and* **Chris** *sit silently.*

It goes on a little longer than it should. Then:

Rob *returns from one direction*

Rob   There you both are

Anne *returns from another.*

Anne   And I'm back too!

Rob   You found the bathroom

Jay   Well, I *hope* so

Rob   Ope! Ha ha ha

Jay   Because I did my business there, so I *hope* it's the bathroom

Anne   Ha ha ha

Jay   Little surprise for later . . .

Rob   Well, cheers to that, oh do you have a

Chris   No I'm

Rob   Lemme just

Rob *gets something caught in his throat.*

He clears his throat—it's still in there. Clears it again.

Everyone waits for him.

Finally it's gone.

Then he lifts his cup.

Rob   Cheers!

Jay   Cheers   **Anne**   Cheers!

Chris   Cheers.

They cheers.

Anne   Quick question vis à vis dinner
And I should have asked earlier, before it was already in the oven, hah, but
Are either of you pescatarian?

Jay   We both are

Chris   We're both pescatarian

Anne   Oh God! No! Oh God no! Because we're having / fish

Jay   Well, that's fine

Anne   Oh it is?

Chris   Sure

Anne   What's, I thought pescatarian was, oh shoot, because our daughter

Rob   She doesn't eat fish

Anne   She's 100 percent opposed to fish
In their dead form

Rob   As food, she's opposed

Jay   This is wonderful

Anne   Oh thank you, those are cheese um

Rob   Cheese blintzes

Chris   "Opposed to fish . . ."

Anne   She claims they're scraping the bottom of the ocean, looking for fish, the fishermen are I mean, (the fish companies?)

Rob   That that's how bad it's gotten

Jay   I can buy it

Chris   Oh I can believe it

Anne   Oh I can definitely believe it but at the same time its like: what are we supposed to do, stop eating fish?

Chris   I'll stop eating fish when they stop selling fish

Anne   And they might! The way things are going . . .

Jay   Because of the environment?

Anne   Yes, on the one hand! And on the other hand the "social justice warriors," banning everything, a step too far (although I'm generally on board, with their, with their—it's the *tactics* that I)

Rob   I hate the idea of scraping, some kind of

Jay   Can a net scrape?

Anne   I think scrape is more of a concept

Jay   Oh like "scrape"

Anne   Like scrape us: "don't scrape me!"

Jay   Like take without consent?

Rob   Without class
Without leaving some for the next guy

Chris   What does it mean to be sustainable?

Rob   When it comes to fish? No idea.
I would bet that it means you leave some behind for the next guy.
I'll look it up.

Anne   Don't—no, we're at a party

Rob   Sorry

Anne   Him and the phone
In your pocket! Bad! Hahaha

Rob   I have a problem
Do you—

Jay   Oh no

Rob   Struggle with this?

Jay   I don't own a phone

Anne   Well that's fascinating

Rob   It's like being um

Anne   My sister, who

Rob   A nomad, a modern nomad

Anne   My sister, she lives on an island

Rob   An "island," it's not an island

Anne   Well, no but it is. It's a piece of land, surrounded by water, and to get there you take a boat.

Rob   Yes but an island implies some kind of lifestyle

Anne   And she lives that lifestyle

Rob   It's a facade. She wants to be thought of as someone who lives on an island.

Anne   But she does, in the most literal sense, live on an island.

Rob   But it's a facade, it's all . . . she's play-acting.

Anne   Okay

Rob   The role of island-dweller

Anne   Okay well

Rob   And the island is the most clichéd, you know, coastal sort of, it's near Seattle

Anne   She's—there's two organic markets on this island
She's a "writer"

Rob   Among other things

Anne   She writes these personal essays, atrocious

Rob   They're very bad

Anne   About birds she sees out her window

Rob   They're very very boring

Anne   And the prose is how would you say

Rob   Florid

Anne   What I want to say to her is: write about something that might be interesting to a reader.

Jay   Yes.

Anne   Write about something that someone might possibly be actually interested in. I mean there's an idea.

Rob   She's very wrapped up in birds and um and what and

Anne   Deer

Rob   Yes, there's

Anne   And she describes them like horses

Rob   She calls them "majestic," which is

Anne   Seems like the wrong adjective

Rob   What I want to say is: it sounds like you're describing a horse
Not a deer

Anne   And I mean if you're going to write about something boring at least write about it well

Rob   Although you love nature

Anne   Being out in it, I don't want to read about it

Rob   So she's always writing, the sister

Anne   She's constantly writing, it's very annoying

Rob   Because she's also very unsuccessful

Anne   She says "published," but she means: by herself

Rob   So at a certain point it's like: why don't you just stop.

Anne   And she says a cell phone would interrupt her flow

Rob   "Her flow"—sounds menstrual

Anne   She can reach *us*? When she wants to

Rob   But we can never reach *her*

Anne   Because she's always out getting massages

Rob   Or giving them

Anne   She's a masseuse

Rob   People pay her to give them massages

Anne   And then she uses the money she makes from that to pay other people to give *her* massages

Rob   It's an insane system

Anne   It's a closed loop

Rob   And when she's not doing that she's a doula

Anne   An aspiring doula

Rob   She's an apprentice, I think, to an established doula

Anne   She delivers babies

Rob   Helps deliver babies

Anne   Well, what do you think about her?

Chris   About who

Anne   About my sister, should she get a phone? Is she under an "obligation" "These days"
To have a phone

Chris   Well, what I think. . . .

Anne   Yes go go

Rob   And you had—these are the people with the ideas
What was the theory, Jay, you were going to, at the party

Anne   Oh yes the theory of why uh was it

Rob   Hey this is crazy but
We should bring them to Aspen with us!

Anne   I love that idea
You would love it

Rob   To the Festival of Ideas, to—

Anne   You would love it

Rob   You can spend the whole day

Anne   In the morning, okay—[*you can*—]

Rob   And she loves this

Anne   You should come with us! Seriously

Chris   Oh no no

Rob   No you should, you should come up with us

Anne   We have season passes

Rob   We have decade-long season passes, so we feel like we have to go

Anne   And we have all these friends there, that we've made, over the years

Rob   And we like them

Anne   Oh we love them

Rob   Some of them

Anne   Some of them we hate

Rob   Others we sort of like

Anne   Who

Rob   Judy and Paul

Anne   I don't like Paul

Rob   Judy is / fantastic

Anne   Fantastic, Judy is fantastic, Judy is incredibly creative

Rob   Paul can be

Anne   Well, you'll see

Rob   It's not that he's

Anne   There's a little

Rob   Cock-swinging, if you don't

Anne   Rob!

Rob   He was a music producer, which
But then he got into real estate
And there's definitely something about people who get into real estate

Anne   And this is a nice guy, in spite of everything he is you know—he just

Rob   He made a shitload off the housing crisis, basically

Anne   When the economy

Jay   Oh the economy

Rob   Couple years ago a shitload yeah

Jay   Right

Rob   Went

Jay   Sure

Rob   Belly up?

Jay   Okay

Rob   And then there's John Grote

Anne   Oh don't talk about John Grote

Rob   Foreign Relations Council, UN, very impressive . . .

Anne   Rob is fascinated with John Grote

Rob   Happened to oversee a *few* massacres in Guatemala

Anne   Let's not talk about John Grote

Rob   *Nicest* guy you'll ever meet. Smart, well educated

Anne   Couple thousand dead peasants

Rob   Some cognitive dissonance there, when you're talking to him.
Charming as hell. But in the back of your mind is just—corpses.
Anyway, point is:
I feel like I'm wearing masks with them, with our Aspen friends, and with you, I
don't know. We don't have to wear masks. And we don't even know you that well!
There's just a comfort here. Between us. Right?

Chris   Definitely

Jay   Yeah I feel that

Rob   I'm still trying to figure out what your deal is, the two of you

Anne   Rob

Rob   What, no, I'm just interested

Anne   Rob has gotten very interested in learning about alternative sexualities

Rob   But that's not, no, that's not where this night is going

Anne   Swingers

Rob   Don't scare the guests

Anne   We have a friend who

Rob   My theory about sexuality is that when you're in your twenties, when you're poor . . . basically there's a link between poverty and sexual satisfaction

Anne   I don't buy this, I think people have more sex when they feel secure

Rob   Although you wouldn't know it from our relationship
Or from the relationships of any of our friends

Anne   Okay, Rob, stop

Rob   No but we have to take you to Aspen.
What are you doing in um / well, next week

Anne   Relax, we'll, let's see if they still like us after tonight

Rob   We just bought, and Anne was against it, we bought this little pied-a-terre, *right* in Aspen Core

Chris   What's that?

Rob   Aspen Core, Aspen Center

Anne   Don't call it "Aspen Core," that's

Rob   What?

Anne   You sound like an asshole

Rob   Well it's in the center of downtown Aspen. The core.
And here's the thing:
It's close to the most wonderful fields, I'm not kidding when I say that Anne and I run through them in the summer, the flowers are blooming, my God when we first got married, shortly thereafter, we took our first trip to Aspen, I mean my God.
Now here's the deal:
We took a little room, right there in Aspen Core, and during the day we would soak up ideas at the festival, new ideas, the most wonderful ideas, about the world, and the way it worked, and what was coming, and where we were going, and what was possible, or desirable, or coming soon, and at night these parties, and we were newly rich, so to be at these parties

Anne   The way people dressed, seemed insane, the things they talked about, seemed insane, and we'd look at each other and giggle, but we kind of liked it, I mean how could you not, these houses, massive, with their own um—ballrooms, some of them

Rob   Ski slopes

Anne   Some of them

Rob   Servants, in black tie

Anne   You'd go: "where'd you get these servants?"

Rob   And there were so many of them

Anne   At each party there'd be at least thirty

Rob   Or forty, if you count the valets, and the men in the kitchen, and the bathroom attendants, in people's private homes

Anne   And the servers, bringing crostinis

Rob   You should *taste* the crackers they serve in Aspen

Anne   And the art, that people would have on the walls, would be an original, you know, whatever, tulip, right there on the walls, and we'd be there, the two of us, imposters, but accepted, you know, fantastic.

Rob   It was really fantastic.

Anne   It was ridiculous, but fantastic.

Rob   The people you run into up there—unbelievable. Bono, like I said. Annie Lennox! Tracy Chapman. Dick Armey, remember him? Henry Kissinger, and co. George W., the son. George Senior, the dad. Anna Deavere Smith! Fascinating. Philip Levine, the great poet. Paul Ryan, when he was just a young buck. We saw Beyoncé, from a distance, through a crowd, as she was gathering her things to go. Martha Stewart, Bill Gates, Steve Jobs, before he croaked, Tim Cook, after that, Tim Ryan, Tony Robbins, people like that. The stars of our time. And then the lesser lights, clustered around them, and then us, on the outskirts, but moving inward, steadily, with each rotation, inward and inward, approaching the center. Inward and inward. Inward and inward and inward.

Anne   The conversations that happen in that context, the chance meetings, the sudden encounters, you'll be saying something—then you'll hear someone near you saying something, so you'll incorporate what they're saying into what you're saying, and it's better. Everyone lifting each other up. Higher and higher. Higher and higher and higher.

Rob   Inward and upward, it's true.

Anne   And listen: the *flowers*.
The flowers, in Aspen, in the summer, are *incredible*.

Rob   They're unnatural!

Anne   They *burst* up out of the ground!

Rob   Shoving up, out of the ground!

Anne   The brightest colors

Rob   Insane, the colors

Chris   A "veritable rainbow"

Rob   Ha ha ha ha—what's that from? "A veritable rainbow"

Chris   Nothing, it's from me

Anne   And the fields! The vast fields, surrounding the buildings, on the top of the mountains.

Rob   In the afternoon, after a lecture, but before a party, we'd pick a field, and just *picnic*

Anne   Lightly

Rob   And drink wine

Anne   And eat crackers

Rob   Aspen is known for its crackers

Anne   And talk about the ideas we'd heard that morning

Rob   And the parties we'd go to that night

Anne   And we'd run through the fields, holding hands, the flowers exploding in color, both of us laughing

Rob   Oh we were laughing

Anne   We could rarely stop

Rob   There may be no experience better than being young, in a field, in Aspen Core. At the Aspen Festival of Ideas.
Newly wealthy.

Anne   And not yet pregnant.

Beat.

Rob   But I suppose we all have stories of being young

Jay   We were all young once

Rob   Indeed.

Anne   And we still go. And the fields are still there. And the flowers are still there.

Rob   And the ideas are still there!

Jay   Wonderful.

The fire alarm goes off in the kitchen.

Anne Oh shit

Rob I guess dinner's ready! Ha ha ha

Anne Oh God

Rob Honey

Anne Oh God, I'll—

Rob I told you with this dish you—

But **Anne** *has already run into the kitchen.*

Rob Are you having a good time?
We haven't hosted in a little while, we've been, having some uh

Jay Yes

Rob Marital difficulties
Yeah?

Jay I'm having a wonderful time

Chris And I am too

Rob Good. Good good.
And how's your week been? I mean what do you two get up to during the—how do you spend your days

Chris Well, it varies.

Rob Uh-huh

Suddenly:

Sound of something very large being pushed or dragged along the floor directly above them.

Rob Oh God that's our daughter

Chris Oh

Rob She's—she can't get comfortable. In her room. She's constantly dragging things around. The furniture, I mean. Rearranging. It's symbolic and also irritating. Completely destroyed the floor.

Jay She should come down and say hi

Rob Let me um, I'll get her to come down

A bang of something falling.

Rob Oh God.

Rob *leaves.*

Jay *and* **Chris** *sit silently.*

Then:
Rob *re-enters with* **Sophie***, who is breathing hard.*

Rob   Say hello

Sophie *waves.*

Rob   Tell them a little about yourself

Sophie   Like what?

Rob   Just—come on.

Chris   I'm Chris

Jay   And I'm Jay. We've met.

Sophie   Um

Rob   Go on

Sophie   I was like born

Rob   Go on

Sophie   I was like born in the early aughts, I don't know. My name is Sophie. I hate my name. It's exactly the kind of name my parents would have named me if I was born in the early aughts. Which I was. It's so cliché.

Jay   It's a nice name.

Sophie   I hate it. I want to change my name. I want to just have an image that represents me, not a word. I want a new body? I hate my body, I feel old in it. I feel—ugh—like I'm already dying. I hate my boobs. They're so small. One is bigger than the other, see?

Anne *has re-entered.*

Anne   Honey

Sophie   What, you guys wanted me to talk.
I hate my legs, I look like a giraffe. My neck is too long from one angle and too short from the other. I hate my posture, I'm always slouching. I try to straighten up but I forget. My "saving grace" is music. My favorite artist is Cutie X. He plays every year at the Aspen Festival of Ideas. He's like an artist in residence. His lyrics will blow your mind.
I'm sixteen. I hate my age, I wish I was younger. I was so much happier and prettier when I was younger. I wish I was fourteen. But I want freedom, I feel trapped under this roof. I want to be twenty-two. That'll be a great age. But with a fourteen-year-old body. I wish I had Mnuchkin's syndrome. What's it called? I wish my body was getting younger but my mind was getting older. I'm already getting these lines, see? Crow's feet.

Rob   Okay, that's probably enough

Sophie   I have a lot of friends but none of them are very close. We mostly connect online and it's weird. We make these images of ourselves but it's not real. I don't see the world like you do. I see only the possibility of images to be posted online. An image is always possible. I wish the colors were brighter in the real world. I wish I could live in my phone and only peek out when I wanted. I wish I had deeper connections and real friends. I feel very lonely. I love my parents but I don't want to be around them, I feel stifled by them, I have contempt for them, and I know one day they'll die. They've made mistakes I'm not going to make. No one really knows me and I have a lot of private thoughts. I have plans for myself. I have big dreams. I'm not suicidal in any way. I feel scared and excited at the same time. I know I'm gonna be a great woman and do great things. And I'm really I guess hopeful about what's to come. What else.

Anne   That's probably good for now.

Sophie   We're going to Aspen next week and I'm not excited. I hate the mountains, I'd rather be on the beach. I love the beach, I love swimming out in the ocean. I like to start on the sand and swim out. I like to get farther and farther from the shore. I like it when my parents are screaming on the shore screaming: come back! And I just get farther and farther from them. I swim out until I'm lost out there. You can't see or hear anything. Just the ocean around you, the waves. I want to swim until I'm gone, until I can't see the shore. Farther and farther. "Bye, Sophie." "Bye," they'll say. But I won't hear them anymore. Just the wind and the waves and the call of the birds. Farther and farther. I'm a good swimmer, I'm strong. I'll swim for days, or even weeks. I'll swim until I'm nothing out there. Until I'm totally gone.

Anne   Honey

Pause.

Chris   It's really nice to meet you.

Scene Three

On the plane to Denver.

Night. The cabin is dark. A few reading lights on.

Faint hum of the engine.

Rob *is sitting next to* **Chris**.

Anne *is sitting next to* **Sophie**.

Jay *is in a row by herself.*

Rob   Perfect

Chris   Yes

Rob   Perfect

Chris   Yes

Rob   Sorry we all couldn't

Chris   Of course

Rob   But
Still, to be

Chris   Yes

Rob   To have you with us! To have you both with us

Chris   Exactly

Rob   On the same flight it's

Chris   Yes

Rob   Feel bad for—[*Jay, sitting all alone*]

Chris   She'll be alright

Rob   Still it's

Chris   She likes a little—[*solitude*]

Jay *has gotten up.*

She approaches **Sophie***, who is on the aisle, listening to her headphones.*

Anne *is in the window seat, asleep.*

Jay   Hello

Sophie   Hi

Jay (*re: the headphones*)   Do you have those in all the time or

Sophie   Most of the time
Do you want to—[*hear what I'm listening to*]?

Jay   Sure if you're, I'd like to

Sophie *hands* **Jay** *one of the earbuds.*

Jay *listens to one while* **Sophie** *listens to the other.*

Jay   Who's this?

Sophie   Cutie X

Jay   I like it

Sophie   Yeah
He was born in China but then he moved to Mali and then I think lived in Germany
for a while? And his mom is full Swedish and his dad is half Indian half Lebanese so
he's like—a citizen of the world

Jay   Cool

The music is loud enough through the earbuds that it wakes **Anne**.

Anne   Oh

Jay   Sorry

Sophie   Headphones

Jay   Sorry sorry

Anne   No that's

Jay   We were just

Anne   No it's fine it's are we still in the air?

Sophie   Yeah

Jay   Thank you for letting me

Sophie   Oh sure it's

Jay *goes back to her seat.*

Anne   You okay?

Sophie   Yeah why

Anne   I don't know
Just checking in

Sophie   I'm okay
Go back to sleep, Mom
It's okay

Anne   Okay, hah
I don't know why I feel so nervous

Anne *falls back into a fitful sleep.*

The plane is dark. Hum of the engine.

Sophie *listens to her music, wide awake.*

Jay *sits in her seat a couple rows back, doing nothing, wide awake, staring out.*

Both of them illuminated by their reading lights as the plane flies through the night.

Rob *and* **Chris**.

Rob *is drinking a vodka tonic. It's his third.*

As **Rob** *talks,* **Chris** *begins to drift off, but* **Rob** *doesn't really notice.*

Rob   I'm a frugal man at heart
God what I wouldn't give

Pause.

To be your age?
God what I wouldn't give
Looking back.
Regrets.
But no it's
But still sometimes you can't
You are right in the thick of it you are
Listen there are some beautiful women up at Aspen, in the bars, we'll—we'll go out. I'll take you out. Jay can come! I don't know if you have that kind of arrangement but—Jay is great. You're a lucky man. I don't know exactly what your arrangement is. But. We'll go out. There's a—the women in Aspen are—they're older, but they look younger. It can be a little creepy. But they're beautiful. If you like fake breasts. Ha ha ha.
There's some younger, ski bum types, God there was one summer where—

He looks back to make sure **Anne** *can't hear him. She's asleep.*

Rob   But no, nothing happened, it's not, but God, we stayed up late, drinking, and I was—don't get me wrong if I'd done it I would have *absolutely* regretted it, you know, it would have *absolutely* destroyed my life, I mean my *God* I love Anne, but that doesn't mean you don't dream, right? I mean my God that's human. Can't judge me for that. Nothing happened. But Jesus Christ it *could have*. We'll get you out there. Out on the field. While you're still young!
I see myself in you. I do. The ambition. To *be*, you know, to *become*. But now I'm—well.
Time.
Passing.
Time passing.
Shame.
Sure you don't.
Ah well.
And she was a looker, she was—let me tell you. The tits on her. Jesus. Can't talk like that anymore. But in every man's mind, I think, lies a goblin. All this rape stuff recently, women speaking out: harassment. It's good. Tear the lid up. See what's underneath the veil. No more masks.
Long flight.
You're not sleepy?
Me neither.
You're a great seatmate. Shipmate. Didn't bring anything to read? Me neither. Good time to think. And drink! Ha ha ha
(*Looks back at* **Anne***:*)   Sleeping like a baby.
(*Looks back at* **Sophie***:*)   On her phone. Classic.
But God I love her. Can't help it.
Jay is fantastic. L'chaim.
The idiot box. One for every seat., of course. Although now they tell us it's culture. Pooh. They're fooling us. We're wasting our lives. Stop watching. Get up! *Do*. What's behind the screen?
Of course look at me. Literally strapped in. Just like the rest of 'em.

Rat in a cage. Hamster on a wheel. The old ball and chain: life.
Good to have a real conversation for once.
Might turn in. Pass out, is more like it.
Just climb over me, if you need to get out.

Rob *sleeps.*

Jay *walks up the aisle to talk to* **Chris**.

Sophie *watches her pass by.*

Jay *whispers so as not to wake* **Rob** *up.*

Jay   Chris.
Wake up.

Chris *wakes up.*

Jay   You're trapped.

Chris   Yes. How's it going over there?

Jay   Oh you know.
Interacted with the girl a bit.
That was nice.

Chris   How many more hours?

Jay   Two.

Chris   And then a little plane to get to Aspen?

Jay   That's what they say.

Chris   When can we go back?

Jay   When it's over.

Chris *sighs.*

Jay   I've always wanted to go to Aspen.
They're nice people.

Chris   They're okay.

Jay   The girl's lovely.

Chris *yawns.*

Chris   Might "turn in"for a bit.

Jay   "Turn in"

Chris   What

Jay   You don't talk like that

Chris   It's WASP-y

Jay   It's affected
Be yourself
Loosen up
We're going to Aspen!
So many *ideas*.

Chris   Hah.
I'll be glad when it's over.
Getting tired of this.

Jay   You losing steam?

Chris   I don't know.
Exhausting.

Jay   But worth it.
Right?
Right, Chris?
Worth it?

Chris   . . .
Right.
I'm going to sleep.

Jay   Alright.

Jay *goes back to her seat, nodding at* **Sophie** *as she passes by.*

Hum of the engine.

Anne *stirs, wakes up again.*

Anne   OH GOD.

She is confused.

Where—
Oh. The plane. Hah.

Sophie *has taken her headphones off.*

Sophie   You okay?

Anne   Yes! Sorry. Lost track of where I was. Sorry. Sorry, honey.

Sophie *puts her headphones back on, closes her eyes.*

Anne   I always have terrible dreams when I fly at night.
Honey?
Oh.
Your headphones are on. Hah.
Well.

She reaches out to touch her daughter.

But **Sophie** *shrugs her off.*

Anne*'s eyes fill with tears.*

She puts her hands back in her lap.

Looks out the window.

After a moment:

Anne   It'll be nice to be in Aspen together, as a family.
I think we'll have a really nice time.

A sound like the seatbelt sign going on: "ding!"

And then, suddenly:

Scene Four

The Aspen Ideas Festival.

Somehow we experience the Aspen Ideas Festival.

It happens onstage, in front of us.

It is somewhere on the spectrum from naturalistic to grotesque.

Everyone is wearing badges.

*There's a lot of optimistic lectures about solving global problems through the power
of technology, cooperation, and empowering people from the bottom up.*

There's artists and scientists.

The Defense Secretary is there, as is the Speaker of the House.

*The head of a private military company like Blackwater is interviewed by a woman
who is renowned for her one-woman shows.*

There are lunches and dinners, people introduce people to other people.

It is both serious and ridiculous.

Is that Bono?

And **Rob***'s friend who got rich off the housing collapse?*

John Grote is definitely there.

It all culminates in one opulent party.

Cutie X plays.

At first there's lots of cocktail party chatter.

But Cutie X's music gets more and more intense.

People start to drift away.

Eventually Cutie X is playing alone.

It gets louder and louder and louder.

And then it's over.

Scene Five

Late at night.

Rob *and* **Anne***'s pied-à-terre in Aspen.*

They're wearing formalwear.

Anne *is collapsed on the sofa, they're drunk and tired and a little delirious.*

Rob *is shaky on his feet.*

Rob   A classic story

Anne   What

Rob   A classic story, a cliché! Man comes home from a party, drunk, rich man

Anne   Robert

Rob   What? Might as well say it, rich man, comes home from a party, drunk

Anne   Sit down

Rob   The wife, the wife, helping

Anne   Don't refer to me as the wife

Rob   The wife! My wife. The woman. The autonomous woman

Anne   Okay stop

Rob   Helping
(*Pouring himself a drink*:) Little bit more—

Anne   Stop

Rob   Might as well, already fucking—

Anne   Okay me too then

Rob   Shree threets to the wind! Ha haha ha, shree threets to the wind
The drunken man

Anne   His accommodating, similarly drunken wife

Rob   We're the ferpect match

Anne   The merfect patch

Rob (*getting close, touching her*)   You're incredible

Anne   Stop

Rob   What

Anne   There's guests

Rob   Wandering eye

Anne   Stop

Rob   Little tickling hands

Anne   Okay stop

Rob (*he stops*)   Blergh

Pause.

Anne   It feels good to be here

Rob   Nature's little patch

Anne   What does that mean

Rob   Nature's little patch of heaven

Anne   It's so godamn beautiful this time of year

Rob   You were fantastic at that party

Anne   Stop

Rob   You were, charming as hell, sexy as all get-out

Anne   Stop
You too
You dirty old man

Pause.

Rob   I like having them here

Anne   Jay and Chris?

Rob   Yes

Anne   Jay is fantastic

Rob   Chris is—I can't put my finger on it

Anne   He's quiet

Rob   I've asked him twenty times now what do you do, where are you from

Anne   He's private
Doesn't talk about himself the whole time
It's nice

Rob   Yes

Anne   What?

Rob   I like him

Anne   Okay

Rob   Still

Anne   Jay is fantastic

Rob   Jay is so funny

Anne   She's great with Sophie

Rob   Yes

Anne   What?

Rob   No, nothing
That party

Anne   Oh God

Rob   The claptrap

Anne   These incredibly wealthy—[*fools*]

Rob   We're incredibly wealthy

Anne   But we have perspective on it

Rob   Talking about Trump, oh what a nightmare oh what a

Anne   We're all holding these cocktails, there's servants everywhere, art on the

Rob   Did you see the

Anne   What

Rob   The painting, of squirrels playing poker

Anne   So tacky!

Rob   These aren't our people

Anne   I like some of them

Rob   Judy was in fine form tonight

Anne   She's getting better

Rob   Paul is atrocious

Anne   Saw you talking to John Grote

Rob   Back of my mind, the whole time: corpses.

Anne   I hope they're having a good time. I mean Jay and Chris.

Rob   They seem to be

Anne   It's hard to tell with them

Rob   That's fucking sure
(*Re: the alcohol*) Little more?

Anne   Why not
They're very easy guests

Rob   You can take them anywhere

Anne   They're so attractive

Rob   People love them, people—Judy was getting a little handsy

Anne   With Chris?

Rob   With Jay!

Anne   Oh God. Too funny. Too funny.
Jay is fantastic

Rob   People love her.

Anne   I hope they're having a good time

Rob   Tomorrow's the last day

Anne   Shame

Rob   Back to the grind

Anne   Wish we could live here

Rob   You wouldn't want that

Anne   I don't know
I'm tired of New York

Rob   We have our whole beautiful house there

Anne   I know

Rob   What do you want?

Anne   I don't know
I feel like I don't have very close friends anymore.
Sophie's going to go off to college
And then it will just be us

Rob   Is that so frightening?

Anne   No
I don't know
What will we do

Rob   We'll come here, we'll go back to New York.

Anne   To what end?

Rob   What do you mean?

Anne   I mean with what purpose in mind?

Rob   I don't know

Anne   I mean what will we be working towards with Sophie gone

Rob   . . . I don't know.

Anne   Thirty years left. You ever think about that? Probly thirty years left.

Rob   We'll live for longer.
Advances in science, etc.
Remember the panel today?

Anne   Exciting stuff.
But to what end, for what purpose.

Pause

Rob   We should take them on a picnic tomorrow, it's our last morning! We should take them to the field, the big field, on the mountain, looking down on Aspen Core

Anne   Alright

Rob   That'll be something to do, a good finale, with Jay and Chris
They'll love that

Anne   I hope so
Maybe we can come back together, the four of us, sometime.

Chris *enters.*

Anne   There you are!

Rob   Thought you'd gone to bed!

Chris   Still up.
Sorry, do you have a phone here?

Rob   Oh

Anne   Of course

Chris   I mean a landline, there's no reception on my cell

Rob   Yes the reception here is abysmal

Anne   There's a phone but it has a cord, so it's

Rob   Here I'll

Anne   Sorry it's very

Rob   Here

Chris Thanks.
Do you mind if I?

Anne Sure

Chris Good party tonight

Anne Oh you had fun?
Wonderful. I'm so glad.

Chris *takes the phone out on the balcony, where* **Anne** *and* **Rob** *can't hear him. Makes a call.*

It's a long call.

We can almost hear what he's saying—but not quite.

Finally it's over. **Chris** *hangs up the phone.*
Rob *joins him out on the balcony.*

Rob Everything okay?

Chris Yes

Rob Good.

. . .

Chris . . .

Rob I really appreciate you guys coming, I know it was a bit of a leap . . .
You get to a certain age, and you just . . . stop making friends.
So I really appreciate you . . . taking the leap.
It's been good for me, and I'll tell you, it's been good for Anne. She just loves you both. She's been having the *best* time. It's been nice to see.
You seem like you've been having fun!

Pause.

Rob Anyway.

Chris It's been an interesting trip

Rob Some great lectures at least, no?
I'm sorry if the parties were—a lot of rich people. But some of them are nice. Judy, tonight, and Frank was a little three sheets to the wind . . . that was funny . . .
You know we have all this space, and Sophie, well she doesn't always appreciate it, so, it's meant so much to us, to have you here. Truly. And I just—we'd love to stay in touch. When we get back to New York. And be friends. I mean *real* friends, you know. You could come back with us. Next year. Here. We could all come back.
If you want, no pressure.

Chris Thank you.

Rob It's been our pleasure.

Tomorrow we'll have a picnic.

Sophie *has snuck out of the house.*

She is outside, listening to her headphones

She hears a sound—who's that? It's **Jay**, *coming to join her.*

They look up at the stars for a moment.

Jay   It's nice out here

Sophie   Yes

Jay   Nice night

Sophie   Yeah really nice

Jay   Do you like it here?

Sophie   Not really.
Do you?

Jay   No, not really.

Sophie   My parents love you guys

Jay   . . .

Sophie   Hah. Yeah.
They love coming here for the festival.
Personally I think most of the lectures are pretty dumb.
The people are always talking about solving these big problems but then you look around and you're like . . . you people created these problems!

Jay   . . ..

Sophie   And actually just all of us not coming here every summer would probably cut down on carbon costs by a lot and that would do more good than like all the talks and panels about global warming. And it's like do you ever think about how much it actually costs to even heat or AC these massive homes? I mean maybe that's the problem maybe we should all just stop doing *that*

Jay   . . .

Sophie   And there's a lot of people here who are honestly evil in my opinion but when you reach a certain level of wealth or celebrity you get forgiven because you're just part of the conversation now of like global elites who have more in common with you than with all of the regular people even if you are evil and I mean these people all hate Trump but that's just because he acts like a poor person and he says the quiet part loud. I mean you hear someone shit-talking Trump and then you turn around and it's Henry Kissinger and it's like: what? How does this even make sense?

Jay   Come here

Sophie   What

Jay   I want to tell you something

Sophie   What

Jay   I need to whisper it

Sophie   What is it

Jay   I need to whisper it in your ear

Sophie   Oh well what is it

Jay   Let me whisper it

Sophie   Um
. . .
Okay

Jay *gets very close to* **Sophie**, *begins whispering in her ear.*

Sophie *laughs, and then she is shocked. And then she is scared.*

She pulls away.

Jay   You got it?

Sophie   Yes

Jay   You up for it?

Sophie   I guess

Jay   You guess?

Sophie   I don't know.
I guess.

Jay   Good.
I thought you might be.

Pause.

Good for you.

Scene Six

Early afternoon.

A field on a hill on the outskirts of Aspen, overlooking Aspen Core.

A picnic blanket. Snacks.

Rob *and* **Anne** *sit near each other,* **Jay** *and* **Chris** *sit near each other,* **Sophie** *sits alone. They're all snacking, except for* **Sophie***. She looks a little shell shocked.* **Jay** *is watching her.* **Sophie** *doesn't meet* **Jay***'s eyes.*

Sunlight. Sound of wind. They snack quietly.

After a moment:

Chris   My God

Rob   Beautiful, no?

Chris   Yes

Anne   We think so

Chris   Well

Anne   Pass the carrot sticks?

Chris *passes them.*

Anne   And would you pass the pretzels and dip?

Chris *passes them.*

Anne   And do you mind throwing me the cheese
Sorry, I'm just
I'm very hungry

Chris   Oh sure

Chris *throws her the cheese.*

It's an aggressive throw.

Anne *doesn't know what to make of that.*

Anne   Careful! Hah

Chris   You said "throw"

Anne   Yes um
Yes I guess I did

Rob   . . .

Anne   . . .
Sophie, you're not eating

Sophie   I'm not hungry

Anne   Do you want me to make you a little plate?

Sophie   I'm not hungry

Rob   How do you like these crackers?

Chris   Fantastic

Rob   These are my favorite crackers
The crunch on them, the little nuts
Seeds too, these crackers have everything

Chris   They are good

Rob   Every year I look forward to these crackers I think
Thank *God* we're going back to Aspen
Where they have, in the grocery store, these wonderful crackers

Chris   Why don't you just buy them online?

Rob   Because I don't want to buy them online I like that you can only get them here

Pause.

You know I was thinking back
To the party where we first met
That awful party
It was a nightmare but we were
So happy to have met you both and the conversation it was fantastic, I mean every
time we see you both we just go go go, the four of us, talking, about everything under
the sun
Although in some ways you remain a mystery
I mean who are you both
I mean we feel so lucky to have found you but
Who are you?
What do you do?
Where are you from?
We spend so much time talking about ideas together that we haven't really
Gotten *down* to it
In terms of that kind of thing and I'm just
Curious.

Chris   So what's your question?

Rob   Well
Just tell us a little, finally, about yourselves
Let's start with work.
Where do you ah—I mean what do you both do for work?

Jay *and* **Chris** *look at each other.*

Chris   Well
We're both consultants

Rob   Consultants!

Annie   Ah, we had you pegged as

Rob   You dress like artists!

Jay   It's a unique consulting firm

Rob   So it's not one of the big guys? BCG, Bain . . . McKinsey . . .

Chris   It's kind of . . . the opposite of that.

Jay   Yes—it's like one of those consulting firms, but the opposite. Whatever it is that they do, you can think of us as doing the opposite.

Rob   Ah

Anne   What does that mean?

Jay *sees something in the sky.*

Jay   Look at that hawk

Anne   Where

Jay   It just landed, way over there

Anne   I don't see it

Jay   Over on that bluff

Chris   Oh I see it

Anne   I don't see it
Do you see it, Rob?

Rob   No

Jay   I'm going to go look at it, it's a beautiful bird

Jay *stands.*

Jay   Sophie? Do you want to come with me?

Sophie   Oh um
Yeah
Okay

Jay   Great.

Sophie *stands.*

Anne   Well, we'll see you in a minute then!

Sophie   Goodbye
Goodbye, Mom

Anne   . . .
We'll see you in a minute.

Jay *and* **Sophie** *leave.*

Anne *is unsettled.*

She watches them go.

Anne (*calling after them*)   Don't get too close to the hawk!
(*To* **Rob**) Are hawks dangerous? I mean to human beings?

Rob   I don't know

Anne   Well, they better be careful.

Chris   Jay has great judgment

They eat more snacks.

Anne *remains unsettled.*

Rob   I'm sorry about all the questions, Chris

Chris   No no

Rob   I shouldn't have pried

Chris   No it's fine, we can get into all that later

Rob   My God what a concert last night—Cutie X? *What* a concert

Anne   I didn't like it

Rob   I think that was his best set yet

Anne   I didn't like it this time, actually

Rob   The drums, I loved it
But it's hard to
I'll tell you I can never understand what Cutie X is saying
It's the accent it's indecipherable

Anne   Where is he from again?

Chris   Look him up

Rob   Oh that's a great idea

Chris   The lyrics, look up the lyrics to one of the songs, to the famous one, so we can see what he's saying

Rob   That's a great idea

Rob *looks up the lyrics on his phone.*

Anne (*re:* **Jay** *and* **Sophie**)   I can't see where they've gone

Rob   Here's the lyrics to the song

Anne   Can you see them? I can't see them

Rob   Here they are

Chris   What do they say

Rob   Well they're kind of repetitive actually
They're kind of dark actually

Anne   I can't see Sophie

Rob   I'll read them out loud:

Anne *stands.*

Anne   Rob, I can't see Sophie

Rob   "This is the end"

Anne   Rob

Rob   "This is the end
This is the end"

Anne   Rob I can't see where they've gone

Rob   "This is the end
This is the end
This is the end
This is the end
It's done now, it's over now
Wake up now
This is the end."

Rob *looks up from his phone, disturbed.*

Rob   Those are the lyrics.

Chris *is staring at him, perfectly still.*

Anne *is standing at the edge of the playing space, looking towards the far point in the distance where her daughter has disappeared.*

Rob   The end of what?

Lights.

End of play.

Kill Floor

Kill Floor opened at Lincoln Center Theater in New York City (Paige Evans, Artistic Director of LCT3; Andre Bishop, Artistic Director of LCT; Adam Siegel, Managing Director), where it had its first performance on October 3, 2015.

Andy	Marin Ireland
Rick	Danny McCarthy
B	Nicholas L. Ashe
Simon	Samuel H. Levine
Sarah	Natalie Gold

Director	Lila Neugebauer
Set	Daniel Zimmerman
Lights	Ben Stanton
Costumes	Jessica Pabst
Sound	Brandon Wolcott
Stage Manager	Megan Schwarz Dickert

Characters

Andy, *female, thirty-four, White.*
Rick, *male, thirty-five, White.*
B, *male, fifteen, biracial. (His father was Black and his mother, Andy, is White.)*
Simon, *male, fifteen, White.*
Sarah, *female, thirties, any race.*

Time

2003.

Location

A small town next to a major highway.

Notes on dialogue

A word that is italicized and in parentheses at the end of a dash, like this . . .

Andy   Really, it's—(*great*)

. . . should be left unsaid. It's what the character would have said had they continued speaking. Actors do not need to leave a pause for this unsaid dialogue. It's for context only.

A forward slash like this / signifies overlapping dialogue. The other actor starts speaking at the slash.

A pause can be any length, from a quick beat to a long silence.

An ellipsis . . . is a silent beat owned by that character.

When two lines are adjacent like this:

Andy   Loved that guy. "Randy."   **Rick**   Lisa Harding.
Moved somewhere. Long gone.   Big, like—(*tits*)

. . . the first word of each line is said at the same time. So "Loved" and "Lisa" are said at the same time, then "Moved" and "Big," etc.

Scene One

Sound of the kill floor. No animal sounds—just metallic clanging, whirring, banging.
It gets louder and louder and louder until:

Lights hard up on a small office.

Rick *and* **Andy**, *both in their mid-thirties.*

Both in cheap business casual.

Rick   So!

Andy   Yeah, so uh thanks for—

Rick's *cell phone rings.*

Rick   Sorry.

Andy   No, that's—

Rick (*answering*)   Hey.
. . .
Yeah.
. . .
Yup.
. . .
I'll pick him up.
. . .
I said I will pick him up.
. . .
I said I heard you, and I will fucking do it.
And don't call me at work. Send me a text.
What?
. . .
That sounds nice.
. . .
I said "Pasta sounds nice."

He hangs up.

Rick   Sorry.

Andy   No, that's—

Rick   Love her! The kid too.
But wish I could kill 'em both, sometimes. Like, you know, strangle.

Andy   Uh-huh.

Rick   My son's four. Got this huge head.

Andy   A what?

Rick   His head is huge. I don't know. It's funny.

Andy   That's funny.
So—

Rick   So how've you been?

Andy   I've been alright.

Rick   Hear from you, it's like—oh yeah! Her! You know.

Andy   Good to think back, sometimes.

Rick   Fun. Man, we had fun.
High school.

Andy   Uh-huh.

Rick   You, on the. . . . .

Andy   What?

Rick   Squad, with the—(*pom poms*)

Andy   Oh, I wasn't—

Rick   No?

Andy   No.
Not my style.

Rick   Huh. Guess I must of—

Andy   It's fine. I wasn't really—

Rick   No, I remember you. Definitely.
Definitely.
Andy . . .
(*Surreptitiously checking the last name on her résumé:*) . . . Weiser.

Andy   That's me.
Down by the—

Rick   Yup.
Huh?

Andy   Oh that's where I used to live. Down by the—

Rick   Down by the old—

Andy   Yup.

Rick   That's right.

Andy   Anyway.
Well.

Rick   "Ruff, ruff!" How'd it go?

Andy   I think that's it.

Rick   "The bulldog bark."

Pause.

So I took a look at your résumé . . .

Andy   Right, yes. Good.

Rick   And I know you've just gotten out of prison—

Andy   Yeah.

Rick   I appreciate you telling that to me, and it's—

Andy   Really trying to—

Rick   Of course.

Andy   And if you're worried about anything, I've got a woman in the uh training program, the job training program there, who knows me. You can call her, she likes me, I never had any—

Rick   We don't have anything, Andy.

Andy   What's that?

Rick   Up here in the office, we don't have anything.

Andy   Oh. I thought—

Rick   I thought maybe—
But I talked to my supervisor up in HQ—and . . .

Andy   Oh.
Sure. No, sure. That's—.
Been looking all over. It's hard. Nothing out there.

Rick   You tried Dairy Queen?

Andy   Can't work fast food.

Rick   No dignity in that.

Andy   No money in that.

Rick   That's for sure.
What about up in Aberdeen?

Andy   Don't have a car. And they cut those buses.
So.
Well, thanks I guess—

Rick   Wait wait.
We do have—I mean—if you want to work down there.

Andy   Down there?

Rick   With the—(*cows*)

Andy   Oh, the—?

Rick   Yeah.
It's hard work.

Andy   I've worked hard.
What's the pay?

Rick   Well, let's see.
We can start you out at—
I can probably get you around, uh—
Would twelve work?

Andy   Holy shit.

Rick   I know it's not—

Andy   No, it's—
Twelve would work fine.

Rick   Great.
Great!
Course there's no benefits. Insurance, all that.

Andy   Psssh. Benefits. "Healthy as an ox."

Rick   So to speak.

Andy   Hah!

Rick   Hahaha.

Andy   That's good. You're good.
Thank you, really.

Rick   It's—(*nothing*)

Andy   Really, it's—(*great*)

Rick   Oh—
How do you feel about Mexicans?

Andy   I don't know. Good?

Rick   Nice people. Really reliable.

Andy   Good.

Rick   Hard working.

Andy   They sound nice.

Rick   Very nice. Calm.
Good.
So I think we're good.

Andy   That's it?

Rick   8 a.m. tomorrow!
Or make it 7. Paperwork and stuff.

Andy   Great.

Rick   Hey.
Sure you wanna do this?

Andy   Uh—

Rick   I mean—

Andy   Yes. No, definitely. Things are—(*tough*)

Rick   Oh yeah. Sure. For a lot of folks.

Andy   Especially since—

Rick   Sure, sure. Hard transition.
We get a lot of people—(*who are just out of prison*)

Andy   Yeah the woman at the, my—I'm living at a halfway-kind of—

Rick   People with your background can be, actually, the—(*best at this kind of job*)

Andy   I've seen it all.

Rick   Exactly. Cuz it can get a little—

Andy   Like I said, everything.

Rick   It can get a little—

Andy   I'll be fine.

Rick   Great.
Let me know, if you start to—
There can be, kind of, an initial—

Andy   I'll be just fine.
Well, how bad is it?

Rick   Not too bad.

Andy   Okay.
Great.

Rick   So did you get married after high school? Or—

Andy   Yeah . . .

Rick   Old ball and chain.

Andy   Divorced now, though.

Rick   Oh yeah?
Huh.
Huh.
I think you'll do great here.

Scene Two

B, *fifteen, waits in the hallway of his high school, eating an apple. He's between classes. He kind of nods at some people passing by but kind of doesn't.*

Simon, *also fifteen, enters, wearing a big set of headphones blasting beats.*

B   Simon

Simon   Woah

B   Hey

Simon   Yeah, pretty much, just . . .
What's up?

B   Not much
"Chillin"

Simon   "Eating an apple"

B   Exactly.

Simon   Cool, cool

Pause.

Simon   Alright   **B**   Are we hanging out this weekend, or—

Simon   What?

B   Are we hanging out again this weekend, or—

Simon   Shhhh.
Dude.

B   Sorry.

Simon   Sometimes you're too quiet and then other times it's like—you're too loud.

B   Are we hanging out again this weekend, or?

Simon   Yeah I'm pretty busy, so, not really sure

B   I got some more of that weed.

Simon   Oh.
Oh yeah?

B   From my cousin.

Simon   Alright.
Well, maybe.
Yeah, maybe.
Maybe tonight?

B   Tonight's good.

Simon   Alright.
I'll call you if I can come by tonight.

B   Awesome.
Yeah so you can take the bus to my house and uh get off at

Simon   I remember how to get there, man.

B   Okay.
So I'll see you.

Simon   What's that?

B   What?

Simon   What are you doing?

B   High-five?

Simon   Shit man
"High-five"
High-five!

They high-five.

B   Cool.

Simon   Cool.

He puts his headphones back on, back in his own world.

Scene Three

Dairy Queen.

B *sits at a table, eating a veggie burger.*

Andy *comes back from the restroom.*

Andy   Have you seen these new hand driers? I mean they had them before but to put your hands in the middle and just—
Like some kind of space thing. Crazy.
So.
Man oh man. Look at all this food.
How's that uh, that uh—veggie burger.

B *shrugs.*

Andy   So what, you're a "vegetarian" now?

B   I'm a vegan.

Andy   Uh-huh. And why's that?

B   Just because.

Andy   But why though?

B   Lots of reasons.

Andy   "Lots of reasons." Alright. Takes all kinds, I guess.
So how's school?

B *shrugs.*

Andy   Classes good, all that?

B *is silent.*

Andy   Your grades are good. That's great.

B   How do you know?

Andy   Trish and John invited me over. While you were at school on Monday.

B   That's weird.

Andy   They say you're doing really good. That's really good.

B   It's easy. You just like . . . (*show up, do the stupid work*)
School is dumb.

Andy   No, but it's good. It's good to do good in school.
You have a girlfriend?

B   No.

Andy   It's good to have a girlfriend, you know, in high school. To practice being with someone. Otherwise you can kind of get stuck alone.
You thinking about college at all?

B   I'm fifteen.

Andy   Yeah but college is really important. Can't do anything without it, these days. Used to be different.
I heard you got a fish. I heard they got you a fish. That's cool. Must be fun to have a fish.

B   It died.

Andy   Oh.
What are you looking at?

B   Nothing.

Andy   You think I look different?
Haven't worn make-up in five years. Feels weird.

B   You look like a clown.

Andy   What?

B   Nothing.

Andy   What'd you say.

B   I said nothing.

Andy   Alright.

Pause.

So uh *and* I got a job today. At Parnell.

B   At the slaughterhouse?

Andy   It's good news.

B   It's disgusting.

Andy   What's wrong with Parnell?

B   It's inhumane.

Andy   What does that mean?

B   It's cruel to animals.

Andy   Oh please.

B   The way they do it is / really really sick.

Andy   It is not "inhumane." They gave me a tour.
Everything is—I mean it's not—
They do everything they can to—
Listen, alright. Here's how it—

B   I know how it—

Andy   They have these tunnels, right?
And they run the cow along the tunnel, this special tunnel with all these curves, so it can't
see what's ahead and it doesn't know what's coming. It can't see anything in front of it
itself, or around itself, so it doesn't even know to get scared. It just sees the next curve.
And then before it knows it—boom. It goes around the last curve and it's dead.

B   Just like the Nazis.

Andy   Okay, you know what? I got a job.
And fine, so, you have an opinion, but you know what they say about them.

B   What.

Andy   What?

B   What do they say about opinions?

Andy   Well, they're like, you know. Buttholes.

B   What?

Andy   Listen, they pay you real well over at Parnell. There's plenty of breaks.
Trying to save up enough for my own place. You can come over and watch TV, or
whatever. Play video games. What is it that you like to do now?

B   You're gonna stink all the time, you know that.

Andy   I am not!

B   Like dead animals.

Andy   Why don't you shut your goddamn mouth.
Christ.

She puts down her burger.

Thing tastes like shit.

Scene Four

B *and* **Simon** *in* **B**'s *room, sharing a joint.*

B   And I started telling her how sick I thought it was—

Simon   Yo, slide me that roach—

B *gives* **Simon** *the joint.*

B   But she like doesn't even care.

Simon   Slide me—

B   Scarfing this hamburger down—

Simon   "Slide me up that roach, nigga, slide me up that roach—"

B   Like a pig. You know. Gobble gobble.
Turkey, whatever.

Simon   Some people just aren't that conscious.

B   Yeah, but like—
It's the whole like—
It's how she thinks. Doesn't. She doesn't think about anything.
She just does something, if it's in front of her, and then screw the consequences, you know?
She's like the stupidest person I've ever met. Or no, she's like most people. If it's in front of their face, they just do it. Not even thinking. Frickin' sleep-walking.

Simon   Exactly. That's how come we're in Iraq.

B   Yeah. Yeah!
And it's like the same thing, it's like people just doing stuff because it's easy, and not even thinking.

Simon   Yo, that shirt looks kinda stupid on you.

B   What?
Oh.
I just got it.

Simon   Kinda fruity.
To be honest.

B   Oh.

Should I take it off?

Simon   Nah, you're good.
I'm just saying. Better watch yourself.

B   Yeah.
I don't know. I kind of like it.

Simon   This town?
Shit.

B   Yeah.

Simon   Rumors are like bullets.

B   No, yeah. / I know.

Simon   Knock you down.
Cut you out. Cut you *out*, nigga.

B   "Nigga."

Simon   You gotta problem, nigga?

B   No.

Simon   This is some strong shit.

B   My cousin's got the hook-up.
I'm like seeing wavy lines.

Simon   What?

B   I don't know, there's all these lines. It's cool.

Simon (*laughing*)   Weed doesn't make you hallucinate. You're crazy.

B   Yes it does.

Simon   Alright.

B   Sometimes it does.

Simon   "Woo! Wavy lines! I'm a fucking . . . pizza!"
Yo, you think you could get me some more of this?

B   Oh.
Um—
I mean, you can come over anytime you want.

Simon   I'll pay you for it.
Think Alex and some of those guys want to buy some too.

B   Isn't that like dealing?

Simon   Uh, no. Not really.
I'll just buy a bunch from you and sell it to them.

B   I don't know.

Simon   Come on.
This stuff is already legal in like, a couple places already, and it's gonna be legal in more probly once people realize it's not that bad, so it's stupid that we're even stuck in this thing where like we're in the past, and other places are in the future, and it's like . . .
Nah, it's cool, I get it.

B   I just don't want to get caught, or whatever.

Simon   By who? You'd just be selling it to me.

B   But you can smoke it here anytime you want, or I guess I can give you some of this stuff.

Simon   Yeah but I told you Alex and a bunch of those guys told me they wanted some too. I basically promised them I'd get them some. So I need, like, more.

Pause.

B   Um yeah I guess I can talk to my cousin about that.

Simon   Look at you. Manning up. I like it.

B   But are you still gonna wanna like—

Simon   What?

B   Hah.
Are you still gonna wanna come over and smoke it here?

Simon   Yeah, man.
Yeah sure.
We're tight.

B   Alright. I'll get some for you.

Simon   Manning up. "B" the man. *Be* the man, B.
B cool.

He freestyles.

(Note: The actor can develop a freestyle in rehearsal if they'd like. Think Eminem with some references to the Iraq War or George W. Bush thrown in—this is 2003.)

Simon *is okay but not great.*

Nonetheless, **B** *loves it.*

B   Hey, that track you dropped at assembly was awesome.

Simon   You liked that? Seemed like everyone thought it was kinda gay.

B   That's cause they didn't get the lyrics and stuff!
I thought it was so frickin' conscious.

And the beats were pretty fresh, too.
I was like dancing a little bit.

Simon   No you weren't.

B   Yeah I was! I was like uh-huh—uh-huh.

Simon   Look at you! "Dancing."

B   Uh. Uh.
Mixing it up.

Simon   Dancing. Look at you.
I saw you, actually.
I was looking at you.
Wanted to see whether you liked it.

B   Yeah I loved it.
I love your stuff.
It's so good.

Simon   Well, don't get sweet about it.

B   I'm not! / Shut up.

Simon   Just wanted to see if you liked it.

B   I did.
I've been listening to your CD. It's pretty fresh.

Simon   "Fresh!" You're like an eighties movie, man.
Like the Fresh Prince of uh—of uh—

B   Fresh Prince of Your Butthole.

Simon   You wish.

B   Shut up.

Simon   Think I'm gonna write a new track about this day. Called "Slide me up that roach." About getting high with your bruthas.

B   Who's the brutha?

Simon   We're bruthas. You and me.

B   Oh you're a brutha now, huh?

Simon   Indeed I am, brutha.

B   Brutha this.

B *shoves* **Simon**, *playfully.*

Simon *shoves* **B**, *less playfully.*

B *goes to shove him back, but* **Simon** *is looking at the joint.*

Simon   This shit is cashed.
Yo, you want to suck me off again?

B   Oh.
Uh . . .
Trish and John are like—(*coming homing soon*)

Simon   But they're not like—

B   No, not yet, but like—

Simon   We're in your room. They're not gonna like barge in or something are they?

B   No.

Simon   Crazy horny today.

B   Okay. Yeah.

Simon   What?

B   Nothing.

Simon   I thought you liked doing that.

B   No yeah I do.

Simon   Sweet.

He starts to unbuckle his belt.

Scene Five

Just off the kill floor.

We hear the hum of machinery waiting to begin.

Rick *knocking on the door of the women's bathroom.*

Rick   Andy? Hey, Andy?

Andy   Yeah?

Rick   Morning ten is over.

Andy   I know. I'm sorry.
Just—
Hang on!

Rick   We can't start the line until you're back at your station.

Andy   No I know.

Sound of vomiting.

Rick   You alright?

Andy   Yup! Just fine!

More vomiting.

Rick   You sure?

Andy   Yup!

Sound of a toilet flushing.

Andy *comes out.*

We see her in her kill floor uniform for the first time.

Andy   Sorry.

Rick   You've been doing so good.

Andy   I know.
Just got to me all of a sudden.

Rick   No, I know. It happens.
Just—you gotta be back when ten's over. You got to. It's just company policy. I could get in real trouble.
Or you could.

Andy   Alright.

She turns to go, but then:

Andy   A lot of those cows are still living, Rick.

Rick   What's that?

Andy   When we skin them. They're still living.

Rick   I told you there were gonna be some like that.

Andy   There's a lot.

Rick   Well . . .

Andy   Makes it harder, is all.

Rick   Sure. No, sure.
That's just part of it, you know.

Andy   I know. Just seems like—
If we could slow down a bit.

Rick   Can't do that.

Andy   Alright.

Rick   You know that.

Andy   I know.
Just feels kind of unsafe, how fast everything is.

Rick   Hey, Andy.
Let me tell you something.
There's about five cameras on us right now.
All those cameras have eyes behind them.
Aberdeen is watching.
You understand?

Andy   Yeah.
I'm sorry.

Rick   You're doing good.
Don't think too much.

Andy   Okay.

Rick   You alright?

Andy   Yup.
Good to go.

Rick   Something on your—

He picks something off her uniform.

Looks at the thing.

Flicks the thing away.

Rick   Okay.
Go. Hustle.
(*Into his walkie-talkie*) We're good to go.

Scene Six

Andy *and* **B** *in* **Andy***'s new apartment.*

The space is not well furnished.

Andy   You like it?

B   It's okay.

Andy   "It's okay." It's a good apartment. Clean, safe, and it's close to that bus.
Yeah, it's pretty small, but soon as I save up enough money I'm gonna get a sofa here,
and definitely you know a divider and another bed, so, for—

B   Why?

Andy   So you can stay here when you want!

B   Uh . . .

Andy   Hey I got you this video game thing too, at Goodwill, and a few games. "Iron
Maiden 4."

B   I'm not into video games anymore.

Andy   Yes you are!

B   Anyway these are really old.

Andy   What, they're gonna wear out?
Tried it earlier. Works fine.
It's fun, too. Actually I couldn't really figure out how to—(*get it going*)
But it seemed fun. Killing Nazis. Or—wait—who do you kill in this game?
Zombies. Zombie Nazis. (*The*) TV sucks, but—

B   Have fun with that.

Andy   You like video games. We used to—

B   Not anymore.

Andy   When you were little! The—the—
Well, what are you into then, B? Christ.

B   Just don't want to waste my time, is all.
Life is short.

Andy   Oh, man.

She starts to put the system away.

B   Don't get upset.

Andy   I'm not upset.

B   We can play it if you want.

Andy   Put your goddamn shit down.
Standing there looking like an idiot.

Pause.

B   I'm into books and stuff.
Music.
Rap, mostly.

Andy   Okay, like Tupac?

B   He's okay.
Like edgier stuff. More political. Stuff with a message. Not just shoot kill
nigga nigga.

Andy   Watch your mouth.

B   I'm allowed to say that.

Andy   Not in *this* house.
Throwing that word around.

B   Whatever.

Andy   I used to be really into music, you know.

B   Yeah, in the eighties.

Andy   In the nineties!

B   Same difference.

Andy   There was some great music back then. I used to put on my headphones and just rock out. Go to concerts sometimes, too. Those were the best. Just lose yourself. Rockin' out.
Your dad was really into music too, we both were. Bunch of local bands.
And then the classics, of course: Nirvana, Soundgarden, Alice in Chains—

B   Pssh.

Andy   Those are good bands.

B   For old people.

Andy   Not back then. Back then, old people hated that stuff. My mom hated that stuff.
That's the way it is, you gotta find the music your parents hate—and *like* it.
So what, who do you like? Give me some names. Of rappers.
I can get funky.

She shows him how to get funky.

B   That's not funny.
I don't know, I like lots of rappers.
There's this guy at my school who's pretty good.

Andy   Yeah?

B   Simon. He's like so frickin' conscious—

Andy (*laughing*)   "Simon"?

B   What?

Andy   Just doesn't sound like a rapper's name. "Simon."
Sounds kind of lame.

B   Shut up!

Andy   What? Sorry. He's white?

B   His rapper name is "D."

Andy   Just D, huh?

B   Yeah.

Andy   You're B! You guys should be friends. B and D.
You should have a group called like "The Alphabet Brothers."
Are you friends?

B   Sort of.

Andy   Who are your friends?

B   I'm not gonna name them for you.
Just people.

Andy   You should write your own raps, is what you should do.
Do you?

B   Nah.

Andy   You should.

B   I'm not good at it.

Andy   So what are you good at?

B   I don't know.
Listening to stuff. Music.

Andy   Well, you can't just listen your whole life.
You should figure out what you're good at. I bet there's lot of things. What kinds of books do you read?
What kind?
Mysteries?
Horror? Stephen King, and stuff?

B   I don't know.

Andy   Come on.

B   Just books.

Andy   That's all you're gonna give me?

B   Well, what else do you want?

Andy   I don't know.
You got crushes on any girls?
Seen any good movies?
You have to practice talking.
It's hard, I know, to put things into words, but you have to try.
So, as for me . . .
I'm back . . .
It was hard being gone . . . but not as hard as I thought, I guess.
It was hard being away from you.
But . . .
No one tried to mess with me.
The food was terrible.
But I made some friends, actually, this woman named Jenny who really—well, she made me laugh, she had like this funny voice, really high, she'd be like—I think she was from Tennessee or something, or North Carolina, one of the states where they

talk weird—she'd be like "How are you doing today, Andy?"
Every morning: "How are you doing today, Andy?"
That always cracked me up.
You would have liked her, if you could have met her. I told her about you.

Pause.

B   I should go.

Andy   B.

B   What?

Andy   You just got here.
Where do you have to be?

B   Just—home.
Not here.
I'm sorry.
It's just basically really depressing here.

Scene Seven

Rick's *office.*

Muted sound of the kill floor.

Rick *has his head on the desk—he's sleeping.*

After a moment, **Andy** *comes in.*

Andy   Hey.

Rick (*a yell*)   AAAAH, sorry, didn't—

Andy   Door was open so I—

Rick   Just taking a little—(*nap*)

Andy   No, that's—(*okay*)

Rick (*collecting himself*)   Uuuuuh . . .
Dreamland, sorry, caught up to me. Weird stuff.
"Sleeping on the job."
So.
How's it—(*going?*)

Andy   Yeah it's—

Rick   Working hard!

Andy   Yeah, I'm sorry about the uh, throwing up thing—

Rick   Oh, yesterday?
Psssh.

Listen, down there I gotta be a little strict, you know.
"Boss man." Because of the—(*he makes an "eyes" gesture*).
But up here I can say whatever I want.
Mostly.
You're doing great though. Head down, speed up. Caught on quick.

Andy   That's good. I'm trying.
Sorry about the—really.

Rick   It's fine.

Andy   Got myself a nose plug, and some ear things, so that's—
Anyway, thanks for inviting me for lunch. Had to wash up in that little room. Didn't want to come up here smelling like—

Rick   Would have been fine. But you look good.

Andy   Yeah?

Rick   Comfortable.

Andy   Screw you!

Rick   No, good, though.

Andy   Sorry.

Rick   It was supposed to be a compliment.
I'm so bad at compliments.

Rick *reaches for his lunchbag.*

Rick   Where's your—(*lunch*)

Andy   What?

Rick   Oh did you—

Andy   Oh I thought we were— (*going out to lunch*)

Rick   Oh no it's—

Andy   I'm a fucking idiot.

Rick   No it's fine it's just—

Andy   Stupid. Of course.

Rick   I should have been more clear.
Not enough time is all.

Andy   No, yeah, of course.

Rick   Gotta get you back down on that floor.
But, hey.
Here.

He holds half his sandwhich out to **Andy**.

Andy   Oh, you don't have to—

Rick   Take it.

Andy   I don't want to—(*take your sandwich*)

Rick   Ruff ruff!

Andy   Okay.

She takes it.

Andy   Thank you. That's really nice of you.

Rick   It's no big deal.
My wife made these. She's not a very good cook.
Bet you're a good cook.

Andy   Not really.

Rick   Bet you are.

Andy   Okay.

Rick   Got those cooking hands.

Pause.

So how you holding up down there?

Andy   Pretty good.
(*Re: the sandwich*) This is good.

Rick (*re: the sandwich*)   Yeah? Good.
(*Re: how you holding up*) Really?

Andy   Yeah.

Rick   It's pretty bad down there.

Andy   I mean . . .
It's terrible.

Rick   Awful.

Andy   Really bad.

Rick   Disgusting.

Andy   Go back to my place stinking like it. Lay in bed there just smelling it.

Rick   Sure, sure. Terrible smell.

Andy   I've been having these dreams too, crazy, like I'm one of them. Running along the path like they do then—shoop, I'm split wide open.

Rick   Yeah, I have some crazy dreams too sometimes like
Well—
Never mind.

Hair in this . . .

Andy   What?

Rick *removes a hair from his sandwich.*

Rick   Plenty of breaks though. Down there.

Andy   Those breaks are good. Been standing outside to smoke.
You ever work down there?

Rick   No way.
Not that I wouldn't. I just didn't.

Andy   Uh-huh.
I'm happy to be working.
I'll get used to it.
It's not so bad.
Money's good.
I mean there could always be more.

Rick   Well, hey.
(*Gesturing around the office*) Play your cards right . . .

Andy   Oh.
Oh yeah?

Rick   White people. I'm telling you. The ones who stay. Do well.
My boss in Aberdeen is racist as all fuck.
You stay around long enough, I'm telling you . . .
And you're a good worker, too. I can see it.

Andy   Isn't easy.

Rick   You're good.
I'll let them know.

Andy   Lot of good workers down there. Been here longer.

Rick   Yeah . . .
Get you off that kill floor.

Andy   Well.
Where?

Rick   Up here!

Andy   That . . . would be nice.

Rick   Pretty nice, right?

Andy   Really nice. It would.

Rick   May take a while. But we'll get you up here, with me.
So how are things going otherwise?

Andy   Good.
You?

Rick   Good good.

Andy   Good.

Scene Eight

B *leaves a message for* **Simon**.

B   Hey, Simon.
Hope you're enjoying that uh stuff I got you, and thanks for the envelope you left in my locker. I counted the money and it's all there so that's good.
Keep looking for you after last period but I haven't seen you.
But maybe we can hang out this week sometime.
I'm free tomorrow after school, and also Wednesday, and Thursday and Friday are looking pretty good too, and also this weekend. Hah. So basically every day. Except Saturday in the morning I have a dentist's appointment.
Anyway let me know what works for you.
Hey on your CD I *really* like track five. I think it's my favorite.
Okay, "brutha."
Bye.

Andy *leaves a message for* **B**.

Andy   B.
Okay you're not answering your phone.
Listen I haven't heard from you in a few days, but I'm assuming we're on for Tuesday, right, at my place?
Just wanted to call and see what sorts of snacks you want. I'm not really sure what you like, so—.
Things are going okay. I mean things are fine at my job, not great, but just fine.
Hope stuff is going okay with you.

She goes to hang up, and then:

It's your mom.

She hangs up.

We see that **Andy** *is is at the grocery store—maybe she's holding a red basket.*

Sarah, *a stranger, approaches.*

Sarah   It's hard, right? So many choices.

Andy   I know.
I usually just go for the cheapest.
But my son's a vegetarian now.
Says he doesn't want to drink milk anymore.

Sarah   A vegan?

Andy   A what?

Sarah   No animal products. He's a vegan.

Andy   Sure, yeah, that.

Sarah   You are really in for it.

Andy   And who knew you could make milk out of nuts now. Crazy.

Sarah   I know, it's like—how do they get the milk out of there?

Andy   Yeah, right!
That's a funny picture, some farmer trying to like . . . milk an almond.

Sarah   Yeah! That's funny.

Pause.

My husband likes the soy milk.

Andy   Oh yeah?

Sarah   Easier on his digestive system. Than regular milk. So that's what I get.
It was hard to make the switch, I think. But he got used to it.

Andy   Maybe that's what I'll try.

Sarah   Yeah, he's uh—well he's an airline pilot, you know, so he kind of comes and
goes.
So when he's back I like to have stuff he likes.

Andy   I hear you.
My son's not around much, so I'm the same way. Just like to have stuff that he likes.

Sarah   Well, and kids are so picky, though, right?
I have three, so, you know how it is.

Andy   Yeah. Little bastards sometimes.

Sarah   I know!

Andy   Love 'em, and you also—

She makes a strangling gesture.

Sarah   Exactly. Sometimes I'm just like—I need one minute, okay? Or an hour.
Like a whole hour. Sometimes I'll just steal some time, like I'll drop my younger one
off at dance, or something, and I know my older one's waiting for me, but I'll just
stop and get a coffee, and just sit with it for a minute by the window. Let him wait.
You have such a nice face, you know.

Andy   I'm sorry?

Sarah   Oh, sorry. I just think you have a really nice face.
Like, I can tell you're a nice person.

Sometimes I can just tell.

Andy   Oh. Thank you.
Did you—

Sarah   Huh?

Andy   Sorry. Are you from here?

Sarah   Oh no, no. Not at all.
My husband's mom is here, and we—
So we just drive over sometimes. From Aberdeen.
Sometimes he comes, and sometimes I just come, when he's off, you know, sailing the skies.
How about you, you're from here, or—?

Andy   Born and raised.

Sarah   It's a nice town.

Andy   It's a shithole.
I mean, it's okay.
Just not a lot going on.

Sarah   Yeah, we just . . . (*come through sometimes*)
Anyway, I'll let you get back to—

Andy   Oh. Alright.
I'm Andy.

Sarah   Andy!

Andy   Andy Weiser.

Sarah   Andy Weiser.
Sarah Miller.
Well, hey. Maybe I'll see you around town.

Andy   That'd be nice.
Sarah Miller.

Sarah   Yes.
Try the soy milk.
It's not bad.
I even drink it now, sometimes, myself.

She leaves.

Andy *watches her go.*

Scene Nine

Night. Sound of a car stopping. **Rick** *and* **Andy** *in* **Rick**'*s car.*

They've stopped just outside **Andy***'s apartment.*

Andy   Thanks for the ride.

Rick   Oh, yeah. Saw you walking.

Andy   That damn bus.

Rick   Seems like it comes when it wants to.

Andy   Whenever the fuck it wants to.
Which is not very often.

Rick   In the morning, too?

Andy   What?

Rick   Is it late in the morning?
Is that why you've been late?

Andy   Oh. Yeah. I'm sorry about that.
It was just once.

Rick   Twice.

Andy   I guess, yeah.
I'm sorry.

Rick   It's alright. You just gotta be on time.

Andy   No, I know. I'm sorry.
That bus.

Rick   The Mexicans are always on time. So.
Just something to be aware of.

Andy   Sure. Sure.

Rick   Trying to get you promoted, you know.

Andy   No, I know. Thank you.
Well, thank you for the ride.

Rick   Hey.
You ever think back about high school?

Andy   Sometimes. Not that much.

Rick   Yeah I was thinking about it—
I don't remember you at all.

Andy   Well, fuck you too!

Rick   Hah.

Andy   Sorry.

Rick   No, it's funny. You're funny.

I feel bad that I don't remember you.

Andy   No reason to. I was kind of just—around.

Rick   I was trying to, I was just—
I couldn't think of anything.

Andy   Oh well.

Rick   Did you have kind of—

Andy   I had like—

Rick   Same color hair?

Andy   Yup.

Rick   What were you into?

Andy   Drugs, mostly.
Music. Loved music.
Fucking. Sorry.

Rick   That's fine.
Me too. I mean—

Andy   I had this boyfriend—

Rick   Oh yeah?
Who?

Andy   Randy / Skilling.

Rick   Randy Hemschauser?

Andy   No. Who's that.

Rick   Oh.
Randy *Skilling*?

Andy   Yeah.
Brown hair?
Used to, like—well I guess he didn't really do that much.
Used to walk around the halls. Like everybody fucking else.

Rick (*i.e. "I don't remember him either"*)   Nope.
No.

Andy   Doesn't matter.
Bastard cheated on me, so—
With Lisa Harding.

Rick   Lisa Harding?

Andy   That bitch.

Rick   Oh man. Yeah. Wow.

She was hot.

Andy   Yeah she was.
Just about ripped my heart out, all that.

Rick   I definitely remember her.

Andy Loved that guy. "Randy."	**Rick** Lisa Harding.
Moved somewhere. Long gone.	Big, like—(*tits*)
Godamn.	Hah.
What an asshole.	Sure.

Pause.

Andy   *You* were pretty popular.

Rick   Thanks.

Andy   Well, I'll see you tomorrow.

Rick   Hey.

Andy   Yeah?

Rick   I don't know.

Andy   What?

Rick   Are you happy?

Andy   For fuck's sake.

Rick   What?

Andy   Nothing.

Rick   No, what.

Andy   "Are you happy."
Shit.

Rick   Sorry.
I just—

Andy   No I'm not happy. Who's happy. Who fucking cares.
I get up. I get a coffee from the store. I get on the goddamn bus. I go to work.
I go back to the place. I wake up the next day. I do it again. I keep going. That's
what I do.
"Are you happy." Fuck you.
Sorry.

Rick   I was gonna tell you that *I'm* not happy.

Andy   Oh. Sorry.
So you're not happy, huh?

Rick   No.
When's the last time you had a happy day?

Andy   Oh, man. What is with you and this—(*happiness bullshit?*)

Rick   I'm serious. The last time.
I want to know.

Pause.

Andy   I took a trip to Florida, with B, with my son. To Miami. Near Miami. To a beach there. Right after my husband left me. I got some money out of that. Not much, but enough to like—and I'd never been to a beach, so. Not a real one.
And it was so beautiful. I mean you see pictures but it was like—being there.
I was like—this is a real place, you know?

Rick   Yeah.

Andy   People live here? Crazy.
We swam in the ocean, me and B, and we were like—
You know, it was like—

Pause.

Rick   I really like you.

Andy   What?

Rick   What?

Andy   What'd you say?

Rick   Nah, nothing.
I really like you.

Andy   That's what I thought you said.
You're my boss.

Rick   I'm not saying it's good to feel this way.

Andy   You're married.

Rick   Yeah . . .

Andy   You don't even know me.

Rick   I'm getting to know you.

Andy   No you're not.

Rick   Well, damnit, I'm trying!

Pause.

Sorry.

Andy   I'm not a cheater.

Rick   Me neither. No way.
You're so pretty.

Andy   Bullshit.

Rick   Got those strong hands.

Andy   That's not a compliment.

Rick   It is. You're strong.
I like it when you swear. It's like—woah. Something going on in there.

Andy   I have anger problems, Rick.

Rick   I like that. Shows you've got a fire in the—in the uh—

Pause.

Andy   You've got a son.

Rick   Yup.

Andy   Wouldn't be right.

Rick   No.

They sit there.

Scene Ten

Afternoon.

B, *with backpack, waits outside his school for* **Simon**.

Andy *approaches.*

Andy   Hey.

B   AAAAH!

Andy   What're you up to?   **B**   Why're you at my school?

Andy   Was thinking you were gonna come by again yesterday. Left you like three messages.

B   What are you doing here?

Andy   You say you're gonna show up, you need to show up. Can't be a deadbeat, B. That's your dad's job. I need to talk to you. You wanna go somewhere?

B   You can't just follow me around.

She grabs his arm.

Andy   Wait.

B   Ow!

Andy   Why are you angry with me?
Are you angry at everyone, or just at me?
I wrote you all those letters, did you get 'em?

B   Yes. Let go of me.

Andy   Did you read 'em?

B   Yes!

Andy   Well, why didn't you write back?

She lets go of his arm.

Andy   Is there anything you want to say to me?

B   You're a frickin' psycho.

Andy   Oh, shut up. I didn't grab you that hard.

B   You're like a stalker. / I should call the police.

Andy   I'm not a stalker. I'm your mom.

B   I'm fifteen.

Andy   So?

B   So it's too late.

Andy   It is not "too late."

B   Five years?

Andy   I know exactly what you were doing during those five years. Trish and John sent me letters, unlike yourself. I know that your paper on the president was good, was really good, I know about the fish you got that died, I know you've been a pretty nice kid and they've enjoyed having you, mostly, except for how quiet you are. Now what they didn't tell me is that you're a vegetarian now, but I learned that from you myself so what's the problem?
What are you laughing about?
If there's something you want to say to me, then say it.
Say it!
Say it.

B   I gotta go.

Andy   Hey wait!
I got you something.

She pulls a bag of water out of her coat pocket. Inside it is a little live fish.

A fish!

B   Why'd you bring me a fish?
I don't want that.

Andy   I got it from Wal-mart, it was fifty cents.
I thought you might like it. To make up for the one that died.

B   That was like two years ago.

Andy   But I would have gotten you one then, if I could.

B   I don't want a fish anymore.

Andy   Yeah, well. But here it is.
This one doesn't have a name yet. You can name it.
Gonna flush it if you don't take it. You know I will.

B *takes it.*

Andy   You know how to take care of a fish?

B   Yes.

Andy   Cuz you killed the last one.

B   I did not.
It committed suicide.

Andy   Hey, maybe you can talk to him. He's a good listener. Talked to him some on the bus here.

B   Stop lying.

Andy   It's true. I whispered. Everyone was looking at me.

She whispers something to the fish.

Like that.
So you want me to walk with you a few blocks?

B   No.

Andy   Alright.
Talk to that fish. He'll listen.

She leaves.

B *puts the fish in a bowl in his room.*

Time passes.

B *makes a phone call.*

B   Hey, Simon.
Uh . . .
You don't have to say hi to me at school. Or afterwards. I totally get it.
But um . . . actually I do want to talk to you though, about your CD, like I've been thinking about some of the lyrics and I think maybe track two should actually be track three, leading into track four, and then track three should be track ten. I think that flow would be awesome. If you come over I'll play them for you that way and we can

talk about it. And I got some more of that weed, so.
Anyway—
Call me, ya frickin jerk.
Just kidding.
Bye.

He hangs up the phone.

B   Stupid.

He walks to the fish.

B   What's your name, fish?
I said, *what is your name*?
Can't talk, huh?
Stupid fish.
Gay-ass fish.
Ugly-ass fuckwad bitch.

He walks to the mirror. Flexes. Not much there.

He punches his own arm disdainfully.

He walks back to the fish, looks at it for a beat.

B   Your name is fish.
Your name is . . . C.
Like the letter.
Like the ocean.
C the fish.
C the Sea.

Pause.

Then **B** *attempts a freestyle.*

B   See the sea flow out of me . . . crazy
Lately I been, I don't know . . . hazy.
baba baba baba . . . ba blah blah
I'm a rapper and I'm . . . amazing.
You're a fish and . . . you are lazy
FUCK YOU, Simon, making me CRAZY!
  . . .
Dang it. I got no skills.

B *'s phone rings.*

He looks at who's calling—it's **Simon**.

B   Hey! Woah.
  . . .
Uh, good! Yeah, not much, just uh . . . hanging out. Chillin'.
  . . .

Friday?
No, that's good. That's great.
So I'll see you then. Friday, after school.

. . .

Awesome. Okay.
See ya, bro.

B *hangs up the phone.*

A beat—a smile.

He gives the fish a thumbs-up.

Scene Eleven

An alley behind the slaughterhouse. Muffled sound of the kill floor, then the machinery wrenches and screeches to a stop.

Andy *comes out the back door. She's shaking. She lights a cigarette and smokes it.*

After a moment, **Rick** *comes out.*

Rick   You alright?

Andy   Yup.

Rick   They got everything cleaned up in there, so—

Andy   Alright.

Rick   I think we're gonna start up the line again pretty soon.

Andy   I'll be in in a minute.

Rick   The Mexicans are ready to go.

Andy   I need. A minute.

Rick   Alright.
Wasn't your fault.

Andy   I could see she was sleepy. Should have said something.

Rick   It wasn't your fault, Andy.

Andy   Yeah I just I should of said something.

Rick   I think she's gonna be okay. I do.

Andy   Hard to keep up in there.
Everything—boom boom boom.
Half those cows are still alive.

Rick   Well—

Andy   They're kicking.

Rick   That can be reflex.

Andy   They're right above me.
I can hear 'em mooing.

Rick   Well—

Andy   Someone should do something.

Rick   Someone probably should.

Andy   It's dangerous to us.
Kind of un—, you know, *humane*, too.

Rick   What?

Andy   Hate to see a thing suffer like that.
Think if things were a little slower, we could do it better.
It's like—stop. Just stop for a second. Everything stop.

Rick   Listen, I don't like it too much either.
But you know, what do you want me to do?
You can't worry too much about the big picture. That's where you get in trouble.
Get distracted.
Like uh—
Like uh—

Andy   Rosalie.

Rick   Like Rosalie in there.
She's gonna be fine. We'll get her some time off.

He looks at his watch.

You alright though?

She says nothing.

A moment.

Then he turns to leave.

She puts out her cigarette and moves towards him, starting to take off her apron.

Andy   Rick, listen. I got something I / gotta say —

Rick   Oh hey, Andy—I almost forgot.
I talked to HQ this AM, and it looks like—
It's looking real good on that promotion.

Andy   Oh.
Oh yeah?

Rick   Yeah! So.

Andy   That's great.
Oh my God. Great.

Rick   Not a done deal yet, but looking pretty good, yeah.
Gonna take a couple months, probably, though.
But good news!

Andy   That's . . . really good. Thank you.

Rick   Get you on that fast track! To uh, to uh—
Hey, we could go celebrate somewhere. After work.

Andy   Oh! Uh—

Rick   My wife's at her mom's, so—
Free man!

Andy   Oh.

Rick   Just as friends.
Sorry. I don't—

Andy   Yeah, I better not.

Rick   I didn't—

Andy   No, I know—
It's just—sorry.
It's not right.
I'm not that kind of person.
I know how it feels to uh—be in the other position, so—no.

Rick   Sure. I understand.
Well.

He turns to go, turns back.

Rick   Hey, what were you going to tell me?

Andy   Oh, uh . . . nothing.
Thank you. For the—for looking out for me.
Really.

Rick *gives her a thumbs-up.*

Scene Twelve

B *in* **Andy***'s apartment.*

He's just come in.

His eyes are closed.

Andy *in the kitchen, offstage.*

Andy   They still closed?

B   Yes!

Andy Keep 'em closed!

B This is dumb.

Andy *runs in from the other room wearing a party hat. She blows a little party buzzer and throws confetti at* **B***, who opens his eyes.*

Andy Surprise! Surprise! Surprise!

B AAAAAAH! Stop! What are you doing? What is this?

Andy It's a surprise party.
For you!
For your birthday!
Surprise!

B It's not my birthday.

Andy Well, this weekend it is.

B Yeah, not now.

Andy Well, I'm not gonna see you until next Tuesday, and your birthday's Saturday, so I figured—sixteen's a big birthday. You gotta celebrate.
Here I got you a birthday hat.

B No.

Andy Put it on.

B It's gonna look retarded.

Andy Watch it.

B What?

Andy That's rude. I don't want you throwing words around.
Now put it on. It's a party! You can't have a party without a party hat! Put it on!
And put your shit down, don't be an asshole.
Jesus.

B *puts on the party hat.*

Andy Awww. You look just like you did when you were five.

B Yeah, dumb.

Andy Very handsome. It suits you.
Anyway sit down I got some uh—
Hang on I got some—
I mean we can have dinner later, I have a plan for dinner, but I got us some snacks.

She brings out some peach rings and a bag of Goldfish.

See? Peach thingies, your favorite.
And goldfish! In honor of your fish.
Try some.

B *tries a snack.*

Andy   Hey, how's that fish?

B   He's okay.

Andy   You named him yet?

B   I named him C.

Andy   What?
Eat some snacks.

B   His name is "C."

Andy   Like the letter?

B   Yeah.

Andy   I don't get it. C. B.
D. Your friend D.
Your name's Brendan, B.

B   I like B better.

Andy   But it's not your name. Maybe you should start using your real name.

B   I said I like B.

Andy   Alright.   **B**   What is up with you?

Andy   Nothing. What do you mean?
What are you trying to say.
I'm excited you're here.
So do you wanna do presents now or later?

B   Uh now I guess.

Andy   Okay, me too.
Here. That's just your first one.

B *opens the present. It's a Tupac CD.*

Andy   I know you said he wasn't your favorite, but I couldn't remember the other ones you said, and I thought maybe you'd still like this. It's supposed to be good. It's all his best songs, it says on the back. I thought you could listen to it on your discman.

B   Okay.

Andy   Have you heard it before?

B   No.

Andy   Okay. Well. Listen to it!

B   Now?

Andy   Try it out!

See if it's good!

B   I'll listen to it when I get home.

Andy   Listen to it now.
You gotta see if it works.

B   I think it's gonna work.

Andy   Well, you never know.
Listen to it.
I wanna make sure you like it.

B *takes his CD player out of his bag.*

Puts in the CD.

We hear the first chords of Tupac's "Changes."

At first **B** *doesn't react.*

Then he kind of gets into it—moves his head a little in time to the beat.

Andy *watches him.*

Andy   Okay, lemme listen.

She pulls the headphones away.

Oh I know this song!

She sings a little bit.

Dances.

He might be kind of amused.

B   Stop

He pulls the headphones off her.

Andy   What?

B   Your dancing sucks.

Andy   "I see no changes, all I see is racist faces."

B   It sucks, you have bad moves.

Andy   Shut up! Dumb-ass. I have good moves. / "I see no changes."

B   That's not how you dance.

Andy   Oh, how do you dance then? How do you dance?

Pause.

B   Like this.

He dances, in a small way.

Andy   Ohoh! Okay . . .
That's all you got?

B   Show's over.

He puts the CD player back in his backpack.

Andy   Wait, I have another present for you though. Well, this is kind of just a stand-in, I'm gonna buy a better one when I can, so this is just like for now.
Hang on.

She wheels out a pretty crappy looking bed on wheels.

Andy   A bed! For you!
Look, it's a little—rickety, sure, but it's—
Huh.
I'll just put some books under that or something.
It's really comfortable, I slept on it earlier. Look. What do you think?
Try it.
Try it!
Not bad, right?

B   I can't sleep on this.

Andy   It's a new bed, B, you'll sleep great there.
Anyway, I wanted to tell you that I talked to Trish and John, and they say it's fine if you want to sleep over here, whenever you want.
And I mapped out the bus lines and there's one that goes right to your school, so it'll be an easy commute.
Anyway you don't have to do it tonight, but you can, if you want to. There's a toothbrush in the bathroom.
So.

Pause.

Feel free to say something.

Pause.

Listen, I know this is hard.
Takes a while, I know, to get back to the way things were.

B   The way things were?

Andy   Things were tough, sure.
But we had some good times. I've been thinking all week about that trip we took to Florida. That was a great time. Man, we had fun. Playing in the water . . .
We should go back there. Maybe we will.
I'm telling you, if I stay at Parnell? We're gonna be able to do things like that.

B   You left me alone for like two straight days on that trip.

Andy   What? What are you talking about.

B   You were frickin' blitzed out on that trip.
You were talking about the dumbest stuff. All this stuff you were gonna do. Buy a house, we were gonna move to the city, get a dog, you were gonna go back to school, become a lawyer or something. Dumb. I was just like laughing. You were high as shit.

Andy   I didn't leave you alone. That is crazy.

B   You don't remember.

Andy   Cuz you're just making shit up.

B (*calm, in control*)   I woke up and you weren't there, and then you didn't come back that whole day, and there was no note or anything, but I didn't want to leave the motel room because I was worried you would get back and not know where I was. Stupid. So I stayed there until the afternoon and then I went to the store and got a tub of ice cream and came back with it and ate the whole thing. And then I went back to the store and got a bunch of chips and candy and ate all that stuff. And then on the way back I started to feel so sick and I threw up on a car in the parking lot and just left it there. And then I just went inside and sat on the bed. I didn't even feel like watching TV.

Pause.

Andy   That's a fucking lie.

B   Okay.

Andy   It is. You are just like your dad. You just make shit up when you don't like the way the world is going for you.
So my plan for tonight—

B   How's the slaughterhouse?

Andy   What?

B   How's it going at Parnell, you murdered a lot of cows?

Andy   Don't be dumb, B.

B   See in my opinion there are two types of people in the world.
There are people who actually do something with their lives?
Who have some kind of values or something?
And then there are people like you.
And people like you are just like, they'll—do anything.
Whatever's easiest.
Doesn't matter whether it's right, wrong, they just do it.   **Andy**
They have like blinders on.   Alright, shut up.
Or no—they're actually blind.
They're down in the dirt.
They're nothing.   **Andy**   I said shut up, B.

They're fucking worms.
I read they shoot the cows in the head.
I read sometimes they don't even die.
I bet you're the one who does it, aren't you?   **Andy**   Why don't you shut up.
I bet it doesn't even bug you.
I bet you're just like—boom, die cow.
Boom—die cow.
Boom—die.
You're dead, cow. Boom.

Andy   WHY DON'T YOU SHUT THE FUCK UP.

B   I thought you wanted me to speak.

Pause.

Andy   So my plan for tonight is we can watch some videos, like something really funny, I want to watch something funny. Alright?
Like that what was that movie we watched with the—when you were little, the—
The guy, the funny man, comedian type.
Don't laugh like that, it's weird.
I figured we could watch some videos and I bought one of those frozen pizzas.
I gotta work tomorrow, so I can't stay up too late, but—

B   I don't eat pizza.

Andy   Some vegetarian pizza.

B   Pizza's got cheese on it. I'm vegan.

Andy (*really trying to stay on track*)   What is the difference between that and vegetarian?
I don't understand.

B   Okay. For the sixteen hundredth time:
It means you don't eat anything made by an animal. Milk, cheese—

Andy   Well, then that's the stupidest thing I ever heard. Trying to starve yourself to death.

B   Yeah, alright.
I gotta go soon.

Andy   Wait, wait, wait.
I wanted you to stay over. I talked to Trish and John about it.

B   You didn't talk to me.

Andy   You're fifteen. I'm not going to ask your permission every time I want to see you.

B   Trish and John don't treat me like I'm fifteen.

Andy   And how do they treat you?

B   Like an adult.

Andy   Oh is that right, huh. Is that right. Well, then, why the hell didn't they tell you that they and I had talked about you spending the night. Why didn't they tell you *that*. If they treat you like such an adult. Jesus Christ.
It's like pulling teeth sometimes to have you here. You don't give me anything.
And enough with Trish and John. I'm sick of hearing about them.

B   I like them. They leave me alone.

Andy   I bet they do. Oh I bet.
You know I had to beg them to take you? They didn't want to. And then the only reason they did was because of that child support money from your dad. Nice big check, every month. Probably why their place is looking so nice now. New sofa, new TV.
Trish and John. Sick of hearing about them. *I'm* your mom, and there's soy milk in the kitchen, and a toothbrush in the bathroom, and I *bought you a bed*.
(*Realizing she shouldn't have said that thing about child support:*) Oh shit.

B   Is that why you want me to come live with you? To get some of that money?

Andy   Don't be fucking ridiculous.

B   Why do you swear so much? Makes me hate being around you.

Andy   You do not hate being around me, you little liar. That is just / bullshit.

B   You talk to me like I'm a kid.

Andy   You are a kid.

B   I'm fifteen.

Andy   Exactly. You're a child, and I'm your mom.

B   Not anymore.

Pause.

Andy   I am so sick of your shit, do you know that?

B   The reason I didn't write you any letters is because I didn't actually miss you.
I just like—forgot about you.
I was happy you were gone.

Andy   Get out of my house.
Get out. Of my house.

B   Okay.

Andy   Get *out*.

He grabs his bag and leaves.

Andy   I'm not going to keep chasing after you!

I am done, I am done chasing after you!

She kicks the bed.

It collapses.

Andy   GODDAMNIT.

Scene Thirteen

Sarah *waiting at the Dairy Queen.*

Andy *enters.*

Andy   Hey!

Sarah   Hey!
So good to see you.

They're not sure whether to hug, or what to do.

Sarah   Got that call from you, and I was like—

Andy   I know it was like—(*out of the blue*)

Sarah   No, it was good. I just, well, it was a surprise.

Andy   Right, I know. Kind of random.

Sarah   Did you find me in the phonebook, or—?

Andy   Yeah, I remembered what you'd said your last name was, so—and the phone book includes numbers for here and for Aberdeen, so—
Hope it's not—

Sarah   No, it's great. I love taking breaks like this, especially when the kids are at school.

Andy   Was it a long drive, or—?

Sarah   Just about half an hour. I listened to the radio.
And I'm going to stop by and visit my mom-in-law, so two birds with one—

Andy   Well, thanks. I hope this place is okay. The coffee is cheap. And I remembered you said you liked coffee.

Sarah   It's nice to take a break from Starbucks.

Andy   Right, I bet. Change is good!

Sarah   I just hate that place. I'm addicted, but I hate it. That terrible jazz. And all those pictures of farmers, to make you feel like you're—like you're—(*helping people when you go there*)

Andy   Hah, yeah.

Sarah   But it's right near my house, so.

Andy   Hey speaking of which I'm going to—(*get us some coffee*)

Sarah   Oh yeah would you get me a

Andy   Just a coffee?

Sarah   Yeah, uh sugar, a little cream, or no it's past two just will you get me a decaf?

Andy   Uh-huh, sure—

Sarah (*digging for her wallet*)   Here—

Andy   Oh no it's—

Sarah   Oh you don't have to—

Andy   No, I'm, it's—I invited you, so. It's my treat.

She goes.

A moment with **Sarah** *at the table alone.*

Andy *returns with two coffees.*

Andy   You said you didn't know anyone in this town and I thought, well, I don't have many friends here—

Sarah   I thought you said you grew up here?

Andy   Yeah but I mean, well, I was pretty different back then.
And a lot of folks have kind of left town.
Or kind of, we're not friends anymore. You know.

Sarah   Oh, sure, I know how that is.

Andy   People change a lot and I'm changing, and it's like—your paths just kind of—.
Basically a lot of my old friends are fucking deadbeats, so—

Sarah   Oh.

Andy   Sorry.

Sarah   No, that's—I mean, I lost touch with most of my friends from high school.
Because it turned out they sucked!

Andy   Hah, yeah.

Sarah   So you said you're a mom?

Andy   Oh yeah, I have a kid. His name is B. He's fifteen.

Sarah   B!

Andy   Well, it's Brendan but he yeah he wants to be called B because well I don't know if it's a kind of rebellion against his dad, Brendan was his dad's name too. Is.

Sarah   And you and his dad are—

Andy   Split up. Long time ago.
He cheated on me, so.

Sarah   Oh wow.

Andy   And there were other problems, but yeah that was the straw that kind of—
(*broke the camel's back*).
Seems to kind of be a pattern with me. Guys think they can—.
I mean I just think that's the worst, you know. I've done a—I haven't lived a perfect life.
But I would fucking never betray someone like that. Not if I loved them. When I love someone, boom, that's it. I would just never do that to someone. That's one thing I know about me.

Sarah   I think trust is really important.

Andy   It's not even that, it's being there, you know? It's being there. Being there. Being there for someone. Being there. Showing up. I may have problems, but I always show up.
How about your husband, you guys get along and all that?

Sarah   Oh he's great. Yeah. We have a great marriage, we do.
I mean the sex is kind of—eh. Sorry.

Andy   That's okay! I know how that is.

Sarah   And there are other problems, sure.

Andy   Hah, yeah.
Like what?

Sarah   What?

Andy   Like what are some of the problems?

Sarah   Well, after, you know, eight years it can kind of—.
But nothing, no, it's nothing big, because yeah we get along really well and so it's—
It's like a friendship at this point but a really good one. I mean I can talk to him about anything.

Andy   That must be nice. Wow.

Sarah   It is, yeah. And we do manage to get away once a year, by ourselves, usually to Italy or something, it's cheap because of the discount, because—he's a pilot, maybe I said that. Although last year we went to Spain and spent a lot of time in Sevilla, you know in the south. Which was really nice. My husband speaks Spanish, so—.
And I'm just like "Tapas. Tapas. Tapas? Tapas."
Do you ever go out of town?

Andy   Oh yeah, yeah sure.
Went to Florida a little while ago.

Sarah   Florida's great.

Andy   It's a great, uh—
It was a good—
Good trip.

Pause.

Sarah   So what do you do for a living, or for—

Andy   Oh, I . . .
I work at Parnell?

Sarah   Oh. The—

Andy   Outside of town, yeah, the

Sarah   Not on the, in the—

Andy   Oh no. No. No.
No I work in the office.

Sarah   Okay. I was like—

Andy   Yeah.

Sarah   Thought you were telling me you worked like killing cows or whatever.

Andy   No I just work in the office as a kind of, doing stuff up there.
Pretty new there, still.

Sarah   What were you doing before?

Andy   Oh I was just—I was—uh—just kind of bouncing around for a while.

Sarah   Oh, with your son or?

Andy   Yeah, with him, and then—kind of without him I guess for a bit.

Sarah   Okay.
That sounds nice.
Well, that must be a pretty good job.

Pause.

Are you alright?

Andy   What?

Sarah   Sorry, you seem—

Andy   I'm alright.
I'm really sorry.

Sarah   For what?

Andy   I'm sorry, I just—

Sarah   Do you need some money?

Andy   What?

Pause.

Sarah   Do you need some money, or something?
Sorry, I just—

Andy   I don't need any money.

Sarah   I didn't know why you—(*called me*)
And I thought maybe it was—

Andy   I didn't call you to ask for money.

Sarah   I'm sorry, I just—I don't know why I—

Andy   Why would you think that?

Sarah   I don't know.

Andy   We don't even know each other.

Sarah   I know, I just—

Andy *packs up her stuff to go.*

Sarah   Hey, Andy, wait. Wait.
I made a mistake.

Andy   Fucking high-class bitch.

Sarah   Woah. Hold on.

Andy   You remind me of some of the bitches I went to high school with.
Man, was I happy to see *them* go.

She leaves.

Scene Fourteen

B *and* **Simon** *in* **B**'s *room, looking at the fish.*

Simon   What's its name?

B   I don't know.

Simon   Serious, nigga? Let's name that fish.
Let's name him Rockwell.

B   Why?

Simon   After Norman Rockwell.
We been studying him in art.

B   Nah. This fish isn't a Rockwell.

Simon   You don't like that name?

B   It's stupid.

Simon   Rockwell? It's awesome! Cuz in all those paintings there's a fish in a bowl. Some guy sitting in a chair smoking a pipe.

B   It's not the right name for him.

Simon   What's up, Rocky?

B   His name is C.

Simon   You *did* name him.

B   Yeah.

Simon   How come you didn't say nothing one second ago.

B   I don't know, cause it's a stupid name?
Just thought of it yesterday.

Simon   C.
Just C?

B   Just like—C. The letter C.
Or Sea, the ocean.
But spelled C. The letter.

Simon   C.
What's up, C?
B, C, D.
Holy shit!

B   Yeah. That too.

Simon   We a trio now!
We half the alphabet!

B   Yup.

Simon   I like it. C.
This fish can roll.
Look at its little cheeks.

B   It's a good fish. I like it.
I just look at it sometimes.

Simon   Hah. Looking at it.
You trying to fuck that fish?

B   No.

Simon   You are!

B   It's a fish!

Simon   So? You're trying to fuck it!

B   I wouldn't have sex with a fish.
It just, like, wouldn't work.

Simon   No, I know.
You're funny, man.

B   Why?

Simon   Just are.
That would be funny though. You trying to fuck a fish.
Like—*uh, fish. Take it fish.*

B   How come you didn't call me back this week?

Simon   I called you yesterday.

B   But I called you like five times before that.

Simon   I was busy, son.

B   With what?

Simon   I just got a shitload of homework this week. Been staying in every night.
So get off my back.

He punches **B***, playfully.*

Simon   Faggot.

B   Ow.

Simon   Hey.

He gets really close to **B***. Something passes between them.*

Simon *shoves* **B***.*

B *shoves* **Simon***.*

They wrestle.

B *starts kissing* **Simon** *all over.*

Simon *shoves him off, for real.*

Simon   Damn, nigga.

B   What?

Simon   Just damn.
Sometimes you're too much, is all. Take it too far.

B   Why do you say nigga so much?

Simon   What?

B   I thought you were a conscious rapper.

Simon   I am.

B   That word's not conscious.

Simon   All the rappers use it. If you listened to more, you'd know.

B   All the Black rappers.

Simon   You think because you're half-Black you can like hold that over me or something?

B   No.
"Nigga" means ". . ."

Simon   Nah, son, the meaning changed.

B   Maybe for you.
I don't like it when you say it.

Simon   So sensitive!
Yo you're my biggest fan, I gotta listen to what you say.
You're my biggest fan, right?
Right?

B   Yeah.

Simon   Alright.
You wanna blow me?

B   Not right now.

Simon   That's cool.
I'm sorry I haven't blown you.

B   It's fine.

Simon   It's not because I think you're disgusting or anything.

B   You wanna listen to some music or something?

Simon   Nah.

B   You wanna smoke that weed?

Simon   I been smoking too much weed this week.

B   I thought you said you had homework all week.

Simon   I did. I've been busy with homework.
And then smoking weed afterwards, to relax. I wasn't lying.
It's just weird. All this.
You know?

B   Yeah.
I know.

Simon   I'm like "what am I doing?"

B   Me too.

Simon   It's good though.

B   Yeah?

Simon   Yeah.
Weird, but good.

B *tries to kiss* **Simon***, but* **Simon** *pulls away.*

Simon   My dick is so hard, son.

B   Yeah.
Okay.

Simon   Not if you don't want to.

B   No, I want to.

Simon   Awesome.

B *starts to blow* **Simon***.*

Simon *raps a little under his breath.*

Simon   Slide me up that roach, slide me up that roach . . .
Uuuh

B   Stop.

Simon   What, you need quiet down there?

B   No I mean with your hands, on my head.

Simon   Yeah, okay.
Come on though.
Feels so good.

B   Okay. But stop though.

Simon   Okay.

B *starts again.*

Simon *puts his hands on the back of* **B***'s head.*

B *chokes.*

B   Ow.

Simon   Sorry.
I just got caught up in it.

B   You said that last time.

Simon   I forgot.

Yo, are you crying, man?

B   No. Shut up.
Let's keep going.

Simon   Dude you're crying.

B   *Shut up.*

He kneels down to continue—

Simon *puts his hand back to steady himself, and knocks the fish bowl off the table. Water and fish on the ground.*

Simon   Oh shit!   **B**   Oh my God!

B *runs over to the fish, picks it up.*

B   It's flopping around!

He drops the fish.

B   No!   **Simon**   Oh shit!

We see **Simon** *accidentally step on the fish as he's pulling up his pants.*

A beat as **Simon** *and* **B** *register this.*

Simon   Whoops.

B   It's not moving.

Simon   Yes it is.

B   *It's not moving.*

Simon   Get some more water it's fine!

B *picks up the fish, runs to the bathroom.*

A long moment with **Simon** *alone onstage.*

Then the toilet flushes.

Simon   Shit.

B *comes back out of the bathroom.*

Simon   I'm sorry, man.

B   That was a good fish.
What is wrong with you?

Simon   What?

B   Why did you knock the bowl over?

Simon   I didn't mean to!

B   I thought you were a conscious rapper.

Simon   I am.

B   I thought you cared about animals.

Simon   I do.

B   Then what is wrong with you?
Why don't you act more careful?

He pushes **Simon***.*

Simon   What are you doing?

B   Why don't you pay more attention?

He pushes **Simon** *again.*

Simon   Come on, man, stop. It was an accident.

B   Why are you so fucking careless?

Simon   Stop pushing me.

B   You fucking jerk.

Simon   Stop it!

B   You fucking worthless piece of shit useless fucking jerk.

He pushes **Simon** *really hard.*

Simon *hits* **B** *in the face.*

B *goes down.*

Simon   Shit, man.
I'm sorry.
But it's just a fish! There are like a thousand of them at Wal-Mart.

He goes to leave, but:

And I don't want to kiss you.
I'm not even like that.

He's gone.

Scene Fifteen

Andy*'s apartment.*

Sound of a shower coming from the bathroom.

Rick *sitting on the bed that* **Andy** *bought for* **B***.*

Shower sounds stop. **Andy** *comes out in a towel.*

Andy   Sorry. Just had to get that smell off me.

Rick   That's fine. Wish I could change out of my monkey suit.

Andy   Do you want to go home first, or—

Rick   Oh no, no. That would be—(*not a good idea, because my wife is there.*)
You look nice.

Andy   Wet.

Rick   Nice though.
Strong.

Andy   You really know how to compliment, don't you?

Rick   Good strong. That's good.
My wife is so small.

Andy   Could you— (*not talk about your wife*)

Rick   Sorry.

Andy   I thought we talked about this.

Rick   Sorry, habit.
Feel like I could crush her sometimes.

Andy   Alright.

Rick   Sometimes I want to.

Andy   You know what?

Rick   Sorry.
We could have gone out for dinner or something. I mean you and me. We still could.

Andy   I think it's better like this.
Just get it done, you know.
Small town.

Rick   Yeah . . .
Thanks for inviting me over. I gotta admit I was kind of surprised.
You got any beer or anything?

Andy   I don't drink, anymore. / Sorry.

Rick   Oh, me neither. Yeah.
Just nice sometimes.

Andy   I have uh—
Do you want a soda?

Rick   No, that's—.
Man, I used to drink so much in high school though.
Did you?

Andy   Oh yeah. Buckets.
Wine, beer, gin.

Rick   *So* much.

Andy   With my boyfriend.
And then alone, mostly, after.

Rick   "Drinking alone."
That's not good.

Andy   I didn't say it was.
Then I met my husband, ex-husband, and we drank together. So that was better, I guess.

Rick   But you stopped, huh? Drinking.

Andy   Well, yeah. In— (*prison*)
I had to. Stop everything.

Rick   Oh. Oh yeah.
I guess—sure.

Andy   And I just kind of lost the taste for it. Then.

Rick   God. Sure. Sure.
Can I ask you—.
What did you—?
I mean why were you—

Andy   Oh. *Well* . . .
My husband hit me, so I sliced his balls off.
Shoop!

Rick   Oh, man.

Pause.

Andy   Just kidding.

Rick   Oh. Man!
See!

Andy   I was selling drugs. Small-time shit.
Bastard's still got his balls.

Rick   See, this is what I love about you. Always keeping it light.
Sometimes I look down at your head on the kill floor. And I think, what is she thinking right now? When she touches those animals. What is she thinking?

Andy   Probably not about much, I bet.

Rick   I don't know.

Andy   Trust me, I'm just—nothing. Zoning out. Trying to.

Rick   I bet you're thinking big things.

Andy   Okay.

Rick   Big dreams.

Andy   Sure.

Rick   Sky's the limit for you, Andy. I can feel it.
You've got grit. Your whole future's ahead of you.

Andy   I just spent five years in prison, Rick.

Rick   Exactly. Nowhere to go but up.
Me, I'm cashed.

Andy   No you're not.

Rick   I am. I'm cashed.

Andy   Seems like a pretty good job you got.

Rick   Seems like.
Do you wanna sit?

Andy   Yeah alright. Sorry. Just feel a little weird or something I guess.

Rick   Me too.
I've put on weight. Since high school, I mean.

Andy   You look fine.

Rick   You too.

Andy   I know.

Rick   I mean, I wasn't— (*making a comment about your weight*)

Andy   Yeah. No.
It's fine.

Rick   You look good.
(*Poking his own belly*) Blub blub.

They kiss for a minute.

It feels awkward and bad.

Andy   Sorry.
Been a while.
Heart is like—(*pounding*)
Don't know why.

Rick   No, that's—
Sure. Sure.

Andy   I'm up on that wall, you know?

Rick　Yeah.

Andy　Not here.

Pause.

Sorry. I'm gonna—
I just gotta—

She goes back into the bathroom.

We hear the water running.

Rick　That's fine.

Pause.

You taking a crap in there?
Hahaha.

He takes something off—his outer shirt? Socks? Belt?

He looks at himself in the mirror. Puffs his stomach out, back in.

I don't know.
It's funny.

Water off.

Pause.

Been waking up a lot, in my sleep.
Weird dreams.

Water on.

Running through the field, hands up . . .
They're chasing me . . .

Andy (*off*)　What?

Rick　Uh . . .

Water off.

Andy *comes out of bathroom.*

She's wearing an undershirt and underwear now.

Her energy is different—she's gonna get this done.

Rick　Haven't been sleeping too well.

Andy　Maybe you're nervous about something.

Rick　I am.
I am nervous.

Andy　That's okay.

Rick   Yeah?
I don't even know about what.

Andy *touches* **Rick***.*

Rick   That's nice.
I like you a lot.

Andy   I think you talk too much and you don't know how to listen.

Rick   I do listen.
Sometimes I talk a lot when I'm nervous.

She keeps touching him. Her hands move lower.

Rick   Stop.

Andy   What?

Rick   Maybe, you know . . . try to be a little gentler.

Andy   Oh.
Sorry.

She touches him again.

He pulls away.

Rick   Jesus!

Andy   I'm sorry.
It's been a while.

Rick   Yeah.
Here.

Andy   What?

Rick   Come here.

Andy   Okay.

She tries to touch him.

Rick   Don't.

Andy   Okay.

Rick   Just let me.

Andy   Okay.

He kisses her, touches her.

She tries to touch him again.

He takes her hands—like "stop."

Rick   Hey.

It's okay.

He resumes touching her, kissing her.

They're on the bed by now. She lays back on the mattress.

He's kissing her neck and her body.

It goes on for a bit.

She's stiff at first. But she relaxes into it.

It does something to her—there is a release.

Andy   That's nice.

Rick   What?

Andy   Nice.

Rick   Oh. Wow. Okay.

But then: her phone beeps.

Andy   Oh shit.

He continues.

After a moment, the phone beeps again.

Andy   Hang on.

Rick   What?

Andy   Could you please stop for a minute?

She gets up.

Reads the text.

Andy   Oh my God.

Rick   Everything okay?

Andy   I don't know.

A beat.

She makes the decision to leave.

I gotta go.

She races to put her clothes on.

Rick   Wait.
What?

Andy   I'm really sorry.

Rick   Where do you have to go?

Andy   It's—I'm—it's important. I'm sorry.

Rick   I don't understand.

Andy   It's an emergency.

Rick   What kind of emergency?

She keeps getting dressed.

Rick   What kind of emergency?

Andy   Can you let yourself out?

She's moving towards the door.

Rick *stops her.*

Rick   Wait wait wait!
You can't just leave me here.
I came all the way over here to meet you.
I really liked doing that. It felt—really nice.

Andy   I know.
(*She means this:*) I'm really sorry.
But I gotta go.
My son texted me.

She leaves.

Rick *is left standing there.*

Scene Sixteen

B *is waiting outside the Dairy Queen.*

He's wearing a hooded sweatshirt. His head is down. We can't see his face very well.

It's night. There's a streetlamp.

Andy *enters, breathing hard—she's been running.*

Andy   I'm here.
Jesus.
I got your text. What's wrong?

He shrugs.

Andy   What's wrong?

He doesn't respond.

Look at me!

B   Don't touch me.

Andy   Well—let's go inside then. Come on. We can get some food and you can tell me what's wrong.

B   They're closed.

Andy   Okay . . .

She smells the back of his head.

Are you *high*?

He shrugs.

Andy   Fucking Christ!

B   Fuck you then. Leave if you want.

Andy   No I'm not going to leave. You just scared me! I get a text from you, I think it's like—thinking you're dead or something. Came running here, buses aren't even going this late! I mean, godamn! Show up, you won't even tell me what's wrong?

Pause.

So you smoke pot now, huh?

B   I don't know.

Andy   You like being high?

B   Sometimes.

Andy   Christ, B, you're sixteen years old, you're way too young for that shit. Do not get started with that shit. I mean I know it's fun but—

B   I didn't call you here to lecture me.

Andy   Well, why'd you call me then?
Why the hell did you call me?

Pause.

I'm sorry.

Pause.

I'm so sorry.

Pause.

I got scared.

Pause.

What can I do?

Pause.

Please.

Pause.

What happened?

After a moment, **B** *pulls his hood off.*

He has a fresh black eye.

Andy   Oh, sweetheart.

B   I got hurt.

Andy *touches* **B**.

B *finally looks at* **Andy**.

Far away, we hear the sound of the cars on the highway.

The streetlight clicks off.

And then the whole stage goes dark.

End of play.

Advance Man

advance man: a person who visits a location before the arrival of an important visitor to make the appropriate arrangements.

(Oxford English Dictionary)

Advance Man opened at UT-Austin's UTNT Festival (Steven Dietz, Curator), where it had its first performance on February 28, 2014.

Marcy	Raquel Watson
Advance Man	Steven Wilson
Frank	Robert Faires
Ella	Pamela Christian
Roger/The President	Cody Edgar
Michael Henry	Patrick Shaw
Science Teacher	Alison Stoos
Exercise Teacher	Cassie Reveles
Baker	Jordan Maranto
Librarian	Arnold Treviño
Local Mom	Diana Small
Director	Will Davis
Set	Michael Krauss
Lights	Andrew Carson
Costumes	Andie Day
Sound	Sam Lipman
Projections	Matt Smith
Stage Manager	Kyle Winkelmann

Characters

Marcy, *a high school student*
Advance Man*, *wearing a suit and dark sunglasses*
Frank, *sixties to seventies, a farmer*
Ella, *sixties to seventies, an art teacher*
Roger *(this actor also plays* **The President***), a loner*
Michael Henry, *editor of the* Bear Creek Bugle, *and Marcy's dad*
Townspeople (a chorus of sorts):
Science Teacher
Exercise Teacher
Baker
Librarian
Local Mom

*Advance Man can be played by an actor of any gender.

Setting

Bear Creek, an island of ten thousand people or so in the Pacific Northwest, accessible only by ferry boat.

A Note about Performance

The townspeople create Bear Creek through a stylized movement that lives somewhere between the sublime, the frightening, the mundane, and the ridiculous.

Ideally, there will be very few props and few set elements.

The sparrows should be beautiful. Dark shapes in the sky.

A Note About Language

(   ) is an implied word, a held moment.

Nonsense words—*humma, shoopa*—carry the same weight as their sensical counterparts. They mean something very specific to these characters.

If there is no punctuation between two or more seemingly unrelated thoughts, they are the same thought.

Scene One

Bare white stage.

In shadow on the back wall, sparrows pick at things on the ground, sometimes rising into the air a little bit before settling back down.

A long moment.

Then the **Townspeople** *run onstage and the sparrows rise into the air and are gone. Woosh!*

Townspeople   I was in the bakery (library/bowling alley/post office/grocery store) when I heard.

The **Townspeople** *switch places.*

Townspeople   I was in the bakery (library/bowling alley/post office/grocery store) when I heard!

Science Teacher   He's coming. THE PRESIDENT.

Exercise Teacher   To Bear Creek?

Science Teacher   Just to visit, I heard. Overnight. He's staying on the ranch.

Exercise Teacher   Bill Shepherd's ranch?

Science Teacher   The only ranch we've got.

Townspeople   It spread around town.

Exercise Teacher   Oh, sure. Heard this morning. They say the whole island's going to be bomb-sniffed.

Librarian   No one's sniffing me. I know my rights.

Exercise Teacher   I wouldn't mind. For this President? Sniff away.

Townspeople   The buzz spread at the bakery, in the video store, and of course at the school, among mothers and fathers as they picked up and dropped off: *hum hum hum.*

Librarian   I heard he's here to raise money.

Local Mom   Big money.

Baker   Money both big and small.

Local Mom   If it's at the ranch, those are big money people. Probably coming over from the city. Get in the car, Sammy!

Librarian   There's going to be an event for large donors, and also an event for small donors, at the bowling alley.

Local Mom   At our bowling alley? I doubt it. Sammy, we're going to be late to ballet!

Baker   That's what this President is like! The kind of President who would hold an event, here, at our bowling alley.

Townspeople   Soon it hit the *Bugle*.

Enter **Michael Henry**, *editor of the* Bear Creek Bugle, **Frank**, *a farmer, and* **Ella**, *an art teacher.*

Michael Henry (*on an invisible phone*)   This is Michael Henry Maloney from the *Bear Creek Bugle*. I'm trying to get in touch with the President.
"P" . . . "R" . . .
Yes, I'll hold.
Bear Creek. No, it's an island. With a creek in it.
Yes I'll keep holding.

Frank   The apples weren't growing right that fall, and I was concerned about the earthworms kind of shifting around wrong under the dirt. And what I wanted to do was to organize a protest for when the President came. I'd pour a bunch of apples out in front of his car, kind of a Tentamin-type Square situation.

Ella   And I, of course, caught wind of this gesture, and it made me insane. To be, you know, to *this* President. Who represented so much that was *right* about this country. So I resolved to organize a counter-protest. The only problem of course was figuring out when he was coming. And then we could make signs that said: "Yes! Yes Mr. President! Yes, Yes, Yes!"

Science Teacher   Some of us felt he was exactly like us. Just, you know, the way he spoke, and kind of all the policies and things, and even the font he used, and even if he wasn't—even if he didn't always—even if there were rumors sometimes that what he was *doing* didn't actually always—

Exercise Teacher   I just think, you know, that even if he sort of, I mean if that STUFF is actually going on that it must be something that—(*Retrieving his/her invisible cell phone, which is ringing:*) oh hold on—I don't think he really believes in it, in all that STUFF, is what I'm—Hey, Carol, I was just texting you—

Roger, *a loner, slinks onstage.*

Roger   And others of us felt that he wasn't like us at all, that in fact everything he was doing was in some way linked to the (   ), and all the (   ), and of course I'm not even going to say it, because you know what I'm talking about.

Baker   And some of us just wanted to thank him.

Librarian   And some of us wanted to say well hey you know fight a little harder, with the uh the uh you know the—go further with that.

Enter **Marcy**, *a high school student, for her internship interview at the* Bear Creek Bugle.

Michael Henry   I'm on hold. With the President. So we'll have to do this INTERNSHIP INTERVIEW verbally. List your qualifications verbally, please.

Marcy   My mind is sharp as a knife, and I have tons of friends, and I'm editor of the high school newspaper.

Michael Henry   It's a very competitive internship.

Marcy   And I'm your daughter.

Michael Henry   You're hired. Get out there and see what you can find out about this presidential visit. And be back by seven if you want a ride home!

He exits.

Marcy *pulls out her reporter's notebook.*

Marcy   First stop: the Bear Creek Bakery, to fuel up with a delicious chocolate chip cookie!

Bakery   We're over here!

Marcy   The President! I'd watched his famous speech, at which he'd said, you know, *a humma humma humma.*

Science Teacher   We all had. There he was, on television, standing atop the (   ), his hair kind of—

Exercise Teacher   It was a late afternoon sunlight kind of situation, the leaves just coming down around him—

Baker   And after all we had been through, the sort of kind of violence, and stuff—

Local Mom   And the wars, all the just the—

Librarian   *Fear*, you know, or lack of fear, the sheer complacency!

Science Teacher   Not to mention the economically, both cresting up and kind of bottoming out.

Exercise Teacher   And then here in Bear Creek, of course, we had great hope.

Librarian   And also great fear, because the Chinese restaurant had shut down, and some people said well everyone who ate there threw up, and others said well it must have been the *economy.*

Local Mom   And *also* the mystery bookshop, and some people said well maybe an island of 8,000 people can't *support* a mystery bookshop, but others said no we were coming to the end of something, something was ending.

Baker   So when the President said it, *a shoopa shoopa shoopa*, standing there, in front of all those cameras, we felt yes, yes, *a shoopa shoopa shoopa.*

Local Mom   Yes, hesitantly, *a shoopa shoopa shoopa*—

Science Teacher   Yes, with total commitment, *a shoopa shoopa* yes.

Librarian   Although I heard a different speech, at which he said *ahumma humma humma*, but it was the same idea.

Science Teacher   The idea being that something was kind of shifting into another thing, was my general sense, or some way in which what was happening now had also happened previously, or was entirely new.
And of course we sensed that.

Baker   *Something* was changing, and it was like well what is this change? Are we going back to a previous time, or are we kind of leaping forward into a new time, because we'll either participate in it or fight it depending on what exactly "it" is!

Science Teacher   I mean we all had our theories, sure we had our theories.

Baker   It's the Mayan kind of with the temples and the lunar moon rocks and etcetera.

Exercise Teacher   I think it has to do with kind of recycling karma consciousness Dalai Lama.

Science Teacher   A mid-90s late 1930s sort of Great Depression type Economic Boom.

Local Mom   You know everything kind of getting warmer, and I know that I was often too warm, just personally.

Librarian   And then of course there were the rumors about the (   ) and all the sorts of things, you know, that we were hearing about, in bits and pieces, from far away.

Local Mom   Hard to hear, sure. Hard to hear, sure.

Exercise Teacher   There was something kind of going on over there, and possibly coming here, and of course that was upsetting, that it could come here, although what it was was, what it *was* was, what it was was—hmmm.

Baker   I think it had to do with the loss of our of uh of uh of uh of uh yeah so uh yeah so uh / yeeah . . . .

Librarian   *Something* was being lost, that much was clear.

Science Teacher   Because there was a time, right? There was a time "back then," right, when uh, when we were, when we would *never*—

Exercise Teacher   It was a really wonderful time, *that* time and we could all kind of look back and be like: *aaah*. And it was like well what happened to *that* time, you know, and what is *this* time we're in now because it seems very very (   )

Baker   It just seemed very very (   )

Local Mom   Nice, sure . . .

Librarian   In *some* ways it was very nice, we had all of our electronically.

Exercise Teacher   And in *other* senses it was like everything's humming everything kind of moving and it was like just *oooh* you know like I mean just what the hell? *You* know.

Baker   And then on a more serious there was the loss of our sort of fundamental kind of—

Librarian   Values, sure, our values sure which we had used to have had back in the time when we all lived in these homes, alright? And here's *mom*, and here's sort of *dad*, and it's—

Frank (*to* **Librarian**)   Bullshit. The time you're talking about, when was that time? Because there was *another* time—

Ella (*to* **Frank**)   Bullshit. I mean during the time that *you're* talking about—I mean let's be clear that there was all this—I mean *that* was hardly the time.

Frank   Well, what time are you talking about then?

Ella   *I'm* talking about the time in the back of the field when you were—that night when we—

Frank   That was in high school, when you and me were in high school. I'm talking about national kinds of times like the Depression, or like—

Ella   Do you remember that night, Frank? In the field? When you and me were in high school? Do you remember that?

Pause.

Frank   No.

Frank *and* **Ella** *exit.*

Local Mom   Raised in a time in which some of us were kind of like "Hey," and others were sort of like *Hey*, and now you could catch nice documentaries on it, and it was like hey! We're not *that* old! Hahaha—

Baker   And I mean we are good people here, most having come from elsewhere, determined to maintain a sort of, whatever our, just kind of to—after all the, in the, and sure we had been part of all the—had kind of now though of course shrunk our sort of you know, had settled for kind of after all the, of the—*big* fans of puppetry, and recycling, *big* fans of vegetables, and hen's eggs!

Science Teacher   And then there were the youth, in whom despite all our failures and our uncertainty and the loss of all the everything we—in spite of all *that*, we'd attempted to cultivate a kind of certainty that we had used to have had and missed now, that we had used to have had and missed now, that things could, that everything could, that if you *did* you *could*.

Marcy (*having arrived at the bakery*)   I'd like one chocolate chip cookie, please, to fuel me up for my internship.

Baker   Sure thing, Marcy.

Librarian   It was fall. Something was changing. The sparrows were everywhere, beautiful if you looked at them close, a nuisance if you passed them by.

Townspeople *exit.*

Advance Man *enters, wearing a dark suit. He joins* **Marcy** *at the bakery counter.*

Advance Man   Cup of coffee, please.

A single sparrow flies across the sky—flap, flap, flap—and settles on the ground.

Advance Man *crosses to the sparrow, puts it in his mouth, and eats it.*

Then he turns, sees **Marcy***, smiles.*

Advance Man   Have to be careful about these birds.

Scene Two

A little later that afternoon. Sunlight; sparrows.

Marcy *onstage. She talks to us.*

Marcy   I couldn't really find out anything about the President's visit, so I was like *hmm*. I really wanted to be a reporter, but I was like how do you gather the facts, like how do you score hot tips? My dad thinks you just get on the phone and ask around, so I tried that.
Ring ring.

Enter **Local Mom***.*

Local Mom   Ring!

Marcy   Hey, Local Mom!

Local Mom   Well, hello there, Marcy. Still in high school?

Marcy   Ninth grade! How's Sammy?

Local Mom   Late to ballet, as usual.

Marcy   Hey, have you heard anything about the President's visit?

Local Mom   What I've heard is very interesting the way people are just *freaking out* when it's like, okay. He's a man, right, and he has power, and that's true. But I'm a woman, and I don't have power, so does that make me any less interesting? Does that make me any less important or whatever? And so it's like apples, and oranges. It's like half a dozen of one! I mean yes the President's coming to town but *I'm* coming to town too! I'm already here!

Marcy   I was more interested in any of the basic reporting facts that a reporter might be interested in, such as who, how, where, what, and when.

Local Mom   Well no, I'm not sure about any of *that*.

Marcy   Alright.

Local Mom   You'll never believe how long Sammy takes to get ready for ballet. Sammy we are going to be LATE!

Marcy   Bye now! Click. Hmm.
Ring ring.

Exit **Local Mom**, *enter* **Roger**.

Roger   I don't own a phone because I live in the woods.

Marcy   Hey, Roger.

Roger   Oh hey, Marcy.

Marcy   Are you still homeless and live in the woods?

Roger   Lately I've been experimenting with methamphetamines do you have any money.

Marcy   I already spent my allowance what's metham-what-a-who?

Roger   Oh nothing I *do* have a beaver that I made friends with in the woods.

Marcy   Uh-huh hey I'm just wondering if you've heard anything about the President's visit.

Roger   Such as why are you asking? I mean yeah they say he's coming but why, why would they announce it in advance, are they trying to do something to us? Or with us? To us or with us or *against* us? And *that's* always the every single thing that comes out of these people's mouths is targeted to sort of tease, and manipulate, or undermine, or fool, to fool, and it's like *are we fools* or do we sort of look at the blank space around the words, what is not said, such as ALL OF THE BAD THINGS, you won't hear them say that, or talk about that, but you can find it in the white space around the words, if you listen, shhh, they're talking about it now . . .

Marcy   Right.
I was wondering more about kind of any facts I could report on to do well in my internship.

Roger   I don't know what an internship is because I didn't learn what it is.

Marcy   Okay well I gotta go I'll see you around!

Roger   Okay well good luck at your internship, Marcy, you're gonna go far unlike me.

Marcy   I appreciate it! Click.
He's a nice guy you can be homeless and sort of threatening and still be a nice guy I think ANYWAY ring ring.

Michael Henry   Michael Henry here, with the *Bear Creek Bugle*!

Marcy   Hey, Dad, I am not having much luck.

Michael Henry   Well, I am driving around in my car looking for a chicken.

Marcy   Why are you doing that?

Michael Henry   The newspaper industry is a growth industry, Marcy, and I made the right decision in my life career-wise.

Marcy   Okay.

Michael Henry   Hey, maybe if you're not finding out much about the President's visit maybe you can— Ella's coming in I was going to interview her for my weekly column called "Interview with an Islander" my WEEKLY COLUMN CALLED "INTERVIEW WITH AN ISLANDER" and then Frank's coming in you can interview him too I have to find this chicken . . .

Marcy   Oh okay alright.

Michael Henry   Don't let any strangers in!

Marcy   I already hung up click hey Ella!

Exit **Michael Henry**, *enter* **Ella**.

Ella   Funny to see you outside of class, Marcy, I do love having you in my art class at high school you're the only one in it because no one else signed up it's like a private class for one person with me teaching it and you're the person in it.

Marcy   I like the glitter and the glue it's fun to play with I like doing collages I like reporting class too which is the class I have after you can sit down if you want.

They look around for a chair—there are none onstage.

Marcy   Or we can just stand.

*A sudden shift—**Ella**'s been talking for a while now.*

Ella   To be out there on the streets just kind of like *Hey Hey Hey* or sort of like just *HEY* or sometimes like *Hey Hey* with our kind of you know we had our signs, and that was well I mean back then you certainly couldn't call me divorced, or a mom, or even a substitute teacher at the high school, a teacher of art, because back then I was just kind of a spirit! Just floating around and I'd sort of alight in San Francisco and make love, and then I'd go back to Boston and set something on fire and then make love, and then we'd all go to DC and just sort of gather together and scream at buildings and then make love.

Marcy   Uh-huh.

Ella   And of course back then it was like at any moment you know things could— there was a real sense that uh in a very *real* way you could, we could, we really *could*, that maybe in some way it *could*, you know it *really could*. And what I worry is that *now* I mean that *now* we're getting ourselves into a situation where there's just not that that that that that that that that there's just not that that that that that that that uh you know that uh that uh you know that uh you know what I mean.

Marcy   Oh look, here comes Frank.

Ella   Well, I just think it's wonderful that you're doing this. "Interview with an Islander." It's a great idea for a column. (*Coldly:*) Hello, Frank.

Ella *leaves.*

Frank   Ella. (*To* **Marcy**) So, huh. Huh, okay. So um so where to start. I mean back then it was like oh Christ sure I mean anything, I thought anything, I'd so I'd be like just out there you know and the sort of big lights shining down on me flying and people going HEY HEY plus my name and the intercourse with Jannie and later Sandra and yes Ella, Ella and I had a sort of, it was, but anyway so and me and my buddies yeah we'd cruise around, sure we'd kind of drive, around in our cars, and then that was over and it was uh well here's this jungle and you better keep your head clean but get your hands dirty and the truth is that sometimes I sit straight up in my bed at night even now and just say to the air—*well am I here or am I there?*

In the distance, **Advance Man** *enters. He's taking notes or measuring something or perhaps speaking quietly into an earpiece.*

Frank   And of course with the farming it's really simple you just gotta work a bunch of days, like all the days your whole life, and make sure the worms are happy, and you can sort of tear at the ground with things, or kind of be like hey, just relax, everyone just relax, and then you can kind of SPRAY IT WITH ALL THESE THINGS, or not, it's up to you, and every Christmas you go to Bermuda.

Marcy   Great, that's great Frank, terrific thanks next?

Advance Man *enters the office as* **Frank** *leaves.*

Marcy *perks up.*

Advance Man (*friendly as hell*)   "The Bear Creek Bugle." Great, great. Really important to have a vibrant press.
Hey maybe you can uh I'm looking for—what I want to kind of get a sense of is just like who everyone is in this town, where you all kind of stand on all the issues, and sort of where you all live, and where you shop, and what you do for fun, and who your pets are, and what are your thoughts, and who are you related to, and what are your middle names, and your nicknames, and your friend's names, and basically are there any kinds of things that someone like me should be aware of.

Marcy   Uh, maybe, I mean my dad just went to look for a chicken, so maybe—

Advance Man   Yes no sure but I'm interested in what *you* have to say. I think young people are really just the kind of—so there's the future, right? And some of us will make it there and others it's quite clear will not, I mean not in any bodily way, so what you have is younger people, and you have older people. And we're all sort of progressing forward in time in a linear manner, ideally, but the difference is that young people were born later and old people were you fill in the blanks and so what we have is a kind of situation where the older people will in all likelihood just kind of die first. And the problem is that one day there will literally be no old people around, not any of the current old people, and all you'll have is young people who've *grown* old, and what kind of people will those young people be? I mean will they honor their elders through their acts or will they I mean as you know there's a kind of "we can do it better" or "totally differently" type situation that has a tendency to so what I'm interested in is just kind of the next generation and young people and humm hummm hummmm hummmm.hummm. So what do you think?

Marcy Uh	Advance Man
I think that like well I think that like	(*Listening very intently:*)
I think that like okay so I don't know	Uh-huh
who you are but if you want to know	
what I think what I think is that like	Uh-huh Uh-huh
young people are like young people	Uh-huh
are like that like young people are like	Uh-huh Uh-huh Uh-huh
it's hard for me to express like usually	UH-HUH
I'm like so like articulate so it's like	UH-HUH UH-HUH

Advance Man   Let's go for a drive.

Marcy   Let me leave a note for my dad?

Advance Man   I'll pay you to leave right now.

Marcy   . . .
Okay.

They leave.

Meanwhile, **Ella** *rides her bike home. This should not involve an actual bike.*

Frank *approaches.*

Frank   Ella.

Ella   Frank.

Frank   What are you doing?

Ella   Well, I am riding my bicycle home.

Frank   Well that's just not uh that's you know *not very safe* out here with the uh—

Ella   Oh and since when do you you know, since when do you *you* know—

Frank   Since well it's just a public safety hazard that uh—I don't you know I don't.

Ella   Right and of course the kind of fossil fuels and all the sort of just oil drilling fracking kind of scraping around down there to get at the last SCRAPS of when it's like okay: just *change* your habits. Just change everything about the way you live and how you are in the world and we'll all be fine!

Frank   I can give you a ride home if my uh my tractor is just uh—

Ella   And what does that get about five miles to the gallon? It's just like and uh . . .

Frank   Since when did you get so angry?

Ella   I'm not so angry! I mean *you're* the angry one, I mean for God's sake to be just so oblivious! Driving around here, and this protest you're planning for the President's visit that I caught wind of which is just like—

Frank   Yeah but democratic! Sort of me speaking out, we're all speaking out, and isn't that the kind of that we all sort of—

Ella   If you're smart about it, *I'm* just saying that—

Frank   Earthworms are not doing well, they're not doing well, and to me the only possible reason for that could be that we, you know, there's something—

Ella   Oh and of course it's the, OF COURSE it's the, you know, the *President*'s fault.

Frank   Well, who else?

Ella   Kind of just like—act globally think locally, you know? Or sort of just open your eyes and look around you for the sort of and take matters into your own and it's like I mean geez!

Frank   Said the woman who spent half the sort of like *back then* kind of out in the street with a—

Ella   But that was different *now* we have a President who he—

Frank   Ella I gotta go and the apples are falling all over the place and I gotta pick them up.

Ella   Yeah well *I* gotta go and get the glitter and fingerpaints ready for my art class so you're not the only one who—

Frank   I'll see you.

Ella   Fascist kind of HEIL HITLER just like—

But **Frank** *is gone.* **Ella***, in a huff, leaves with her bike.*

A dance beat begins. Enter **Librarian** *and* **Science Teacher***: they are trying to keep up in a difficult exercise class led by* **Exercise Teacher***. Lots of moves.*

They're simultaneously talking about what it means to live a good life.

Librarian   I mean I think I *am* good I think I have lived a good life so and it's just like—

Science Teacher   Right but so and how do you define that so and I mean how do you define that?

Librarian   Well, I'm very good at my job.

Science Teacher   Right . . .

Librarian   And I think that my job is important, you know, I think that my job *is* important, such as libraries.

Science Teacher   And you think that without you there wouldn't be libraries, or?

Librarian   No, but I think I am helping the library grow, and helping make it a welcoming place, and a special place, and helping people get excited about uh you know all the kind of knowledge and things, and teasing that out, so I think that's pretty good, I mean I guess I could have had kids, and that probably would have done more good, maybe, but I never I never I mean sometimes sure I regret kind of—I am very lonely.

Science Teacher   As for me: as a teacher, *all* the kids are my kids and I definitely try and teach them about science, and some such, and values and such, scientific values and such, the environment, and some such, and I think I'm having an impact, I do, and yeah I make sure I mean what I do is I make sure when I go to the grocery store that I only get things I believe in, such as products. Such as gentle eggs.

Librarian   And I definitely vote.

Science Teacher   Oh, I always vote in the elections for candidates.

Exercise Teacher *bounces over.*

Exercise Teacher   As for me I think it's all about awareness for example the body, and the mind, and just sort of calm, and relax, and *release*, and relax, and push it, and push it, and release, and let's move!

Scene Three

An enormous flock of sparrows flies quick across the sky, pausing briefly to make a strange formation. Then they're gone. Woosh.

Advance Man *and* **Marcy** *in the car.* **Advance Man** *is driving.*

Advance Man   Ticking bomb type scenario the bomb in this case being the fact that the President is arriving tomorrow and I was supposed to I mean the situation was that I was supposed to be around here a week ago sort of checking things out and getting things set up but I fell asleep and I woke up a week later and it's like holy shit you know so I caught a ferry out here and it's like there's not enough time to make sure it's so I really need your help or I could get fired and the President could die and the economy would collapse sending the whole world into a depression leading to global nuclear war full-scale destruction the annihilation of the human species and the literal implosion of the physical planet.

Marcy   One time I left my backpack at home and I didn't have any of my books but then it was fine because I just looked over people's shoulders.

Advance Man   I'm going to need you to steer.

Marcy   Oh. Okay.

Advance Man   I'll keep my foot on the gas.

Marcy   This is kind of fun but also I hope I don't hit anyone!

Advance Man   So what do you do, Marcy?

Marcy   I'm in high school.

Advance Man   Me too. I mean I was. So what kind of subjects are you studying over there, history and all that?

Marcy   Yeah, history and English and I'm taking this journalism class—

Advance Man   Yeah history is really important it's really important to know your history I'm a big history buff, me I'm big into it, The President is too, we're all into history in a way I mean for God's sake, all the stuff that happened? Kind of getting it in order and just sort of sorting it out and figuring out well this is history, and this is perhaps not history, and kind of prioritizing and things, very important, sure sure no sure sure sure, sure sure sure sure sure, no suuure suuuure suuuure suuuure suuuuure suuuuure no definitely sure uh-huh yup yeah no sure I bet uh-huh suuuure.

Pause.

Marcy   I actually have to be back at the office pretty soon because my dad is getting back so—

Advance Man   Stop right here.

In one swift single clean motion, **Advance Man** *kneels and put his ear to the ground, listening.*

He's found a whisper hole.

Advance Man   Uh hmmm. Okay, wait hmm. Ah yes, okay, yes yes yes. Uh-huh. Yup. No—wait.
Okay, wait. Okay go go go go go go go put your own ear to the ground and then— yes?

Advance Man *raises his hand like a tuning fork.*

The whispers of the **Townspeople** *rise and rise and rise.*

Townspeople   Whisper whisper whisper whisper WHISPER WHISPER!

Librarian   A kind of scented flesh blanket with all the eyes in it just hmmm ahhh—

Baker   Apples everywhere, or honeydew melons, or even little chairs, or sumsquatch a willy-nilly—

Exercise Teacher   Zuchinnis, uh-huh and sort of, sure, lots of geese—

Local Mom   School board election and a lumber rain helmet oooh—

Science Teacher   Sweet little hens eggs with kind of their cheep cheap butts in the air—

Roger   All the wires all the whispers and it's like THE PRESIDENT, said Roger—

Advance Man   You heard that?

Roger   All the wires all the whispers and it's like THE PRESIDENT, said Roger—

The whispers fade.

Marcy   I think that was Roger, he's homeless and he enjoys drugs I believe but he's pretty nice. This is a weird hole.

Advance Man   Roger. Yes. Interesting. Making a little note of it, writing, done. And that's the sort of—democratically? Definitely. Freedom of—and you know it's just that okay, here is this person, right? The President. Very special person. And here we have all these other people, namely you and the sort of villagers in this place, the kind of settlers here, all of you people, and any one if you if we I'm not but *that's* the problem is that okay I'm thinking that what we have here is a—where you will just sniff around, Marcy, and I will be sort of and you can find me and yes yes hum hum hum in my ear.
(*Explaining something obvious*:) I want you to come work for me.

Marcy   Uh I don't know if I'm qualified to like and I'm pretty busy so uh sounds kind of weird?

Advance Man   Okay, put your eyes on mine.
I'm inviting you to sit in the History Chair, which certain people choose to sit in, and others kind of get invited to sit in, and most people are just kind of like well we'll just stand over here by this wall and maybe write a book about the History Chair or kind of criticize it for being, you know, whatever. But the History Chair, you have to understand, the History Chair is high and firm and it supports your buttocks. But to sit in it in the first place you have to be like: well do I sit in this chair, or do I stand up against the wall? And you can't kind of stand *between* the History Chair and the wall, you have to sort of *choose*, do you understand? Let's listen some more are you in are we is it sure sure suuuure, right?

Marcy   I don't know . . .

Advance Man   Great, good, sure.

Flap, flap, flap—a sparrow lopes by overhead.

Advance Man   And then we'll deal with those birds.

Advance Man *slumps over, asleep.*

Marcy   On the car ride home he slept soundly and my thoughts tumbled. On the one hand I thought well this is my town, I love these people, I trust these people, and I'm just in high school, I mean what the heck! But on the other hand I was thinking about the History Chair and how it might be nice to place my buttocks in it and get out of this old place called Bear Creek, and maybe they'll have a job for me in the White House as special assistant for recycling because I already know a lot about recycling because I run the recycling club at school. And so that sounded pretty good and I was like sure, whatever, I'll do it. But then I got confused, and I was like if the chair is history, then is the floor kind of non-history, or is the whole room history, and what are all those people doing up against that wall, and why am I in the Advance Man's lap? And then I fell asleep.

From the sky come the deep dulcet tones of **The President***.*

The President   Marcy.

Marcy   Mr. President!

The President   Very proud. Very excellent. Spectacular. Rewarding you.

Marcy   But I'm still deciding. I've got a lot on my plate. I'm events coordinator for the recycling club, and I'm in the musical, and I—

The President   Highly deserving. Of all people, you: inspiring. The kind of more of, these days. Young people and all the sort of just the kind of you know, so, yes, rewards in your future, honors and recognition and special secret access and my ear. Giving you my ear. You tilt your mouth to the right, I'll bring my ear around to the left. We'll talk! You talk, I'll listen. Very promising. Very exciting. / A golden bird covered in jewels, resplendent.

Marcy   But Mr. President? You won't—I mean will you—I mean what if we, uh—

The President   Not to worry!

Pause.

Marcy   I need a little time to decide.

The President   Take all the time you need.
And Marcy? Advance Man. Be careful there. Keep an eye out. Let me know.

Marcy   I thought he worked for you.

The President   Tentative. We'll see. It's all tentative it's all—

The President *disappears.*

Advance Man *wakes up, rubbing his eyes.*

Advance Man   Something wrong?

Marcy   No.

They walk.

Marcy   It seemed strange to have left the car behind, to be walking through the forest, but the Advance Man held my hand, and there were no apparent wolves, and all seemed well, although the worms were shifting mumbling in the soil. Along the way—

We see **Ella** *eating dinner alone,* **Frank** *eating dinner alone,* **Roger** *eating dinner alone,* **Science Teacher** *and* **Local Mom** *staring at each other across a vast expanse, other townspeople doing various evening things.*

Ella   Ella.

Frank   Frank.

Roger   Me.

Science Teacher & Local Mom   Us.

Everyone Else   We.

Advance Man (*to* **Marcy**)   Until soon.

And he's gone.

Marcy *joins* **Michael Henry** *at the dinner table.*

Michael Henry Dinner time	**Marcy** Dinner time I'm thinking if I want to tell
eating dinner	my dad what happened
dinner time yum.	

Marcy   Dad?

Michael Henry   Yum.

Marcy   Do you ever worry that maybe your life that like—you've lived the wrong kind of life?

Michael Henry   What do you mean?

Marcy   Like Bear Creak is like, and yeah like we have a good life but like—

Michael Henry   Are you worried about—

Marcy   I just like—

Michael Henry   You're fifteen, Marcy, there's plenty of time to you know—

Marcy   When Mom left I was like—

Michael Henry   But that was a whole different sort of—

Marcy (*an explosion*)   That your life doesn't matter? That you're just like—nobody? I mean our lives are so so so I mean *your* life is just so—small.

Pause.

Michael Henry   I'm proud of my life.

Marcy   I know . . .

Michael Henry   I've lived a good life.

Marcy   But yeah but like—

Michael Henry   I have a great job.

Marcy   I know.

Michael Henry   I have you.

Pause.

I'm proud of my life.

Marcy   But don't you ever feel like you're just standing up against the wall? Kind of all bunched up? I mean didn't you ever want to sit in the History Chair?

Michael Henry   The what?

Marcy   The History—Chair. Nevermind.

Michael Henry   Like a historical chair?

Marcy   No . . .

Michael Henry   Are you interested in antiques now? Because I would love to go antiquing this weekend if you—

Marcy   No. Never mind.

Michael Henry   It's like what's bugging you? It's hard for me to you never I'm struggling to—

Marcy   Never mind nothing no I'm mmm yum this is a delicious—sigh.

Michael Henry   Are you sexually active?

Marcy   AAAH I gotta do my homework I gotta sleep I'm tired I gotta clean my room I gotta find my shoes not these shoes my other ones I think they're in my room so night!

She flees the dinner table.

Michael Henry   You didn't finish your dinner!
Sigh.
Sigh.

He picks up an imaginary phone, dials.

Ring ring.

Marcy   I walked up the stairs to my room.
Time felt very slow for me everything was
stretched out the stairs were kind of vibrating   **Michael Henry**
it was a BIG MOMENT for me, a decision moment.   Ring ring.
On the one hand, Bear Creek. On the other hand, History.

Exercise Teacher   Ring.
Hello.

Michael Henry   Who is this?

Exercise Teacher   Um who is *this*? You called me, so—
And it's like . . .

Michael Henry   This is . . .
Another resident of Bear Creek.
I opened the phone book and I just dialed.

Exercise Teacher   Okay . . .

Michael Henry   It's nighttime over here and I'm just about to have my sleepytime tea so . . .

Exercise Teacher   That sounds good so—?

Michael Henry   Do you want to come over and have some with me?
It's very good tea.

Exercise Teacher   . . .
Who is this?

Michael Henry   This is . . . nobody. Nothing. Nevermind. Night.
Click.

Exercise Teacher   Wait!
. . .
Click.

Michael Henry   Sigh.

Advance Man *walks on and hands* **Michael Henry** *his tea, almost absent-mindedly.*

Michael Henry   My tea! Thank you. Mmmm.
This sleepytime tea is very good. It has valerian root in it. It always makes me so
sleepy makes me so sleepy so . . . sleepy . . .

He sleeps.

From her room, **Marcy** *calls* **Advance Man** *on the phone.*

Marcy   Ring ring.

Advance Man   Hello.

Marcy   It's me. It's Marcy.

Advance Man   I can certainly tell—by your voice.

Marcy   By my voice yeah I—

Advance Man   I recognize your voice because we spent time together earlier today.

Marcy   That's right.

Advance Man   So I know it's you.

Pause.

Advance Man   It's nice out here it's nighttime it's so peaceful now I am not
working now I'm off hours I wouldn't eat a bird now I'm not a bad guy I like trees.

Marcy   Uh . . .
Yeah so uh so uh—that sounds good. Everything sounds good. The History Chair. I'll
sit in it. What you were saying today. I'm into it. I'll come work for you. I'll do—
whatever you want.

Advance Man   Oh.
Right.
Fantastic.

Marcy   Yeah?

Advance Man   Yes. Of course. Fantastic, yes.
It's a good choice.

He leaves.

Townspeople   Slump! Everyone slump! It's night!

The **Townspeople** *sleep.*

Marcy *is still awake.*

Marcy (*spoken*)   Bear Creek? Get out of town! I'm a big deal now! I'm getting
out of this old cracker joint! I work—for the President now! He saw me and
he said you're special he said you're special he said—you're not like them.

(*Sings*) Glistening in the—and I climb the stairs!
They're running they the people with the notebooks they they're running they.
Say here comes Marcy here comes Marcy here comes here she comes here comes
Marcy here she comes—hey.
She's too busy to respond to your emails.
Send her a text! Oooh send her a text—she's busy!
She is the President.
She's President Marcy.

Everyone sings!

Townspeople   We-are-sleeping-this-is-a-dream!

Baker   Glistening oooh yeah I became the President oooh yeah.
Got my President pants on and I'm wearing my President mind thinking President
thoughts oooh yeah.
Yes I live in the White House yes you can call me Mr.
Mr. President. I'm the President.

Townspeople (except Roger & Frank)
In our white houses we live in a white house glistening
We too have people running we too have secret phones we too
We keep our thoughts clear we keep our mind clean
We think President thoughts
We're the President, we are the President
We're President—We!

Roger & Frank   Alone in the woods.

End of musical number. Everyone sleeps, except for **Advance Man**.

He is alone in the dark woods. He is off the clock.

Advance Man   Did I want to be a bird? Yes.
There have been times when I considered becoming a tree. Yes.

From the sky, we hear the deep dulcet tones of **The President**.

The President   Do you think of me as . . . large?

Advance Man   Mr. President! Ah . . . yes.

The President   Do you think of me as . . . also small?

Advance Man   Yes, sometimes yes.

The President   Do you suspect that I contain multitudes?

Advance Man   Multitudes, yes.

The President   And yet am singular.

Advance Man   The one and only, yes.

The President   When you see me out on the street, do you say . . . hello?

Advance Man   Yes.

The President   If someone insults me at a party, do you say . . . he's a good guy.

Advance Man   Yes.

The President   What would these woods be like without me?

Advance Man   Dark and cold.

The President   The child Marcy—be careful there. Keep an eye out. Let me know.

The night sky is suddenly alive with sparrows. They're everywhere. They come together in patterns, fly apart again. The noise is overwhelming.

Scene Four

Morning. A few sparrows. They flit around—anxious, erratic.

Townspeople   Morning time!

Marcy *tries to wake her dad up. He's looking very cozy, perhaps snoring.*

Librarian   I go to the library!

Frank   Me, to the farm.

Everyone Else   Us to our various other locations—

Ella & Science Teacher   And we, to school!

Marcy   Dad?

Marcy   Dad, I'm going to school?

Marcy   Dad?

Michael Henry   Sleepytime tea gonna sleep in I'm sleepy today.

Marcy   I'm going to school.

Michael Henry   Have a good day and I'll—I—zzzz.

He's snoring again.

Marcy *shrugs, leaves.*

Baker & Local Mom   We're at a coffee shop.

They are, indeed, at a coffee shop. This should not involve any actual furniture or props.

Baker   I mean he's a good guy. The President.

Local Mom   Oh, sure. Well. I mean how do you know?

Baker   Know what.

Local Mom   That he's, you know, that he's—

Baker   Well, there's all the policies.

Local Mom   Like . . . .

Baker   Well there's the you know he's very very just—I mean look at the guy! And there's all the kind of where he comes from and his background, that uh that uh—

Local Mom   No, I feel that. I agree with you there. But then there's all the stuff *now* that uh I mean if you look kind of at what's *actually happening now*, or at least some of it—

Baker   Uh-huh. But that isn't, I mean you can hardly, I mean—

Local Mom   Well.

Baker   You know? I mean there was already so much kind of and you can't expect him to just like I mean—patience! You know. "Patience, my son," or whatever.

Local Mom   Yeah . . . but it's like okay. So it's like, uh, yes. So no, yes, I understand what you're saying but, and hear me out here, but I feel like, I mean, we judge, like okay so we judge *you* based on what you *do*, right? Like if you like if you like, okay. If there's this thing that you're kind of secretly doing or not doing that is bad, then like *that's bad*. You're doing a bad thing. But then there's like all this other stuff that's *good*, then like—and I know you, you know? And I know that you're like *good*. But then there's also all this other stuff that you're doing that's *bad*. And the good. And so there's kind of the good, and the bad.

Baker   But I'm good.

Local Mom   Right.

Baker   I do good things.

Local Mom   No, right. But also like—you killed that thing, you know, you killed it, for example, it's dead, you smashed it you jumped on it you kind of just like—you *ate* it, you know. Let's say you ate it.

Baker   My friend ate it.

Local Mom   Let's say your friend ate it. But like, you know—you gave her permission. Or you told her to. You told her to eat that thing.

Baker   Well, she was hungry.

Local Mom   Yeah but that's a given! I mean I get hungry I mean we all get hungry I mean for God's sake, *sure.* I mean I'll give you *that.* But it's like you can't—it's what you *do* with that you know is like what I'm is all that I'm and I'm just like—"good person"? I mean what does that even, I mean how do we even—

Baker   Yeah . . .
I just like him. You know? "The President." I like saying his name, you know: "The President." And there was that thing he did.

Local Mom   Which thing?

Baker   The thing. You know. *That* was good.

Local Mom   No, sure. Yeah, no, sure. Sure. Uh-huh.

Advance Man *and* **Marcy** *enter.* **Advance Man** *whispers in* **Marcy**'s *ear, telling her how to spy on the* **Townspeople**. *During the following section, she does just that— sneaking around and note-taking as* **Advance Man** *watches approvingly.*

The **Townspeople** *do their thing:*

Exercise Teacher   And smack it! And swing it! And push it punch it tease it! Aaaand rest.

Exercise Teacher *slumps over in "resting pose" as* **Frank** *enters.*

Frank   And pick up an apple. And pick up an apple. And check up on the worms. And do a little weeding.

Science Teacher *teaches:*

Science Teacher   Protozoa, right? And kind of alright, so next. Floating along, right? Boom, explosion. Chaos. And just like mitochondria, and photosynthesis. Next, periodic table of the elements. Monkey bones. Dissection, yes. Hypothesis, other hypothesis, synthesis, conclusion. Taking care of the environment. Paying attention to your environment. Proving it, you know? Prove it. Prove it to me. Take an idea? Bam—experiment on it. Do some science on it. Mix it up. This is science, people. It's fun.
Questions.
Mmm. Mmm-hmm. Great. So check it out.

Science Teacher *diagrams the answer on the board.*

Librarian *shushes several sections of the audience in turn.*

Librarian   Sssssssssh.
Hey, guys? Sssssshhh.
Hey, guys? I'm gonna need you to—shhhh. We're in a—yeah.
Hey, uh, ahahaha, yup. You guessed it. Plenty of places outside if you want to—
Ahem.

Baker *enters with a piping hot tray of cookies that no one seems to want.*

Baker   COOKIES!

COOKIES!
COOKIES!
. . .
Bread.

Marcy *joins* **Ella** *in art class.*

Ella   Art class! Art class! Art class!
So yes, what is art? Is the great question is the great question, I mean—what do *you* think art is?

Marcy   I mean to me art is like art is like

Ella   Take this glitter and throw it. Throw it. Throw it higher! Uh-huh! See we're *doing* it! This is what it means to make art is just like the *doing* of it!

Marcy   I mean to me I guess art is like art is like uh, I mean it's like—so there's all this weird stuff, right? Like let's say for example there's a guy who comes to your newspaper office when your dad is out and he gives you twenty dollars to go with him in the car and he works for the President you find out and then you stop at this kind of whisper hole and listen to all these whispers and *then* he's like hmm you should come work for me and you're sort of but he's and it's and the President's and like and now it's . . . and so maybe art is just like you shove people's faces in that kind of thing and kind of grind it around until their faces are all mashed.

Ella   I guess . . . uh-huh, yes no sure I think you're right in a sense, although but to *me* I guess art is . . . I mean there is so much SO MUCH just kind of like you know and I mean the sun on the trees? And kind of—yes even the birds are beautiful and I bike home along the water everything bright in the just kind of like wow.

Marcy *sees* **Advance Man** *through the window.*

Advance Man   I watched her through the window quivering yes ask her ask her ask her!

Marcy   Ella? I'm just wondering if you've heard anything else about THE PRESIDENT'S VISIT.

Ella   Oh my God Marcy it's exciting it's I mean do you know when he's coming because I oooh and you'll never believe what that do you know what Frank is oh BUT.

Marcy   Yeah, I'm just wondering kind of how you feel about it and everything.

Ella   I remember when *many decades ago* the similar but also
kind of glowing in his sort of—and that smile!
Big the hair, and of course we know he's and it's but still it's—.
And on the one hand if I see a—if there's a cereal box
on the television that is very pretty very nice, I mean we all
know it's, there are people who, there's a lot of thought that—.   **Marcy**
And of course I know about the and I listen to all the on   Yeah but
the kind of more radical and I know I know, but you know   Hmmm

270 Abe Koogler Selected Plays

nothing in my life I mean I'm not no church and it's	
like a man in the sky? A MAN?	
And so *what I want* is to not dumb or hopeless or delusional but	Hey, uh
that actually has a chance of—	Ooooh
And at one point he did say Hey with us! and even if now	
he's saying Hey in a different tone of voice or sort of in	
a weird tone of voice where I'm like Hmmm?	
And he's kind of like Ho.	
And I'm like Hey?	My question is
And he's like Ha.	Sure, no, but
Even then I know that in his heart is Hey, and maybe in	
his mind is Hey, but he has to say Ha because people	No, but sure
like Ha more than Hey, and someday he'll say Hey,	
and if he never does then maybe for fuck's sake it	
was never sayable in the first place, and for God's sake	Yeah
what the hell were we doing all those years, just what the	
hell were we doing all those years screaming at buildings	
and kind of making love like Hey when in fact what there	Okay here's the
is, is Ha. Ha, ha, ha, ha, ha.	You're not

Marcy *gives up, frustrated.*

Advance Man   I met her outside.

Marcy   It's really hard it's—she won't stop talking it—

Advance Man   Excellent no this is excellent I think we can she seems—bing! Cross her off and move on. Oh here comes another I'm hiding!

Advance Man *hides as* **Roger** *enters.*

Roger   Oh, uh, nothing.

Marcy   Oh yeah um hmmm sure no hey Roger I was wondering—

Roger Yeah I mean sure I wonder why the wires why the	
whispers is that a wig is that your real hair? I'm	
concerned about the sparrows Marcy I am concerned	**Marcy**
where are they going why they're not so bad sparrows	Uh-huh, sure uh
and sure I live behind the Thriftway sure I'm on food	
stamps sure I enrolled in an	Dang it
online university once and sometimes I hitchhike	Yeah but
around the island carrying a chainsaw but that's	The question I
just because I'm good at chopping trees, sometimes	want
people need firewood out of trees, and it doesn't mean	to ask you is uh
I'm none of this means I'm what are you looking at who's	Is uh is uh
behind that tree?	Is uh

Advance Man *steps out from behind a tree.*

Marcy   Oh.

Advance Man   This is an interesting man an interesting person I'd like to get to know *this* person better you have led me to this most interesting person and I appreciate that I love to meet new people and just find out how they're doing and what they're into.

Roger   No.

Marcy   Oh—but—you're fine, right Roger? You're fine. Everything's fine. He's fine.

Advance Man   No I don't think so I we we should go for a walk him and me is what we should—

Marcy   He's really he's—

Roger   See this was I always told you that no one listened to me but I was the wires YES the whispers YES the birds the birds something with the birds I don't know what but I can see the outlines of it / I can I can I can see the outlines of it things missing changing it's not right it's it's not right is it's not right it's MISSING GONE MISSING GONE MISSING GONE MISSING GONE

Advance Man (*overlapping*)   Is what you should be quiet is you should be quiet you should be quiet is you shouldn't speak so loud you shouldn't I'll shhh, I'll shush you, I'll make you quiet, it's so nice to be quiet IT'S SO NICE TO BE QUIET BE QUIET BE

*In one swift motion—***Advance Man** *puts his hand over* **Roger***'s face.*

A beat.

Then **Marcy** *screams at the top of her lungs.*

Roger *runs.*

Advance Man *looks at* **Marcy**. *He's furious.*

Marcy   I mean I don't know I think there's like a lot of factors that we should consider I mean isn't it kind of a grey area like it's nice to like it's nice to like it's nice to like isn't there a way we can kind of like talk to people first to kind of see how they I'd say there's a lot of factors at play here and it might be nice to like get consent from like all involved parties or just kind of ask everyone if they're cool with like I don't know I'm only fifteen so—

Pause.

I mean what exactly did I sign up for here?

Advance Man   Listen, Marcy. I'm gonna need to go deep incognito for the next few hours, part of the deep background just sink into the earth kind of deal, but and so I need you to not slack but actually redouble? And what I need is a sort of nap, I'm going to nap, and here's a twenty dollars when you what I a full report is what I'm go get to it no time to the President's calling.

Advance Man *runs offstage.*

Marcy   Had I done something wrong? The Advance Man seemed so mad at me and I thought well maybe he's right maybe I should maybe I'll just maybe I'm not trying hard enough is what it's—the History Chair would be nice on my buttocks . . .

A sparrow flies in, lands.

Hey. Pretty pretty pretty pretty. (**Marcy** *tries to put the sparrow in her mouth, but it struggles and she takes it out.*) That's—oh I've hurt you! Here I'll—why don't you oh here rest in my pocket just kind of sleep sure and I'll be hmm.

Advance Man   I came back.

Marcy   OH MY GOD YOU SCARED ME!

Advance Man   I came back because I smelled a bird. I heard a bird, I saw a bird land, and then the bird was gone. Question being where did the bird go? Now if it got eaten it's—I mean, sure it's sad, sure—but do I know any birds? No, not personally. And so while I'm sad when there's one less bird, it's also like, okay: so here you have these *us* kind of clear skies fruit in the trees unmolested and here you have all these *them*. And that's a tough language, bird, not speaking allegorically I've studied bird, they sent me to a special—and I've flown, sure I've flown, it's great yeah, but I mean, to be on the ground? Two feet I mean there's the happy with what I've—sniff, sniff, sniff.

He sniffs her, stopping at the pocket where she put the bird.

Advance Man   You didn't eat it.

Marcy   I wasn't hungry? I was going to eat it later I was I was I swear I was—

Advance Man   Eat it now.

Marcy   No.

Advance Man   Eat it now.

Marcy   I can't.

Advance Man   Eat it now.

Marcy   It's not right.

Advance Man   Eat it now.

Marcy   But I like birds!

Advance Man   Eat it now.

Marcy   I'm not hungry I had a big lunch it's—

Advance Man   Eat it now.

Marcy   It's a bird.

Advance Man   It's food.

Marcy   It's a bird.

Advance Man   It's food though. It's food. It is food. It's food now.

Marcy   It's a bird.

Advance Man   It *is* food.

Eat it now.

Marcy *puts the bird in her mouth, eats it.*

It's really hard for her to do. Perhaps she retches, keeps going—swallows.

Advance Man   Now come with me.

Advance Man *holds his hand out.* **Marcy** *takes it. They leave.*

Roger *emerges from behind a tree.*

Roger   Marcy?
Marcy in high school?
Marcy?

He hears whispering from a hole. He puts his ear to it, raises his arm like a tuning fork, and listens, just as **Advance Man** *did earlier. He hears:*

Marcy   The trees everywhere now darkness everywhere now the sky.

Advance Man & Marcy   Yes indeed sure of course sure finally now yes now indeed now yes.

Roger *runs.*

Suddenly a helicopter can be heard overhead. Its dark shadow passes over the stage. The **Townspeople** *hear it and run off and onstage, agitated. Chaos from the birds.*

Librarian   No!

Local Mom   No!

Exercise Teacher   Yes!

The helicopter circles—noise of blades—

Science Teacher   Yes!

Local Mom   No!

Baker   Yes!

Then everyone's onstage, looking up at the sky.

Baker   The President's coming!

Baker, Exercise Teacher, Local Mom   The President's coming!

Townspeople   The President's coming—

Librarian   He's here!

A held beat—then—

Townspeople   Everyone get ready!

Frenetic activity—everyone runs on and offstage, getting ready.

Maybe the helicopter is still passing overhead but farther away.

Ella   I raced home to grab my signs, they said "yes Mr. President, yes yes yes!"

Local Mom   The sparrows were agitated, or excited, or frightened, it was hard to tell.

Frank   Real quick I loaded up my truck up with apples so I could kind of just spray them all over the road.

Baker   I baked extra cookies I—

Librarian   Shut down the library I—

Science Teacher   Cancelled classes I—

Local Mom   Put Sammy in the car I—

Exercise Teacher   Said everyone let's move!

Townspeople, **Ella** and **Frank** *form an expectant line onstage.*

Then, a whispered chant:

Science Teacher   Hey.

Science Teacher & Exercise Teacher   Hey HEY.

Science Teacher, Exercise Teacher, & Librarian   Hey*hey*heyhey.

Everyone Else Except Frank   HEYHEYHEY*HEY*HEYHEY!

A yell, pulled up deep from the earth:

Local Mom   Oooha!

Everyone Else Except Frank   Ooooha oooha!! Shoopa Shoopa Shoopa Shoopa! Aha ha ha!

In perfect harmony:

Everyone Else Except Frank   And a llama llama llama and a llama llama llama and a llama llama llama llama oooooh.

Everyone looks around for **The President**.

The birds are gone.

The "oooh" hangs in the golden air.

A held moment of incredible expectation and possibility. **The President** *could show up at any moment.*

But **Ella** *is distracted by* **Frank**'s *presence.*

Ella   Frank.

Frank   Ella.

Ella   What are you doing with those goddamn apples?

Frank   Well, I'm going to spray them all over the road.

Ella   Now that's just a stupid idea.

Frank   You know being over in the jungle really fucked up my life and I've had just about enough of you people telling me I'm stupid.

Ella   Well, maybe you, I mean that was your choice to—

Frank   And just what are you, and what were you—

Ella   We were—you were leaving, to go fight in the jungle, and we were dating, we had been dating, eighteen, I mean can you remember? And we had no idea, I mean *not to know*, to stand there on the kind of bright night in the field behind your house—I mean *do you remember*? You must remember you—

Frank   No.

Ella   You must remember you—

Frank   No!

Ella   Time shift.

Frank   No.

Ella   Forty years ago.

Frank   *No.*

Ella   High school.

Frank   No I don't want to go I have to go!

Time shifts. **Townspeople** *recede.*

Frank *and* **Ella** *are in a field, forty years earlier.*

They laugh. They touch each other. They can't believe it.

Ella   Sleep with me one night, I'm making a castle we'll sleep in a field don't mind the horses—they won't think we're hay, we're people! We're human beings, we live here on this island!

Frank   I'm not afraid of horses.

Ella   What are you afraid of then, what are you afraid of?

Frank   You have the most beautiful long hair.

Ella   You're just trying to get in my pants, aren't you, Frankie?

Frank   Don't call me that, my dad calls me that. Call me Frank, just Frank.

Ella   Then call me Ella, just Ella.

Ella   Frank   **Frank**   Ella.

Ella   There's a place where we can live where they won't find us of course, there's castles there of course, we can live there with a horse!

Frank   They'll hear us whispering they'll—

Ella   They won't. We won't speak, we won't whisper even, we'll just be quiet, we'll plant fruit trees, we'll have candles a warm bed at night, we'll sign stories to each other with our hands. Who needs words? We'll say it with our hands!

Frank   But history, my dad says history—

Ella   Fuck history, I don't—what's history, history is what they tell you when the big man wants you to—

Frank   I like that big man, we need a big man.

Ella   Man, man, always a man, who's that man to me? I got you and I got my own two hands and let them come here—I'll fight 'em with my hands. I'll give 'em fruit from the garden. We'll confuse 'em and then feed 'em. Everything's going to be—

Frank   History, history, history.

Ella   Me! Bear Creek. You and me. My hands. You. The horses in this field. We'll give them apples. What more do you need? This is it. Wake up. Wake up. Wake up. Wake up. *Wake up.*
And then we were asleep.

They sleep in the field.

After a moment, **Frank** *awakes.*

From the sky we hear the **The President**.

He speaks just to **Frank**—*softly at first, but with growing intensity.*

The President   You're no one special, you, you're like the rest of them, you, don't think you there's nothing you they'll find you they'll you'll whisper you'll—*why run from the chair?* Is . . . sit in it, stand in it, lots of us over here in the—, all your friends everyone it's obvious so obvious its so obvious shouldn't even be saying it no need to even speak it's a given its given *so much given* asking a little. Not selfish are you, aren't selfish are you, I'll be here you know I'm I wouldn't ask if I *not asking* commanding to you stand stand stand stand up like your dad would have grandpa would have brother mother even in factories wagons even in uniforms even rowing in boats the bottoms of boats even then on the prairie in over the ocean over through the mountains under on top of the dark fields stand stand stand stand stand stand up now STAND STAND STAND.

Frank *stands.*

Frank   But what if I—? Mr. President. Are you sure I'll—?

The President   Not to worry!

The President *is gone.*

Frank *looks at sleeping* **Ella**, *leaves.*

Ella *wakes up in the field, alone.*

Ella   Frank?

Nothing.

Ella *is in past time, speeding towards the present.*

The **Townspeople** *re-enter in present time, waiting for* **The President**. *The day is ending—it's twilight.*

Ella   I waited and waited and waited.

Townspeople   We waited and waited.

Ella   That day into the next and the next. No word from Frank—not nothing, no nothing, not nothing.

Science Teacher   We waited in the road for the President. No nothing, not nothing, no President no—not.

Ella   I waited by the phone for a—, by the mailbox for a—, I took a job at the—, I moved to California. Time passed. The 60s, 70s. The 1980s, the 90s. Moved back to Bear Creek, and there was Frank. Two thousand one, two thousand two. Oh-five, oh-six, oh-nine. 2010. Today.

Librarian   Night came, still nothing.

Baker   I closed the bakery and put the cookies in the—

Science Teacher   We drove home the route we always drive looking out the window at the like always we—

Exercise Teacher   I closed my phone and felt strange somehow as if I, as if somehow I—

Ella   You know the hopes you—. You imagine you'll—. And then when you get there you—. And looking back thinking: *well why didn't I just it's so obvious what the hell was I wake up! Why didn't I wake up, what was I sleeping about, what was I—* Anyway.
The day the President didn't come, I put my signs in the trash and walked over to the Rusty Bear Bar.

She does, fully back in present time now.

Frank *is also at the Rusty Bear Bar.*

Frank   Ella.

Ella   Frank.

Frank   Beer?

Ella   I'm drinking wine.

They sit near but not too near each other, drinking.

Frank   "The President."
He's not coming, I guess. Guess I'm going to have to deal with that earthworm problem myself.

Ella (*as she sees something in the sky*)   Frank. Look up there.

Frank   Looks like a 'copter to me.

Science Teacher   A tiny dot, the whirring of blades. It hovered and dipped dark patterns in the sky. And then floating down, from way up high—something like words.

Ella (*trying to repeat what she hears*)   Sssp sssp spp a ssspp ssspp sppp

Science Teacher   They rose and fell, rised and falled. But we couldn't—

Ella   I can't. Can you?

Frank   Not quite.

Townspeople   We can't. Can you?

Science Teacher   I can't. Not quite.

Everyone strains to hear the sound.

The faintest of whispers.

Then it's gone.

Townspeople   Surely we'd surely there'd be another we'd—

A held moment.

Frank   Ah well.

An exhale.

Frank   Hey, Ella.

Ella   What, Frank?

Beat.

Frank   No, nothing. Nothing. It's always nice to see you.

Frank *leaves one way,* **Ella** *leaves another.*

Roger *enters.*

It's deep twilight now—almost dark.

Roger I came down from the forest the streets empty now the skies empty now no birds anywhere now no birds.

And perhaps this is the first time the **Townspeople** *notice this too.*

Michael Henry *enters, yawning. He's missed the whole thing.*

Michael Henry Late in the day. Must have slept.
Marcy?

Baker No birds now. It was strange. But we were—maybe it was the 'copter maybe the blades of the 'copter.

Michael Henry Marcy?

Librarian No birds now anywhere, those pesky birds gone now everywhere, come and gone, those pesky birds at least gone now, that was good now gone now quiet now nice now, although although—

Local Mom Quiet now and nice now, in a way, nice now, in a way, nice now.
In a way.

Michael Henry Marcy?
Marcy?
MARCY!

Scene Five

Morning—bright and clear. The sky is empty. No sparrows.

Marcy *and* **Advance Man** *in the car.*

Marcy *is driving. Something is very different about her.*

Marcy Sure no SURE—

Advance Man Careful.

Marcy Yes and yes and so if you this was here and of course this was there and that's the really I mean who's to and yes yes no sure sure.
Can I go home now?

Advance Man (*relaxing*) Aaaah. This is why, you know. Clear air, kind of the— look at that blue sky, that blue sky, that clear blue sky, clear as air the clear air, just us here now, just us here now, juuuuuust us.

Marcy Maybe we can just drive me home now.

Advance Man "The Advance People." Never had kids but still and not in any weird way just proud.

But be careful there's kind of grabbing at you hold tight and all your friends bring your friends you'll get there you will and it's President very proud and I so sleepy is it—am I dying?

Although to be honest I do wonder sometimes about those birds. Do they have houses?

What's it like to speak bird? What does the earth look like from up there, and how's it, how do we, what's it like to be a tree? And how do the earthworms but it's—NO it's two feet on the ground and I'm very firm and but NO my arms up and it's like hello! I'm a cloud! But it's *no no no no no* very firm, on the ground, HUMAN BEING, not kind of drifting everywhere potentially everything, two eyes, no more eyes than that, feet on the ground, eyes clear, my history very clear, my future very clear, and it's—

So sleepy . . .

Although to be honest I did wonder I do wonder I always did wonder . . .

Advance Man *waves at* **Marcy**. *Then he's gone.*

Marcy *stops the car and sneaks out. She's home.*

Michael Henry *enters.*

Michael Henry   Marcy. Where have you been?

Marcy   Yeah, I got lost in the I was calling for you but yeah uh so I guess hmmm it's all I mean you could have well no never mind its done. I'm older now. I've shoop—changed. My eyes have kind of—ope, different. My mind. It's firm now. Very clear. Everything, particular perspective just—shoop. Like a beam of light—ping! Particular. Clear. Everything outside dark inside shoop! Yes. Light. Clear.

Michael Henry   Are you alright?

Marcy   Sure sure no sure, sure sure sure sure no sure absolutely sure sure yes sure yes I'm sure sure sure sure sure sure sure sure s—

Marcy *chokes on something, pulls it out of her mouth.*

It's a bird feather.

Michael Henry   Do you want to—uh, should I make us some—

Marcy   Sure.

The **Townspeople** *emerge from the shadows—they have been watching.*

Librarian   Yeah, but like—

Baker   Yeah, I don't know, but like—

Local Mom   Yeah but uh, but I don't know, but like—

Exercise Teacher   It's like uh, it's like—

Science Teacher   Yeah, so it's like—

Exercise Teacher   Uh yeah it was a—I mean sure we thought, we *thought*—

Local Mom   We thought that uh, we *wondered* sure, I mean sure we *wondered*, we should we have could we still—

Baker   Yeah.

Beat.

And then, to the audience, as if in answer to a question:

Science Teacher   And so it was, it was it was, no it was, sure it was, and sure we did, sure sure we did, sure we *voted*.

Baker   We *voted*, sure.

Exercise Teacher   Sure sure we *voted* that fall, sure.

Librarian   We *voted* that fall, sure we *voted*, and it was like, but I don't know, but we all kind of, and there was a sort of, that it wasn't—

Townspeople   It wasn't—

Science Teacher   And we felt kind of—sure it was important, absolutely, but there was an unsettled kind of—the sparrows used to be everywhere, a nuisance if you ignored them but so beautiful up close, but now no sparrows, no sparrows anywhere no just sometimes we'd—and sure we *voted*, sure we *voted*, sure sure we *voted* that year like every year we voted sure, but—

The **Townspeople** *leave.*

Marcy *is alone onstage.*

Then she hears something—the faintest of whispers, coming from downstage.

In one swift single clean motion **Marcy** *walks downstage, falls to the ground, and raises one hand like a tuning fork, just as* **Advance Man** *did at the beginning of the play.*

Whispers rise and rise and rise.

They're deafening.

End of play.